THE NATURE OF
BORNEO

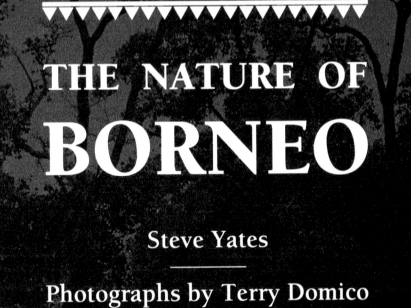

THE NATURE OF
BORNEO

Steve Yates

Photographs by Terry Domico

Facts On File
New York • Oxford

The Nature of Borneo

Text copyright © 1992 by Steve Yates
Photographs copyright © 1992 by Terry Domico

Facts On File, Inc.
460 Park Avenue South
New York, NY 10016
USA

Facts On File Limited
c/o Roundhouse Publishing Ltd.
P.O. Box 140
Oxford OX2 7SF
United Kingdom

Library of Congress Cataloging-in-Publication Data
Yates, Steve.
The nature of Borneo / Steve Yates ; photographs by Terry
Domico.
p. cm.
Includes bibliographical references and index.
ISBN 0-8160-2428-6
1. Natural history—Borneo. 2. Natural history—Borneo—Pictorial
works. I. Domico, Terry. II. Title.
QH193.B65Y37   1992
508.598′3—dc20   91-37722

A British CIP catalogue record for this book is available from the British Library.

Facts On File books are available at special discounts when purchased in bulk
quantities for businesses, associations, institutions or sales promotions.
Please call our Special Sales Department in New York at 212/683-2244
(dial 800/322-8755 except in NY, AK or HI) or in Oxford at 865/728399.

Text design by Ron Monteleone
Jacket design by Catherine Hyman
Composition by Facts On File, Inc.
Manufactured by Trilogy S.A.S.
Printed in Italy

10 9 8 7 6 5 4 3 2 1

This book is printed on acid-free paper.

To David and Kathryn Yates
for your help and encouragement

CONTENTS

A NOTE FROM
TERRY DOMICO

Few places on this planet seem as mysterious to the would-be traveler as Borneo. The mere mention of the area conjures up images of impenetrable jungles, wild ape-men, headhunters and leech-infested swamps. These things are certainly here, to be sure, but Borneo has also been deeply affected by the trappings of the late 20th century: modern shopping malls, video halls, traffic congestion, deforestation and urban sprawl.

I had no idea what to expect when I first arrived in Borneo in 1986. At that time we were seeking information about a small jungle bear that we feared was approaching extinction. We eventually found the bear and at the same time became spellbound by the sheer variety of life in this wonderful place.

Borneo itself does not feel like an island. It really seems too vast, especially when inland travel is measured in days or weeks instead of miles. Borneo also feels more "centrally located" than I could have imagined before going there. I've heard other people, visitors and residents alike, attempt to comment on this odd impression, but it was a British traveler whom I met on a forest trail who expressed it most succinctly. He said he felt as if he had finally "arrived at the center of the earth." After five years of exploring and contemplation of Borneo's many facets, I think he was right.

There were so many adventures and experiences I would like to share with you that I hardly know where to begin. A few stand out like beacons, though. There were hair-raising incidents such as meeting the enraged orangutan that might have killed us when it suddenly began throwing huge branches down at us from the tree canopy, and there were lovely moments such as when I discovered a stunning array of orchid blossoms that simply wasn't there the night before and which withered and vanished before midday.

Then there was the surprise of the "leaf" that suddenly became a butterfly before my eyes, the fiercely adorned natives who gleefully offered us their incredibly generous hospitality, and the primal heartache of a sobbing man sitting next to me on a ramshackle bus with his dead baby lying across his lap. There were the falls, the bruises and the exhaustion of hiking tortuous trails, there was the rustle of leaves as the mouse deer that I had been stalking all evening suddenly bolted. There was the incredible electric-blue light that infuses the rainforest as dawn approaches, the sparkling coral reefs, the muddy mangrove swamps, pristine forest streams—the beauty and power of the life in Borneo is almost too much to bear. I hope my photographs are able to communicate some of these feelings.

—Terry Domico
Penang, Malaysia

PREFACE

The mystique of Borneo has fascinated European naturalists and travelers for the past century and a half. Long before that, Chinese traders and Arab sailors brought back fantastic tales along with valuable exotic products from Borneo's rainforest and seacoast. This mystique brought me to Borneo, but I quickly found that reality was more interesting than fiction.

Southeast Asia's tropical rainforest was once the most magnificent on earth. What's left of it still is, but the pace of deforestation has been fierce, as the Philippines, Indonesia, Malaysia, Thailand, Cambodia and now even Burma have tried to modernize or to balance their budgets through log exports or conversion of forest lands to more "modern uses." In some places this desire for diversification is real—forced by unprecedented population growth. Often, though, it is simply a rationalization for quick fortunes to be made from mining the forest on a grand scale—driven and financed by the plywood markets of Japan and Europe.

Despite this, Borneo still possesses large remnants of rainforest. The policies of Indonesian Kalimantan and of Malaysian Sarawak and Sabah—semi-independent nations in terms of land use—will determine whether or not enough forest is preserved to support the island's incredible diversity of wildlife. And to support the peoples who depend on wild fish, game, fruits and such critical plants as rattan and bamboo. In the meantime, Borneo's wild places can still overwhelm the most energetic explorer.

Though the wildlife and habitat types described in this book are found throughout Borneo, most of my travels and research occurred in Sarawak and Sabah, primarily in designated parks or wildlife reserves. The principal reasons for this limitation are language and access and, one hopes, the permanence of these preserves.

During the late 19th and early 20th centuries Sarawak and Sabah were de facto British colonies, whereas Kalimantan was part of the Dutch East Indies. Thus, while most Kalimantan research material is in Dutch, English has been the language of most published research in Malaysia since the advent of Rajah James Brooke in Sarawak and the British North Borneo Company in Sabah, allowing the fortunate English-speaking naturalist easy access to the scientific literature. In fact, one of the primary tasks for those working to create a pan-Borneo research center will be to translate important Dutch research papers into English—and the papers of both languages into Bahasa Malaysia or its very similar Indonesian equivalent.

Bahasa Malaysia has only recently replaced English in schools and courts of law in Sarawak and Sabah. Meanwhile, Hollywood movies, American and British television shows and popular music, and advertising aimed at the prosperous Chinese community all give English a continuing strong cultural presence. The people of Sabah and Sarawak are remarkably multilingual, and

Opposite:
Few flowering plants live below the shade of the primary rainforest. This Butterfly pea is common in cleared areas.

English remains the second or third language of many. Only in remote Malay *kampongs* (villages), Dayak longhouses or Penan settlements is it liable to be absent. For visitors from the United States or the British Commonwealth nations this widespread use of English greatly facilitates travel in Malaysian Borneo.

Borneo is a vast island of swamps, mountains, steep valleys, flooding rivers and dense rainforest. Paved roads are limited mostly to the coast, and railroads are almost nonexistent. It takes both a commitment by state governments and a steady flow of passengers to justify air routes or the expense of building roads through difficult terrain. Adventure tourism is seen as a growing source of income to Malaysia, and the parks are recognized as Borneo's chief attractions; thus air or boat transport can be arranged, food and lodging are available, and red tape is minimal (though it should be pointed out that Sarawak's government is rather touchy about visitors who resemble journalists). Kalimantan, on the other hand, though it covers three-fourths of Borneo and has reserves of impressive size (on paper, at least), makes up just a minor portion of far-flung Indonesia. The Indonesian government considers it more valuable as a source of timber and oil and a population safety valve for crowded Java than as a tourist destination that could compete with Java or Bali.

Borneo's parks and reserves (listed at the end of Chapter Ten) contain good examples of all the island's habitat types and most of the island's incredible variety of plant and animal species. For the present, they remain oases within the frantic pace of rainforest logging and agricultural transformation, offering even the casual visitor the chance to experience Borneo's natural wonders.

My own travels were made easier and much more enjoyable by the kind assistance and boundless hospitality of the following people, many of whom offered insights into Borneo's intricate ecosystems and diverse cultures.

In Sabah, I would like to thank Lamri Ali, director of Sabah Parks; Patrick Andau, Sabah Wildlife Department; Junaidi Payne, World Wildlife Fund Malaysia; C. L. Chan, botanical artist and authority on Borneo's stick insects; the entire Kinabalu Park staff, especially technician/naturalist Tan Fui Lian, Head Naturalist Jamili Nais, Chief Warden Eric Wong and Assistant Warden Gabriel Sinit; Rob Stuebing, biology professor at Universiti Kebangsaan Malaysia, Kota Kinabalu campus; Anthea Phillips, former head naturalist at Kinabalu Park and now a free-lance writer; Clive Marsh, research director for the Sabah Foundation and director of the Danum Valley Field Research Centre; the staff and scientists at Danum Valley, especially ornithologist Frank Lambert, soil ecologist Theo Burghouts and hydrologist Tony Greer; Sylvia Alsisto, naturalist at Sepilok Orangutan Rehabilitation Center; Neil Antrum and Clement Lee of Borneo Divers. Also: Ian Douglas, hydrology professor, University of Manchester, U.K.; Robert Inger, curator of amphibians and reptiles, Field Museum of Natural History; John MacKinnon, World Wildlife Fund, Hong Kong; Kathy MacKinnon, EMDI Project, Jakarta.

In Kota Kinabalu I was fortunate to share an apartment with Steve "Jungle-man" Pinfield, director of Borneo Endeavor Expeditions, who guided me through the Crocker Range. In Sandakan, I experienced Borneo's overwhelming hospitality in the persons of Patrick and Elizabeth Seah, who put us up (complete with meals and transportation) and put up with us and all our gear for days at a time on less notice than that. In Likas I stayed for weeks at a time at Cecelia and Denny Chew's Bed & Breakfast, rest stop for most Western naturalists and scientists passing through Sabah.

In Sarawak I would like to thank the following in Kuching: Elizabeth Bennett, New York Zoological Society and WWF; Director Lucas Chin and the staff of the Sarawak Museum; the owners and staff of the Orchid Inn; the helpful staff at Bako National Park. In Miri, thanks go to the kind folks at Alo

Doda Travel Services (Diana Yap, Elizabeth Deng, Danny Lawai, Nilong Man, Robert Sim, Michael Wan-Nilong, George Ngau, James Laing, Henry Nilong and Magdelene Ping Nilong); Jeffrey and Caleena Pasang and family; and the owners and staff of Ku's Inn. At Mulu Park: guides Simon Lagang and Philip Lawang. In Bario: Andreas and Jane Tapang; the Terawai family; the people of Ramudu and Pa Barang.

In Kalimantan: Birute Galdikas, director of the Orangutan Research Centre, Central Kalimantan, and the Orangutan Foundation, Los Angeles; Mark Leighton of Harvard University, director of the Gunung Palung Rainforest Project, West Kalimantan.

In Peninsula Malaysia: WWF Malaysia Executive Director Mikaail Kavanagh; MAS "Wings Of Gold" editor Khalilah Mohd Talha; Jane Vong, Malaysia TDC, who was most helpful in a pinch; the libraries of the Universiti Malaya, Petaling Jaya.

Others who made my journeys more enjoyable include traveling companion Dave McCargo (presently mending his broken ribs in a longhouse in the Kelabit Highlands after a fall from a slippery log bridge); Mark Newman, M.D./photographer (who should have been along); Jade and Kumar—housemates and friends; orangutan behaviorist Isabel Gilloux; orangutan geneticist Dianne Janczewski; and the mermaid who danced into my dreams.

Special thanks go to photographer Terry Domico and editors Gerry Helferich and Gary Krebs of Facts On File for making this book possible.

I gratefully acknowledge the assistance of Malaysian Airlines System for discount airline tickets and the Malaysian Tourist Development Corporation for sponsoring our Mulu explorations.

In addition, Terry Domico would like to thank David Goh and his staff at the Penang Butterfly Farm for their help in photographing the life cycles of several Bornean butterflies, and Sylvester Tan of Sarawak's Forestry Department.

—Steve Yates

THE NATURE OF
BORNEO

INTRODUCTION: VOYAGE TO SUNDALAND

With a roar the Boeing 737 takes off from Johor Bahru, on the southern tip of the Malay Peninsula, heading east across the South China Sea toward Borneo. Situated on the equator just south of the Philippines and in the center of the Malay/Indonesian Archipelago hat stretches from Sumatra to New Guinea, Borneo is the world's third-largest island. Always one of the earth's most intriguing places, it is now one of its most controversial. Borneo—last masterpiece of Southeast Asia's magnificent tropical rainforest, possessor of Southeast Asia's tallest mountain and largest caves, and home to some of its most fascinating native cultures—is now under siege from a world hungry for its fabled resources.

Below us, the plane's shadow floats over a dark green sea of palm oil plantations. Geometric rows of palm oil trees cover the once-forested flatlands of West Malaysia; they stretch northward along the west coast, up past historic Malacca to the open tin mines and rubber plantations surrounding Kuala Lumpur, Malaysia's expansive, modern capital. South of us, a busy causeway links the Malaysian city of Johor Bahru to the tiny island-nation of Singapore.

Malaysia and Singapore are booming. Singapore, founded as a British colony by Sir Stamford Raffles in 1819 and separated from Malaysia two years after Malaysian independence in 1963, has overcome its lack of size and natural resources to become the commerce and transport hub of Southeast Asia. Malaysia's prosperity, on the other hand, comes in part from the Malay Peninsula's raw materials (palm oil, rubber, tin) and from manufactured goods (electronics, textiles and latex goods). A full quarter of its export earnings, though, are derived from offshore oil and rainforest timber from the East Malaysian states of Sarawak and Sabah on Borneo.

Though Bornean East Malaysia's population is less than a tenth that of West Malaysia, its size is more than 50 percent greater than all 11 peninsular states combined. Yet Sabah and Sarawak together—with the tiny, oil-rich Sultanate of Brunei tossed in—take up just the northwest quarter of Borneo. The remainder is divided into the four Indonesian states of West, South, Central and East Kalimantan (Kalimantan being the Indonesian designation for Borneo).

The same Bornean oil and timber that contribute so heavily to the Malaysian economy also drive the economy of Indonesia. East Kalimantan's oil-rich coastal city, Balikpapan, has been called "a suburb of Houston" and timber barges dominate the river traffic along that state's mighty Mahakam River.

Kalimantan is governed from Jakarta, Indonesia's sprawling capital on the western tip of Java, 500 miles to the south of Singapore. As residents of the

Opposite:
Tall sandstone cliffs overlook the Sulu Sea near Sandakan in eastern Sabah.

world's most densely populated island, Javans are well aware of thinly populated Kalimantan's rich natural resources. The popular saying goes "Sumatra for us; Kalimantan for our children; Irian Jaya (western New Guinea) for our grandchildren." Sumatra, not much smaller than Borneo and now largely deforested, stretches northwestward from Java, past Singapore, and halfway up along the west coast of the Malay Peninsula. Between lies the long, narrow, strategic Strait of Malacca, the critical central passageway of the enduring coastal trade route connecting the Mediterranean and Mideast to India, China and Japan.

Below us now on the East China Sea just east of the strait where Arabian dhows and Chinese junks once sailed, only an occasional freighter or oil tanker spreads its wake like a comet tail across the endless parallel waves. The seas are flat now, during the lull between the region-wide monsoons. Monsoons (derived from Arabic *musim*, or "season") are the prime climatic events of southern Asia, driven by two massive low-pressure areas shifting between central Asia and the southern Indian Ocean.

During the middle of each year the sun beats heavily on the high deserts of central Asia, creating a rising cell of hot, dry air. This continental low-pressure zone draws wet surface weather northward from the Indian Ocean. The resulting Southwest Monsoon rains annually devastate the flat floodplains of Bangladesh as they run off the deforested foothills of the Himalayas. The monsoon rain is also intercepted by the mountainous islands of Southeast Asia; fortunately, much of it is soaked up by the lush rainforests still covering most of Borneo and New Guinea. But these equatorial islands are losing their protective forest cover; their thin soils are being washed downriver into once-clear tropical seas.

In October and November the climatic situation reverses, creating the winter's Northeast Monsoon. Central Asia turns frigid; dense, sinking air creates a high-pressure zone pushing the winds outward. The low-pressure center shifts to the relatively warm Indian Ocean west of Australia, drawing weather from the north. For India and Thailand this means an influx of dry continental air. For Borneo and nearby islands it simply means that wet oceanic air now comes from a different direction and, if anything, is even wetter.

The predictability of these alternating monsoon winds allowed early downwind-sailing ships to travel back and forth from the Red Sea and India to China and Japan. Coastal trade began as early as Roman times and was well established by the third century A.D. The monsoon-based trade reached its zenith during the "Golden Age of Arab Shipping" (eighth to 16th centuries) before being dominated by the expanding European powers: Portugal and Spain, then Holland and Britain.

The major coastal route reached northwestward as far as Venice and Alexandria on the Mediterranean, through the Red Sea to Muscat (in Oman—home of the legendary Sinbad the Sailor), Karachi and Bombay on the Arabian Sea; to Madras and Phukat (western Thailand) on the eastern Indian Ocean; through the Strait of Malacca past Kelang (west coast of Malaysia) and Jambi (eastern Sumatra); and from Bangkok north along the Indochina coast to Guangzhou and Shanghai in China, and the seaports of southern Japan.

Along this route passed Chinese silks and pottery; Greek olive oil and Egyptian cotton; frankincense and myrrh for perfumes and incense; Indian bronze, Chinese iron, and Sumatran gold; fragrant and decorative woods such as sandalwood and ebony; Bornean camphor and sago flour. Spices, which had the power to turn bland, repetitive fare into a stimulating feast, were especially valued: Sumatran pepper; cinnamon from Borneo; nutmeg and cloves from the fabled "Spice Islands" (the Moluccas) west of New Guinea.

Of even more lasting significance were the trade route's less tangible legacies: Indian Hinduism and Buddhism, still the cornerstones of the Indones-

The Sabah Foundation's ultramodern Sabah Tower dominates a bay north of the booming state capital, Kota Kinabalu.

ian island of Bali; Chinese technology—ceramics, metallurgy, and gunpowder; Arabic culture—mathematics, astronomy, and especially Islam, the religion of scholars and sailors.

By the 14th century, at the height of the Hindu/Buddhist Majapahit Empire based on Java, Islam had already reached the Malay Peninsula and was spreading along the trade routes to the Spice Islands. It was soon adopted by the Sulu Sultanate of the southern Philippines, and by the extensive Borneo-based coastal empire centered in Brunei. Thus, coastal Malays are Muslim; Islam is the official religion of Malaysia and Brunei; and Indonesia has become the world's most populous Islamic country.

Important links had been forged between Borneo and China as early as the ninth century. By the 11th century there is evidence of thriving Chinese-dominated trade centers at Santubong on the southern coast of Sarawak, and at Sandakan on Sabah's east coast. China sent huge stoneware "dragon" jars,

colored glass beads and elaborate bronze gongs to Borneo. In return, Borneo offered the exotic treasures of its inland forests: cinnamon bark and camphor; rhinoceros horn for magic medicine; hornbill ivory (worth more than elephant ivory or jade) for carvings; Cave swiftlet nests (worth their weight in gold) to infuse soup with aphrodisiac power; gutta-percha latex and damar resin; bezoar (gallstones from monkey bladders), considered medicinal by the Chinese and reputed by later Europeans to reveal poison in wine; beeswax for candles; decorative feathers from kingfishers and hornbills; tortoiseshell, deer antler, and pangolin scales.

With this movement of goods from Borneo's mysterious inland forests came the seafarer's stories that gave the island its mystique: sophisticated sultanates surrounded by primitive jungle; rivers of gold; a mountain so tall that a dragon lived in its summit lake far above the clouds; mysterious caves; humanlike apes;

A hillside Chinese cemetery overlooks Kota Kinabalu. The Borneo-China connection has been strong for centuries.

man-eating crocodiles and snakes; merciless pirates. And, of course, Borneo's dreaded headhunters.

Except for the dragon, perhaps, all these tales were true.

As the plane drones on, I try to liven up the seascape below by imagining that the sea isn't there. Ten to 15 millennia ago this was so. And even now, a ship can anchor anywhere in the shallow southern half of the South China Sea. During periods when vast ice caps covering northern Europe, Asia and North America locked up much of the earth's water, sea levels were lowered by as much as 600 feet (180 m). For periods lasting thousands of years the world's continental shelves were exposed as dry land.

The Sunda Shelf off Southeast Asia is the most extensive of all the world's shallow continental edges. Its uplands remain above water as the present islands of Sumatra, Java and Borneo. Its flooded lowlands form the straits between these islands, along with the southern South China Sea. Geologists refer to this vast region as Sundaland.

The South China Sea between Borneo and the mainland of Asia was then a broad, forested valley, drained by a huge "Sunda River," the only Southeast Asian river on the scale of the Amazon or Mississippi. As it passed through the chain of mountains that then connected the Malay Peninsula to the western end of Borneo, the Sunda was joined by extensions of the mighty Kapuas River West of Kalimantan and the Baram River of Sarawak. It emptied into the sea midway between Borneo and the southern tip of Vietnam.

At least 20 times during the 2-million-year Pleistocene ice ages (of which we are still part) this broad "land bridge" connected Borneo's forests to the 100-million-year-old rainforests of Indochina, the Malay Peninsula and the neighboring Sundaland islands. These alternating periods of connection and isolation—along with Borneo's tremendous diversity of habitats, ranging from 13,500-foot (4,100-m) Mount Kinabalu to coastal swamplands (plus the equatorial sun, continuous rainfall, and absence of harsh winter)—have combined to give Borneo a unique flora and fauna that is impressively diverse. Perhaps one in every 20 of earth's plant species lives on this single island, as well as one in every 25 terrestrial animal species.

Tropical rainforests, mangrove forests and coral reefs are the earth's three most productive habitats. Borneo's coastal mangrove forests are more floristically rich than anywhere else in the tropics. Its fringing reefs are at the evolutionary center of the ocean's most spectacular collection of corals and reef fishes. Its rainforest has been called the grandest and richest on earth.

BORNEO'S ETHNIC DIVERSITY

Borneo's human societies are equally diverse. Anthropologists recognize more than 25 language groups on this single island. Its native peoples, conscious of the finer points of dialect, custom and worldview, consider themselves even more diverse than that, their kinships and loyalties sometimes restricted to a single river valley. But four major groupings are obvious even to an outsider.

The primarily coastal Malays and other Islamic peoples (about 40 percent of the population) range from Sarawak's native Melanau (who have adopted Malay dress and customs) to more recent immigrants from neighboring islands: Kalimantan's Bugis (of Sulawesi descent); Sabah's Bajau (originating centuries ago from the southern Philippines); and 20th-century Javanese and Madurese settlers (some spontaneous migrants, some brought over under Indonesian government transmigration schemes).

Ethnic Chinese (about 20 percent of the population) dominate the commerce of most Bornean towns. Most families originate from the provinces of southeastern China. A majority came during the past century as gold miners, farmers or shopkeepers; their descendants started up most of the island's manufacturing, financial and service industries. As Kuching and Miri, Kota Kinabalu and Sandakan, Pontianak and Banjarmasin have grown into substantial cities over the past decades, bicycle shops have developed into automobile dealerships and bus lines; sons of small-town moneychangers now manage large branches of Hong Kong–based banks; and Chinese timber merchants now control huge logging operations.

At the other end of the economic spectrum are the Penan and Punan: settled or seminomadic forest-dwellers inhabiting the upper watersheds of the dwindling rainforest. They harvest wild sago palm instead of dryland rice, hunt pigs

and deer, and barter forest products such as rattan and wild rubber to Dayak traders.

A typical longboat, now commonly powered by outboard motor, on the Baram River, Sarawak.

The two dozen or so diverse native groups lumped together as "Dayaks" contribute about 40 percent of Borneo's population. Dayaks speak dozens of separate languages or distinct dialects and probably represent many waves of migrants from many parts of Southeast Asia over the past 50,000 years. Yet interior Borneo's extraordinary rainfall, mountainous or swampy terrain, daunting forests and difficult soils have combined to force a certain uniformity of life-style. All the groups practiced (and often still practice) variants of a generalized Dayak culture. Rural Dayaks typically reside in a longhouse—a string of individual "condominiums" strung together under one defensible thatched roof—raised high off the ground on ironwood poles and fronted by a wide communal veranda.

Dayak groups hunt wild pig and deer from the forest; they net and spear fish from the rivers. Borneo's staple crop has long been dryland rice *padi*, grown on shifting, slash-and-burn forest plots, though Sarawak's upland Kelabit irrigate their rice plots and use domesticated water buffalo. In earlier times, wild sago provided carbohydrate (and still may in hard times). Taro, cassava, sweet potato, tapioca and maize were the main cultivated vegetables. Fruits include cultivated durian, papaya, bananas and rambutan, along with a dozen seasonal wild fruits such as langsat and longan. For sweets there is wild honey and cultivated sugarcane. Cash crops include cultivated pepper, rubber and coffee, along with wild illipe nuts, cinnamon-bark and damar resin.

For transport, most Dayak groups are masters of narrow, shallow-draft longboats, now powered mostly by outboard engines through deep water but still paddled, poled and pushed along the shallows. For crafts, Dayaks developed ingenious uses of bamboo, rattan and palms; gained various degrees of

A Kayan musician plays the traditional sape *while his wife dances.*

expertise with wood and beadwork; and were masters of forged iron, used for parangs (slender, curved machetes) and spear points.

Arts center around the two- to four-stringed, mandolinlike *sape* and bronze gongs; a slow, meditative dance emphasizing balance but punctuated by abandoned leaps and shouts; intricate motifs of jungle animals and the many-tendriled tree of life; decorative hornbill feathers, carved deerhorn and hornbill ornaments; cloaks and hats from the patterned skin of the Clouded leopard. And before the coming of Rajah James Brooke, or the later corps of Christian evangelicals, there were bird omens, elaborate funeral celebrations, ritualized headhunting and plenty of potent rice wine.

I met one day in Kuching a man with a doctorate in headhunting—more precisely, the philosophy of headhunting. Julian Davison, a British anthropologist, has spent the past few years unraveling the religious basis of Iban headhunting (rather than the practical effect, which was to intimidate neighboring groups into welcoming the Iban into their valleys to clear new ricefields). We discussed his and others' theories over perhaps too many beers in a noisy open-air Chinese restaurant, and so I cannot repeat them verbatim. Nor would that be fair in advance of the book that he decided that night to write.

The gist of it is that the original grain of rice was stolen from the bird-god by a hero who secreted it under his foreskin. Men still plant the seed after poking a hole in the ground, and it is still nurtured, like an embryo, by the women who cultivate the fields. A severed head, like the original rice grain, was acquired by manly daring. It refreshed the vitality and fertility of the longhouse that acquired it—to the detriment of the community that lost it. And if the successful warrior was a potential groom, acquiring a head proved his virility, courage and skills, as preparation for planting his own human seed. As Tom Harrisson points out in his *World Within*, slicing off a head in a surprise attack on a bathing villager is not that difficult a task, but getting back home alive with it definitely is.

If the head had been taken for a funeral rite, it (or many heads if the deceased was powerful) compensated for the longhouse's loss and jeered in the face of ever-imminent death. There is more to the tale; it is full of sex and blood and heroics and tragedy—perfect to spice up a life of hard farming—but we will just have to wait for Mr. Davison's book.

Dayak communities have managed to adapt first to British or Dutch colonial rule, then to Christian missionaries, and finally to modern Islamic Malaysia or Indonesia—often within a single lifetime. There are Kelabit doctors whose fathers were headhunters, Iban lawyers and senators from isolated jungle longhouses, and Kadazan and Ngaju chief ministers, along with inland villagers whose lives, despite airplane flights and Walkmans, follow the same agricultural rhythms as centuries before: felling and clearing secondary jungle or virgin rainforest from April to early June; burning the dead trees and brush during the dry season in July and August; planting many varieties of rice by hand soon thereafter; weeding the ricefields from mid- September to early December; driving off the "ricebirds" (Munias), deer, pigs and other pests; harvesting the rice from late December to early February.

At least a dozen Dayak groups still flourish, including the aggressive, democratic Iban—called "Sea Dayaks" by the first Europeans, who encountered those who had reached Sarawak's lower rivers and paddled their formidable longboats along the coast of the South China Sea. Perhaps originally from Sumatra, Iban settlers had during the past few centuries pushed eastward up West Kalimantan's Kapuas River and down the river valleys of Sarawak to become Borneo's largest ethnic group (about 350,000 people in Sarawak plus 50,000 in West Kalimantan).

The Bidayuh, or "Land Dayaks," were gradually pushed from along the rivers into the hills of West Kalimantan and western Sarawak by the advancing Iban. They alone erected special houses to honor and display their captured heads. Now numbering about 150,000, many live in and around Sarawak's capital, Kuching.

The Kenyah and the Kayan (of separate origins but similar culture) had reputations as fierce as the Iban but were far more settled and socially stratified. Consummate artists and artisans, they farm along rivers running from Borneo's central highlands, inhabiting longhouses holding up to hundreds of families. During the period of Iban expansion, Kayan and Kenyah populations moved from the uplands of East Kalimantan down the Baram drainage in Sarawak. They were checked by the punitive Great Kayan Expedition of 1862, consisting of 15,000 Ibans led by Sarawak's second rajah, Charles Brooke. Together, the Kenyah and Kayan now number about 80,000.

The remarkable Kelabit inhabit the "Kelabit Uplands," the isolated Plain of Bah behind the Tama Abu Range along the Sarawak–East Kalimantan border. Unknown to Europeans prior to 1945, they alone among Dayaks developed irrigated rice from dryland varieties and domesticated the water buffalo. Though one of the smallest of the Dayak groups (numbering fewer than 5,000), the Kelabit remain one of the most successful; many now live and work in the Miri area on the coast just west of Brunei. Their scattered relatives, the Lun Bawang (numbering about 40,000, mostly in upland East Kalimantan), are also called Muruts, but this confuses them with the unrelated Muruts who inhabit the mountainous region across the border in southern Sabah.

The adaptable Kadazan (Duzan) are Sabah's largest Dayak group (about 25,000), and now dominate its political system as well. The Ngaju occupy Central Kalimantan's formidable swamp forests and have become that state's most powerful political force.

Along with these are a host of more localized Dayak groups: Lun Dayeh, Maloh, Desa, Taman, Tebidah, Kantu, Limbai, Modong, Tunjung, Ma'anyan and Lawangan.

Magdalene Ping Nilong, a young Kenyah woman in traditional garb. Her earlobes have been stretched with weights since childhood, a practice now dying out among young Dayaks.

THE ENGLISH CONNECTION: JAMES BROOKE AND ALFRED WALLACE

Into this polyglot of peoples sailed, in 1839, one James Brooke, a young Englishman with a yen for adventure and money enough to support his own well-armed sloop. The British had by then established the "Straits Settlements"—Penang, Malacca and Singapore—on the Malay Peninsula's west coast. But there was no British presence in Borneo (nor, though they theoretically controlled Kalimantan, much Dutch influence in southern Borneo beyond desultory tribute from the sultans of coastal Banjarmasin and Samarinda).

Brooke was the right man in the right place at the right time. The Brunei Sultanate during its height in the 15th and 16th centuries had controlled coastal Borneo (whose very name is derived from Brunei), as well as the entire coastal region from Sumatra to the Philippines; its wealth had dazzled early Portuguese chroniclers. But following a century of feeble rulers and venal courtiers, the kingdom barely functioned. It lacked the power to protect and tax trade or to exact tribute from nearby states. It had, in short, lost both its sources of revenue and its claim to empire.

Brooke was offered a deal he couldn't refuse: For a moderate annual fee (a bird in hand compared to the uncollectible ones out in the headhunter- and pirate-infested bush), the Englishman was granted a goodly portion of what is now western Sarawak. The only hitch was that he had first to make peace between the warring Dayak tribes. To conduct local trade, he next had to break up the unholy alliance between local Malay pirates and Ibans (booty for the Malays, heads for the Ibans). Finally, to restore commerce with the outside world, he had to destroy the feared Sulu pirates who preyed so successfully on larger merchant ships.

Brooke sailed up the Sarawak River to found his capital, Kuching. By using skillful diplomacy and Borneo's only modern warship, he managed within two years to pacify the area and subdue the pirates. Later, in 1857, he barely

A Melanau man, member of a coastal Dayak group which long ago adopted Malay customs and the Islamic religion.

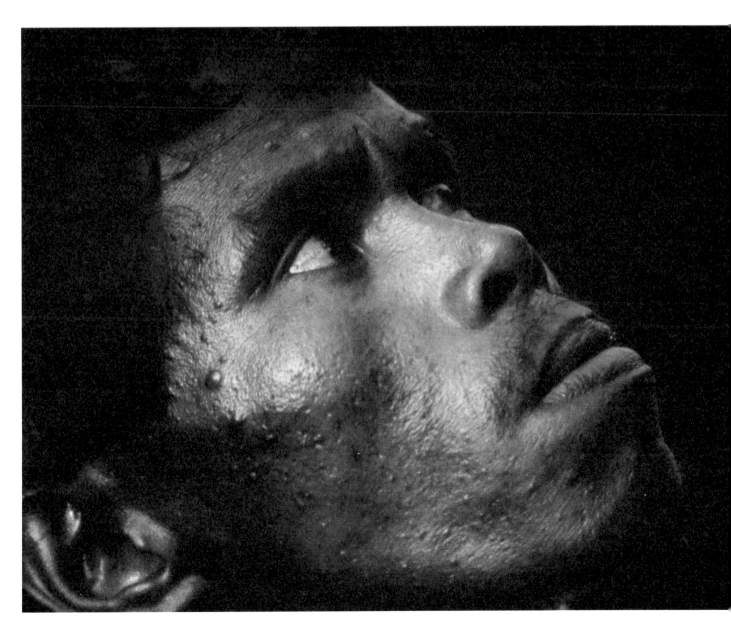

survived an armed rebellion by Chinese gold miners who had settled the Bau district upriver from Kuching. Brooke was now hailed as the "White Rajah" of Sarawak. (As indication that this accomplishment took more than simple firepower is the tale of adventurer Erskine Murray. In 1843, seeking to emulate Brooke, Murray sailed a two-brig British task force up the Mahakam River in East Kalimantan to intimidate the Sultan of Kutai. But Murray misread the local politics. The Bugis remained loyal to the sultan and overpowered Murray's ships, rewarding his ambitions with an ignominious death.)

Brooke eliminated the largest source of intertribal friction by banning the practice of headhunting. For all Dayak groups other than the Iban, this loss of cultural freedom was well compensated by relief from the daily anxieties engendered by the Iban ritual need for innumerable heads for funerals, weddings and other public ceremonies. Aside from this singular custom, Brooke admired Dayak culture and worked hard to protect the *ulu* (upriver, or interior) tribes from outsiders. To keep Iban war parties from paddling downriver to the coast, or the agents of the Malay sultans (whom he believed exploited the Dayaks) from traveling upriver, he built a series of forts at the upriver end of the tidal reaches of Sarawak's major rivers, and these eventually became its principal cities. The forts also allowed Brooke to control the Chinese-dominated inland trade. For the traders, increased personal security and safer commerce were well worth the taxes.

The Brooke system proved so successful that he soon was able to enlarge his domain, piece by piece and treaty by treaty, until the Brooke Raj had swallowed up all but a small bit of Brunei.

Near the end of his life Brooke tried, without success, to get Britain to accept Sarawak as a colony. (The island of Labuan, just off Brunei Bay, had been ceded by the Sultan of Brunei directly to the British in 1847; the British North Borneo Company had effectively taken control of Sabah by 1877.) Sarawak was eventually adopted as a British "protectorate" in 1888 but continued under his descendants, Charles Brooke and Charles Vyner Brooke, as a family fiefdom until the Japanese invasion during World War II.

By the early years of the 20th century, the Dutch—by putting local sultans on their payroll, by veiled threats, and by eventual successes in long-festering wars—had finally been able to assert their authority from the coastal cities inland: up the Barito River from Banjarmasin in the south, up the Mahakam River from Samarinda on the east, and up the Kapuas River from Pontianak on the west. Kalimantan was now Dutch, if only tenuously; while Sarawak, Brunei and North Borneo (Sabah) were de facto British colonies.

During his reign, Sir James Brooke encouraged European naturalists to visit Sarawak. For two of these visitors, Sarawak marked the beginning of illustrious careers. Both men were energetic travelers, keen observers, tireless collectors and scientists of great insight. And both wrote classic accounts of their travels.

Odoardo Beccari arrived in Borneo in 1865 as a promising young botanist. He returned to Italy three years later as a renowned scientist with a hard-won collection of thousands of previously undescribed plants and a profound grasp of rainforest ecology. Beccari's 1904 classic, *Wanderings in the Great Forests of Borneo*, recounts his work and adventures with the perspective of almost 40 years but no loss of enthusiasm for the island.

"The Bornean forest," he wrote, "is so varied and so different at different hours and seasons that no description can possibly convey of it to those who have not known it. Infinite and ever changing are its aspects,

Dawn in the primary rainforest.

as are the treasures it hides. Its beauties are as inexhaustible as the variety of its productions . . . The more one wanders in it the greater grows the sense of profound admiration before Nature in one of its grandest aspects. The more one endeavors to study it, the more one finds in it to study."

An earlier guest of Rajah Brooke's was a young British naturalist, Alfred Russel Wallace, whose eight-year journey through the Malay Archipelago proved as fruitful and important as Darwin's voyage on the *Beagle* a decade earlier. And with the same effect. While at Brooke's estate in Sarawak in February 1855, Wallace wrote an important (but at the time largely unnoticed) paper, "On the Law Which Has Regulated the Introduction of New Species." In it he stated that every species has come into existence "both in space and time with a pre-existing closely-allied species." Three years later, while in the Moluccas, he followed it with the famed "On the Tendency of Varieties to

Depart Indefinitely from the Original Type" in which he explained the principle of natural selection. Wallace thus independently developed the theory of evolution and presented it, together with Darwin's similar paper, on his return to England in 1858.

Like Beccari, Wallace was a prodigious collector. In Sarawak alone, he collected more than 1,500 species of butterflies and 2,000 of beetles, most of them new to science. His 1869 book, *The Malay Archipelago: Land of the Orang-utan and the Bird of Paradise*, is considered the first great travel book on the region and ranks among the 19th century's most important books on natural history.

A full century before the acceptance of the theory of plate tectonics and continental drift, Wallace discovered a clear division between Indo-Malayan and Austro-Malayan regions of the archipelago that we now know to be the result of the colliding, 10 to 15 million years ago, of the Asian and Australian continental plates. He noted that the animals of Sumatra, Java and Borneo were closely allied with those of the Asian mainland but that the animals of the eastern archipelago were almost entirely allied with Australia.

The line between the two regions ran north-south, east of the Philippines, down between Borneo and Sulawesi (and between the much smaller islands of Bali and Lombok). "If we travel from Borneo to [Sulawesi]," he wrote,

> the difference is still more striking. In [Borneo] the forests abound in monkeys of many kinds, wild-cats, deer, civets, and otters, and numerous varieties of squirrels are constantly met with. In the latter none of these occur . . . The birds that are most abundant in the Western Islands are woodpeckers, barbets, trogons, fruit-thrushes, and leaf-thrushes . . . In the Eastern Islands these are absolutely unknown, so that the naturalist feels himself in a new world, and can hardly realize that he has passed from the one region to the other . . . without ever being out of sight of land . . . Borneo and New Guinea, as alike physically as two distinct countries can be, are zoologically wide as the poles asunder.

This line separating the Asian and Australian faunal regions came to be known as Wallace's Line, and earned Wallace the title "Father of Zoogeography."

FROM SARAWAK TO SABAH

Though much of Borneo would still be easily recognized by Wallace and Beccari, their romantic, treacherous sail from Singapore was a far cry from my own quick but uneventful trip by jet. After only an hour of clouds and sea, Cape Datu at the western tip of Borneo comes into view. West of the cape, the coast of West Kalimantan curves southward toward its capital, Pontianak, directly on the equator. Before us the coast of Sarawak runs northeastward for 400 miles toward Brunei and Sabah.

Beneath our flight path along the short stretch of coast between Cape Datu and Kuching lie a series of Sarawak's most important ecological reserves: Sumunsam Wildlife Sanctuary, created to protect Borneo's "Cyrano of the Swamps," the endemic Proboscis monkey; the Talang Talang Islands, where most of Sarawak's sea turtles come to breed; Santubong, on the coast north of Kuching, noted both for its wildlife and as the site for one of the earliest trade centers on Borneo (Indian-type pottery from the first millenium A.D. has been found, along with massive amounts of Chinese pottery and ironware from as early as the eighth-century T'ang Dynasty); and Bako National Park, a small gem containing seven different types of forest habitat.

Sandstone cliffs and beach at Bako National Park, Sarawak.

We touch down briefly in Kuching, considered Borneo's most attractive city. Unmarked by the Japanese occupation during World War II, Kuching still hosts most of the colonial monuments of the Brooke era: the Istana (palace), the Court House, Fort Marguarita and Brooke's most important scientific contribution—the Sarawak Museum. Designed by Wallace, the museum is one of Southeast Asia's finest, and, under a series of gifted European curator/naturalists, it flourished from before the turn of the century until just before the Japanese occupation in World War II. After the war it and its well-respected *Sarawak Museum Journal* were revitalized by its most colorful curator, Tom Harrisson.

Harrisson first came to Borneo as the brash undergraduate leader of the Oxford Expedition of 1932. He returned in 1944 by parachuting into the previously unknown Kelabit Uplands with a group of Australian commandos—

his mission: to organize the upland Dayaks to drive out the Japanese from Borneo.

Harrisson's wartime adventures, along with a lively portrait of the Kelabit people, are detailed in his *World Within: A Borneo Story*, upon which was very loosely based the 1989 movie *Farewell to the King*.

Aside from his interests in the Kelabit, and in Bornean birds, sea turtles and cave bats, Harrisson organized the archaeological dig at Niah Cave that was to uncover the earliest human remains in Southeast Asia. He and his second wife, Barbara Harrisson, also started Sarawak's pioneering orangutan rehabilitation program.

Flying from Kuching to Miri, at the northern end of Sarawak our plane crosses the broad mangrove-edged estuaries of the Sadong and Lupar rivers, and the multiple winding branches of the Rajang, whose Amazonian outflow from Sarawak's rainforest belies its moderate length. Pulau Bruit, the largest of the Rajang's deltaic islands, hosts massive flocks of dozens of species of migrating shorebirds (and is presently being considered by the Sarawak state government for recognition as a wildlife sanctuary).

Between these huge tidal inlets, sunlight glitters on blackwater rivers issuing from uninterrupted miles of peat swamp forests that cover one-eighth of Sarawak. Among the coastal mangroves, plumes of smoke rise from charcoal kilns near small clumps of houses perched on stilts, or from land being cleared and burned for expanding villages. The booming timber city of Sibu, center of

The imposing National Mosque, which dominates Brunei's capital, Bandar Seri Begawan, is considered the world's largest.

Sarawak's timber industry, creates the first large hole in the forest. Site of a Brooke fort, the city is strategically located at the junction of the Rajang's two largest tidal outlets.

The presence of civilization here is jarring: smoke rises from a dozen places; patches of cleared forest stretch from here all the way to Bintulu, a hundred miles farther up the coast. Bintulu itself is another boom-town. Under the Bintulu Development Authority it has become the site for a huge new port facility with a liquefied natural gas plant, an ammonia/urea factory, a new airport and deep-water port. Ringing the town are large oil palm plantations directed by the Sarawak Land Development Board.

On the coast near Bintulu, Similajau National Park stretches for miles along the sandy beach. Such beaches, except where they are interrupted by river mouths, extend up along the entire coast to Miri, the tidy Shell Oil–dominated city where the first Bornean oil well was discovered as early as 1904.

The greatest oil fields, though, lie just beyond Miri. Though James Brooke (and the later North Borneo Company of Sabah) dismantled most of Brunei, the last tiny remnant of the empire—now called the Sultanate of Negeri Brunei Darussalam—turned out to be as valuable as the entire region it lost. Oil was discovered in quantity in 1929, and still flows like a rainforest river. The present Sultan of Brunei, considered the world's richest individual, is worth an estimated $30 billion.

Brunei's capital, Bandar Seri Begawan, whose sumptuous palace, huge, ultramodern State Mosque and Brunei Shell buildings are surrounded by a native water village on stilts, expands over the flatlands surrounding Brunei Bay. The city has consumed the nearby jungle (and in the process seems to be silting in the reefs of Brunei Bay). But rivers flowing out of the rainforest to the north still run clear, glinting like gunmetal instead of the usual muddy brown of most Bornean rivers. Sustained by its oil wealth, Brunei can afford to leave its rainforest intact, protecting its rivers from sedimentation and floods.

Crossing Brunei Bay, the plane sets down on the Malaysian Federal Territory of Labuan. Before Malaysian independence, Labuan Island was center of official British colonial presence on Borneo, its main town then called Victoria. Hugh Lowe, the first consul-general on Labuan, figured prominently in the exploration of Sabah's Mount Kinabalu in the late 1850s and in the study of Borneo's natural history in general. The island, formerly part of Sabah, was donated (controversially) to the federal government by a previous chief minister of Sabah and is in the process of becoming an "offshore finance center." Labuan's coral reefs look good from the air as we take off again, but surveys done by marine biologists confirm that the corals have been extensively mined and polluted, perhaps beyond repair.

Continuing northeast into Sabah, we fly over the Klias Peninsula. The Klias area is still fairly wild, as indicated by a recent survey of local Estuarine crocodiles: Populations on the peninsula's Paduas River approach those along the rivers of northern Australia.

Between the coast and the Crocker Range, Borneo's only railway runs from Beaufort toward Sabah's capital, Kota Kinabalu. From Beaufort a track also runs inland, up the winding scenic gorge of the Paduas River to the fertile farmland of Tenom Valley. From the Paduas gorge northward, 540 square miles (140,000 ha) of the Crocker Range have recently been gazetted as a national park, protecting, at least in theory and for the near future, its orchids and monkeys, and its rafflesias—largest and rarest of the world's flowers.

At the north end of the Klias Peninsula, unspoiled Pulau Tiga (Tiga Island) and its surrounding reefs and islets have also been gazetted as a national park, as have the islands of Tunku Abdul Rahman National Park, 30 miles farther up the coast. Tiga is also the site of a research station supported by Sabah Parks and the National University's Kota Kinabalu campus.

A vendor's stall in Sarawak.

Below us, the sea is still flat, though by afternoon the offshore winds will have whipped up a stiff chop. We are now six degrees north of the equator—the same latitude as northern peninsular Malaysia and of the southernmost islands of the Philippines—but still south of the zone of furious typhoons that annually wrack the northern Philippines and neighboring portions of the South China Sea. This freedom from tropical storms, appreciated first by sailors and now by tourist bureaus, has given Sabah the sobriquet "Land Below the Wind."

As we approach the airport at Kota Kinabalu, Malay water villages sprawl on rickety stilts over the mudflats, alongside the geometric splendor of the Tanjung Aru Beach Hotel. Beyond the lines of light surf, circular patches of reef lead out to Tunku Abdul Rahman's forested islands. From the air, the islands' fringing reefs are just dark shadows in the clear, aquamarine water—barely hinting at the fantasy world of sculpted corals and technicolor fishes just below the surface.

Gaya, largest of the nearshore islands, is a miniature model of Borneo. Its inland hills are still hidden under a rough carpet of broad-leaved evergreen trees—a forest typical of the one that once stretched unbroken across Sabah.

The eastern end of the island, facing Kota Kinabalu, however, is now covered by a dense jumble of shacks on stilts. The sprawling water village is home to an unknown number of Islamic refugees, legal and otherwise, from a generation of bloody warfare in the southern Philippines. Its inhabitants cling to the economic fringes of an otherwise prosperous Sabah, making do as best they can: fishing the reefs, ferrying into the city to sell wild fruits and cigarettes in makeshift booths along the streets across from the Pasar Beser ("Big Market") and working as domestics in city hotels and suburban homes.

Kota Kinabalu greets us with a contrasting mix of the not-quite-old and the very new. Called Jesselton before being captured by the Japanese during World War II, and subsequently leveled by Allied bombers, "KK" is experiencing a second rebirth. The dusty Filipino market and crowded blocks of postwar concrete shops of Chinese and Malay merchants snuggle against the imposing

Kampong *(village) in northern Borneo.*

Hyatt International Hotel. At the expanding southern edge of the city, glassy modern high-rise shopping complexes (the latest heralded as "the largest in Southeast Asia") compete for upscale dollars. But despite the inroads of multistory, air-conditioned malls, KK's outdoor "night market" still prospers, and on Sundays one of its main streets, closed to traffic, assumes the carnival air of an outdoor bazaar.

KK is also typical of Borneo's other booming cities in its environmental effects: open sewers leading to polluted beaches; clouds of dust and diesel from the streets; deafening noise from construction, heavy traffic and heavy metal music. Its population swells faster than the construction, as droves of rural kampong dwellers, especially the young, are drawn by the city's schools and college, jobs, malls, movie houses and discos. Typical, too, is the city's aggressive consumption of forest and wetland as it spreads out over the countryside. Clusters of suburban shop-complexes are surrounded by small factories and by tracts of handsome tile-roofed houses interspersed with rusted tin roofs of humbler homes, around which sprout neat green gardens and groves of banana and coconut trees.

Beyond the suburbs and outlying kampongs, dirt roads lead to blocks of freshly burnt-over *padi* (rice) fields carved from the secondary forest along the riverbanks. Mountainous western Sabah has neither the flat land nor deep soils of eastern Sabah, and so has been spared large-scale agricultural schemes. There is relatively little forestry either, since much of the potential forest land of western Sabah has long been cleared by Kadazan smallholders for rice and for cash crops such as rubber and coconuts. The mountains of south-central Sabah hold the state's last virgin forests. Within a few years the remnants will either be preserved or felled.

Heading eastward across Sabah toward the coastal city of Sandakan, the tin roofs become sparser. Only along the narrow cross-Sabah road are the effects of slash-and-burn agriculture noticeable as scars of red erosion on the steeper slopes.

On a map, Borneo vaguely resembles a fat little dog, standing on its hind legs. Sabah is its head, with two tiny ears at the top separated by Marudu Bay. Sandakan is its eye; the Dent Peninsula, at Sabah's easternmost tip, its snout; and Darvel Bay its barking mouth. We are crossing at eye level, just below Borneo's tallest patch of mountains. To the north, the jagged peaks of 13,500-foot (4,100-m) Mount Kinabalu, highest mountain in Southeast Asia and site of Sabah's world-class Kinabalu National Park; to the south, 8,700-foot (2,640-m) Trus Madi, south of which a spine of forested, river-sculpted peaks and plateaus lead down to Borneo's mountainous center.

The hills subside and we are soon flying above a wide band of flat coastal plains fronting the Sulu Sea. Like those covering the entire southwestern portion of Borneo, the extensive swamp forests are edged by thick swaths of mangroves and dissected by meandering tidal estuaries.

Passing over Sepilok Wildlife Reserve, containing Sabah's showcase orangutan rehabilitation center, we descend to Sandakan.

Long before it was capital of the prewar British colony of North Borneo, Sandakan was a thriving trade center run by Chinese merchants. Archaeologists have found remains of trade goods dating back to the ninth century. More recently, the city was a booming export center for timber and cocoa; but as the timber runs out and cocoa prices slide on the world market, Sandakan has lost its boom image, and a fast-growing population of impoverished refugees from the Philippines and Kalimantan have swelled its seaside neighborhoods. Despite this, Sandakan's prosperous middle-class housing, its variety of excellent Chinese restaurants, and its new mosque and impressive new Chinese temple on a hill overlooking the city give the town an air of solidity that Kota Kinabalu lacks. From KK, seat of state power and facing the Asian mainland, Sandakan

Oil palm fruits being hauled to the processing plant. Palm oil plantations have replaced large tracts of rainforest in eastern Sabah and elsewhere.

seems provincial, but from here Sandakan remains the center of the universe, and KK a rather crass upstart.

Flying south from Sandakan toward Tawau on the east Kalimantan border, the plane crosses Sabah's two major rivers—the Kinabatangan and the Segama. The Kinabatangan snakes across a vast coastal plain. On both sides the coastal forest is being mowed down for palm oil plantations in huge, neat rectangles 10 miles (16 k) or more on a side. The flat lowlands of eastern Sabah, between the hills and the coastal swamp forests, have been the focus of most of the state's agricultural schemes. Oil palm plantations began here about 1960, planted by Unilever and other large corporations. By 1970, when Sarawak was just beginning its palm oil plantations, Sabah already had 140 square miles (36,000 ha) under cultivation; this had more than doubled by 1980, and shows no signs of abating. As prices have dropped on rubber and cocoa, they, too, are being replaced by oil palms.

Beyond the plantations, the land becomes steeper again among the Banjaran Brassey hills, where the logging roads and partial cuts assume a less geometric mode. Along the Segama River, within the huge timber concession of the state-run Sabah Foundation, a large patch of unlogged forest—the Danum Valley Conservation Area, one of the last remaining protected areas in eastern Sabah.

It was here, in the late 1960s, before there was a field station and before logging had penetrated this far upriver, that the young British zoologist John MacKinnon carried out his pioneering study of wild orangutans. His book *In Search of the Red Ape* gives a vivid description not only of the orangutan but of rainforest life just a generation ago. MacKinnon later studied the Sumatran orangutan and Malayan gibbons; he now designs primate conservation programs for the World Wildlife Fund in conjunction with Southeast Asian governments. Kathy MacKinnon, John's wife and partner on the primate studies (aside from her own doctoral work on Malaysian squirrels), has worked extensively on conservation projects in Kalimantan.

As the land flattens to dense cocoa, coconut and palm oil plantations, we descend to the tiny airfield at Tawau, near Sabah's border with East Kalimantan.

Today's Borneo is not the Borneo of Wallace or Beccari. Former headhunters travel by scheduled airplane down to their retirement homes in the city. Their grandchildren, educated in government boarding schools, compete for space in the best universities, recreate in discos and video parlors, and collect

Langsats (tan, on left) and mangosteens (opened, in center) are two of the many tasty Bornean rainforest fruits available in local markets.

cassettes of the latest American and European pop singers. The forests have shrunk, and rivers now run brown.

Yet behind the mystique, and the obvious recent environmental damage, remain large patches of "Nature in its grandest aspect"—a Southeast Asian rainforest that ranks with the Amazon Basin as the world's richest terrestrial habitats. These natural areas are comparable in size to American national parks and wildlife refuges—seemingly larger because of their lush vegetation and overwhelming diversity—and they are huge compared with natural areas remaining in Europe. Despite the logging, urbanization and agricultural schemes, Borneo still offers naturalists and curious visitors a window on ancient ecosystems that are awesome in scale and complex beyond comprehension.

Borneo's treasures can be truly experienced only at ground level—trekking the forest, exploring its caves, climbing above the clouds, wrestling a longboat through a shallow rapid or wading in the estuarine mud. My own explorations began on the very edge of Borneo.

THE COAST OF BORNEO

Measured roughly, Borneo's coastline is approximately 4,000 miles (7,000 km); if traced with a finer pen, following each estuarine indentation, it would be much, much longer. Islands merge with peninsulas; reefs merge with sandy beach and muddy beach with mangrove forests. Broad beaches stretch out toward the receding surf for half a mile, making it possible at low tide to wade out to forested, reef-fringed islands. Saltwater tidal bores sweep up meandering rivers; coastal dolphins and estuarine mangroves penetrate into the heart of Borneo. It is often difficult to tell where the sea ends and Borneo begins.

At the very edge of the land and just below the surface of the sea lie one of Borneo's most complex habitats, and certainly its most colorful—the shallow fringing reef. On Gaya Island's rocky shore I don mask, snorkel fins, tennis shoes and a thin lycra body suit—less for insulation than for protection from the sun, the sharp coral and the occasional stinging jellyfish—and slide into the clear equatorial sea. Shafts of sunlight refracted by the undulating surface dance over the sandy seabed, seeming to come from every direction at once.

Striped blennies rest sluggishly on their pectoral fins, camouflaged against the colorful encrusting algae covering the rocks and the dead coral washed in by winter storms. Sea cucumbers—once a valuable trade item (*trepang*) and still served as a delicacy in Chinese restaurants—vacuum the sand with sticky tentacles surrounding their mouths, cleaning the seafloor of diatoms and organic waste. A few kicks of my fins whisk me past the rubble, and soon I'm floating above the living coral gardens—a world of incredible shapes and kaleidoscopic color.

Visually, there are few waking experiences with which to compare a coral reef. Perhaps the nearest analogy would be to imagine hang-gliding low over a flowering tropical rainforest above which flocks of hornbills, parrots and sunbirds rise and settle. Yet that would slight the reef. It would take incredibly large mixed flocks of birds to match the schools of fish drifting through the coral. Unlike the green forest canopy, corals take on an infinite variety of shapes and colors: from branching staghorns to huge, spiny plates; round, convoluted brain-shaped boulders to feathery fingers of crimson fire.

REEF CORALS

Borneo is in the very center of the world's richest diversity of coral types, boasting perhaps 300 species in 70 genera. Looking down at an area just a few body lengths in diameter I can easily count two dozen types.

Opposite:
Sandstone beach and wind-sculptured cliffs along the South China Sea at Bako National Park Sarawak.

Staghorn corals dominate large patches of reef. They range in form from branching, bumpy horns to massive plates covered with tall protuberances. Staghorns provide a forestlike structure that shelters innumerable small fishes. The related, platelike cabbage corals and rose corals, with their beautiful vertical "flowers," are fast-growing and help rejuvenate damaged reefs.

The fissured brain corals, though, may take centuries to form massive heads that can measure 6 feet to more than 30 feet (2–10 m) across. The heads provide a solid substrate for dozens of species of colorful sponges, encrusting algae and "soft" corals such as the red Organ pipe and blue *Helipora*. Fanworms, their multicolored spiraling plumes extended outward to filter plankton from the water, zip back into their protective tubes as I approach. A thick, bright-blue mantle covers the wavy lip of a Boring clam (related to the Giant clam of deeper waters), growing embedded in the coral with just enough room to open. Beautiful tubular sponges, which appear motionless, are actively extracting tiny organisms from the stream of water they suck in and expel.

Corals are colonial animals. Yet each tiny coral polyp is a separate animal and begins its life as a single-celled, free-swimming planula. At two weeks—still smaller than a pinhead—it tests potential substrates before settling on the surface of a bare rock or of a coral cleared of older polyps and algae by grazing fishes. After growing to full size, the lone polyp begins to clone itself into thousands of similar polyps, each of which secretes a six- or eight-sided framework from its outer layer. If it is a species of stony, or "true," coral, it secretes limestone (calcium carbonate) from the seawater to harden its six-sided skeleton. Soft corals (octocorals) are reinforced not by limestone but by internal sclerites similar to those that stiffen sponges. Fan and whip corals have a second skeleton of hard but flexible material called gorgonin.

Staghorn coral dominates fringing reefs.

It is the stony corals that create the reef structure. A honeycomb of polyps gradually covers the old coral skeleton, adding another layer to the surface, in characteristic patterns of stars or ridges or bumps. Though each polyp can feed and spawn on its own, each is connected to its neighbors by strands of jelly-like tissue extending through minute holes between the enclosing skeletons.

Although corals look static from our viewpoint, they are actually highly dynamic. Time-lapse film footage of two corals that have grown too close together shows the more aggressive species (in this case a slow-growing brain coral) sending out specialized poison tentacles to attack a neighboring star coral. Over the course of two or three days, the brain coral kills the defenseless polyps on the adjacent portion of the star coral, preventing its competitor from growing closer, and thus giving the brain coral more room to expand.

Each polyp mouth—like that of the related anemones and jellyfishes—is ringed with tentacles containing tiny stinging organs called nematocysts. With these tentacles the coral polyp actively captures microscopic plankton (tiny animals such as copepods and larvaceans, and the spawn of fish and shellfish). Most corals feed at night, while polyp-nipping fishes sleep. When extended to feed, the tiny polyps appear like brightly colored flowers, but they, like their jellyfish relatives, are basically colorless. The varied colors of the coral garden are provided by photosynthetic algae—called zooxanthellae—living symbiotically within the polyps.

The microscopic zooxanthellae make up in numbers what they lack in size: There may be 9 million per square inch (1.5 million/sq cm) of coral surface. The algae produce nitrogen, sugars and oxygen during day; at night, they thrive on the coral's waste carbon dioxide and nitrogen. The added nutrients—and perhaps more importantly the extra oxygen—provided by the zooxanthellae are critical to the polyp's growth. In turn, the algae depend on the corals for living space and protection. It is a classic case of mutualism. The importance of the zooxanthellae, as well as their contribution to the reef's color, becomes

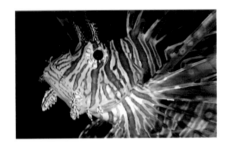

Its striking shape and markings advertise the venomous nature of this lionfish.

This stonefish lies motionless and camouflaged on coral, waiting for prey. If disturbed, it erects a poisonous dorsal spine to pierce the hand or foot of an unwary reef explorer.

obvious when corals expel them due to a rise in water temperatures or pollution. The bleached corals are unable to grow and may even die.

Tropical seas are so strikingly translucent because they are low in nutrients and dissolved oxygen, and thus low in plankton. It is the zooxanthellae, along with the coraline algae, which form crusts on boulders and rubble, that make the coral reef a highly productive habitat (rivaling the tropical rainforest) in an otherwise rather barren tropical sea.

Because of their algal partners, reef-building corals are limited to tropical seas. Outside the tropics, seawater is both too cold and too turbid. When the temperature drops below 73°F (23°C), few reef-building coral thrive; below 68°F (20°C) none survive. In murky, plankton-rich waters, the zooxanthellae can no longer convert minerals to sugars and proteins, or carbon dioxide to oxygen. This need for sunlight limits living corals to the top 150 feet (40 m) in even the clearest tropical seas and restricts them from areas silted by the outflow of turbid rainforest rivers. Beccari wrote of Sarawak: "It is notable that all along the coast, from Cape Datu to Brunei, there are no coral banks, so frequent elsewhere in Malaysia." Wherever large rivers and swampy coastal swamps are absent, though—as along Sabah's coasts—reefs are spectacularly rich.

DENIZENS OF THE REEF

Snorkeling the shallow reef is like swimming in a giant aquarium. The sheer diversity and incredible coloration of the fishes is boggling. Aggregations of coral fishes (also called butterfly fishes and angelfishes) swim over and through the coral plates and staghorn branches. Most of them take tiny worms and crustaceans or nip off the soft coral polyps as they extend to feed.

Two strikingly beautiful coral fishes are highly adapted for picking out tiny crustaceans coral crevices: the bright yellow, black and silver Long-snouted, or Forceps, butterfly fish, and the squarer, orange-and-white (to greatly simplify the pattern) Beaked butterfly fish. Another species, the spectacular Pennant coral fish, with its bright yellow fins, broad curving black stripes on a white body and an elongated curved pennant of a dorsal fin, is known as "the poor-man's Moorish idol."

The real Moorish idol, mascot of Sabah's marine parks, also hovers over the reef, too shy to be approached. It resembles a coral fish, but the beautiful idol is placed in a family of its own. Found throughout the Pacific and Indian oceans, from the Red Sea to Mexico, it is one of the world's best-known reef fish—and one of the most popular saltwater aquarium fishes. According to my field guide (Carcasson's *Coral Reef Fishes of the Indian and West Pacific Oceans*), the Moorish idol is "regarded as an object of considerable reverence by some Moslem populations." Its body color is alternately velvet black, pure white and bright yellow, with a patch of scarlet at the base of its slender snout. Topping it all off is a long body-length trailing extension to its already vertically elongated dorsal fin. It swims equally well in all directions, keeping its distance with a dreamy motion.

Here and there among the corals are giant anemones, deceptively flowerlike animals related to corals. Their long, fingerlike tentacles also have microscopic stinging cells, which feel merely prickly to us but are deadly to any small fish wandering into them. There is one notable exception, however—a small pugnacious fish that darts up at me and then retreats among the tentacles. When I dive down for a closer look, the cheeky red-orange fish comes right up to my mask with a fearless stare before retreating again. Nestled inside the

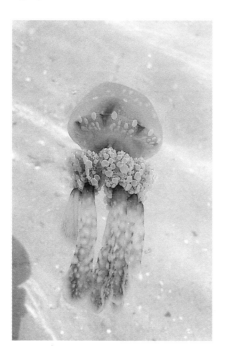

Ornate Mastigias *jellyfishes are found throughout the South Pacific. They feed on plankton but also harbor the same symbiotic algae found in corals.*

waving field of finger-like tentacles is a smaller one. Both are anemone fish, or clown fish, the larger probably being a female, the smaller one her mate.

Clown fishes are unique in that they have adapted to live among the sea anemone's stinging tentacles, covering themselves with the same mucous secreted by the anemone to inhibit it from stinging itself. With this refuge, deadly to other small fishes, clown fish can afford to act so bravely. They even lay their eggs among the anemone's wavy tentacles. In return, scraps from the fish's meals fall into the anemone, providing it with food; in the aquarium, clown fish have even been seen "feeding" their anemone partners. Popular with aquarists, they are among the few marine fishes that have been bred in captivity.

Passing slowly and deliberately but always unwilling to let me follow very closely are some of the largest and most colorful of reef fishes—the spectacular parrot fishes—arrayed in the most striking patterns, with color combinations encompassing an entire rainbow. Their mouths are small but the teeth are thick and horny, forming a parrotlike beak for crushing mollusk shells, grazing on encrusting algae or even nipping out chunks of coral to get at the polyps inside. One large individual swimming away from me trails a cloud of fine sand, the crushed remains of coral skeleton. By this process, in fact, parrot fishes create much of the reef's sand.

The closely related wrasses—whose larger members look like parrot fish without the prominent "lips"—have teeth that are partly adapted for crushing mollusks but are also used for nipping softer algae. Both wrasses and parrot

A Tomato clown fish and its refuge, an anemone. This cheeky fish often rises to challenge a snorkeler many times its size.

fishes sleep at night in coral crevices or buried in sand or wrapped in seaweed. The parrot fish, in addition, secretes a loose "sleeping bag" of mucous that is thought to protect it from nocturnal moray eels, which hunt mainly by smell.

Fierce-looking morays zip out of crevices to grab passing fishes with a snap of their pointed jaws. Most species are rather retiring, but the field guide cautions: "Large eels are dangerous and may attack without provocation; divers should be careful not to poke their hands into blind crevices and holes." Okay. There are more than two dozen moray species in this region, mostly dark green to gray, some striped, some patterned with variously shaped spots. They are generally nocturnal, but I have seen them slithering along outside their holes during the day. The commonest medium-sized morays grow a yard or so long, but one species, in Kalimantan called the Poma, can reach 10 feet (3 m).

SEA TURTLES

One day on a scuba dive off Sabah, far below the surface of the Sulawesi Sea, I met a Green sea turtle napping in a coral cavern. I turned clumsily in my scuba gear, drifting too close. She—for it was a gravid (egg-bearing) female—opened one rather pretty, heavy-lidded eye and slid from the cave, pushing off from the cliff with her short rear flippers. A few slow, powerful strokes of her long flagstone-patterned foreflippers and she faded like a ghost into the green shafts of sunlight.

I felt elated to have stumbled across this magnificent turtle and the opportunity to see her underwater, at her graceful best. But at the same time I felt a bit guilty for disturbing her. She may just have navigated a thousand miles back to this tiny island, having left it more than 30 years before, and knowing it only for the brief time it took to scramble down the sandy beach immediately after her hatching.

This particular turtle was one in a thousand. Aside from the amazing feat of navigation, the prodigious swim and her tenacious desire to return, she had survived predaceous seabirds and fishes eager to snack on turtle babies; sharks who chomp off flippers of adult turtles; the fishermen who hook sea turtles for their tasty meat and valuable oil, or inadvertently drown them in nearshore shrimp nets; or, even worse, the 40-mile-long "curtain of death" drift nets set each night on the open Pacific. She would be one of the dozen turtles who would haul her 200-300-pound (90-140-kg) body laboriously out of the sea that evening to lay her hundred or so soft, leathery eggs in the upper beach above high tide.

The Green turtle's shell or carapace is not actually green—that is the color of its fat—but olive-brown, with sun-rayed patterns on the 13 large polygonal scutes. Its head and flippers show a rock-wall pattern of dark leathery scales separated by light connecting tissue. Its diet is mostly vegetarian: sea grasses and algae with a bit of sponge on the side.

Early in this century, Sarawak Museum curator Robert Shelford found the Green turtle "very abundant in seas around Borneo." Its numbers have decreased alarmingly during the past decades: annual nestings off Sarawak have dropped from an average of 13,000 to about 2,000 over the past three decades. But it still breeds every month in Sarawak, primarily on the Talang Talang Islands near Cape Datu and West Kalimantan's Natuna Archipelago, which stretches northward from Cape Datu into the South China Sea. In Sabah, a few Greens come to the Tunku Abdul Rahman islands and to Tiga Island farther south, but the main breeding areas are the sandy Turtle Islands National

Park and neighboring Philippine islands in the Sulu Sea north of Sandakan and at tiny Sipadan Island near the East Kalimantan border.

Hawksbill sea turtles also breed in Sabah and Sarawak in small numbers. Unfortunately for the species its "tortoiseshell" is highly valued for jewelry, especially by the Japanese (who have just now agreed to end imports). Intensively harvested, Hawksbill populations have plummeted locally and worldwide. The equally endangered Olive ridley, smallest of the marine turtles at about 2 feet (60-65 cm) in length and 80 pounds (35–40 kg) is harvested for its meat and leather. It feeds on shrimps and jellyfishes (and the deadly "false jellyfish," the discarded polyethylene baggie) along with some crabs and snails.

The Leatherback sea turtle, named after its leathery, ridged carapace, is the world's largest turtle, weighing in at up to a ton (900 kg). During nonbreeding season, the Leatherback forages in cold, temperate seas and can dive to depths of 4,000 feet (1,200 m). It also feeds primarily on jellyfishes and so is particularly vulnerable to the exploding populations of plastic bags and other clear plastic trash that collect at the edges of currents (exactly where jellyfish collect) throughout the world's seas. Leatherbacks sighted in Sabah are probably vagrants from the main migration to breeding beaches of Terengganu on the east coast of peninsular Malaysia. There, offshore fishing nets, beach development, egg collecting and overzealous turtle-watching tours have reduced populations from almost 2,000 egg-laying females a year in the mid-1950s to an average of under 100 since the mid-1980s. The Loggerhead sea turtle, once found in southern Borneo, is now nonexistent here.

Thus the Green turtle I encountered represents the future of sea turtles in Borneo; and Borneo's beaches are critical to the future of the Green. If not too badly disturbed on land (especially before she starts to lay), this particular female may return a half-dozen times to this beach, at intervals of eight to 15 days.

A Green sea turtle glides over the staghorn coral of a shallow reef.

A Ghost crab is perfectly camouflaged against the sandy beach as it consumes a dead fish. The round pellets are made by the crabs as they glean the sand for diatoms.

Her life in the sea between departure as a hatchling and return decades later, is virtually unknown. By contrast, her beach sojourn is now famous thanks to wildlife films on television. But it never ceases to inspire: the laborious crawl, the digging of the sand, the rest stops to recover energy, eyes dripping copious tears to wash out the gritty sand (all the while perhaps crowded by tourists or by collectors taking the eggs as they are laid), the slow drag down the beach back to the sea. And then, two months later, the surviving baby turtles, tiny and vulnerable, scrambling down the moonlit beach toward the bright, shark-infested water . . .

SEA SNAKES

Most of Borneo's sandy beaches are found on peninsulas or islands—far enough from the massive sediment loads major rivers carry down from the uplands. The sand beaches often alternate with headlands of resistant rock: Currents sweep the headland clean of sand and deposit it in the sheltered bays behind the points of land. If an island or peninsula is unprotected from strong winds and currents, the sand may be washed away, exposing the underlying bedrock.

These rocky beaches are the hunting grounds for the only common species of the half-dozen heron-type birds seen along Borneo's coastline: the small, ubiquitous Pacific Reef heron. Tom Harrisson mentions one in a delightful description of a visit to Sarawak's Talang Talang Islands while monitoring Green turtle breeding: "On one occasion a shoal of fish were moving in the channel off Talang Talang pursued and plagued by some hundreds of terns. Amongst them, as well as a school of unidentified large dolphins dancing attendance, a Reef heron swooped, stalled, plunged his head, and looked for all the world like a trick-flying helicopter."

Opposite:
The Amphibious sea snake (Yellow-lipped krait) returns to the sea after spending the night under leaf debris along the shore. Sea snakes are extremely poisonous but are not aggressive.

On such rocky islets is found another animal that has broken the land/sea barrier: the Amphibious sea snake (Yellow-lipped sea krait). Sea snakes are well adapted to marine life. The tail is laterally flattened like an oar to scull from side. The upturned nostrils have a valve-like closure to keep out water. And since they do not need tough, overlapping scales for traction or protection on land, the skin is thinned, the better to absorb oxygen; large blood vessels run between the widely spaced scales.

Found only in the tropics, sea snakes make up a rather compact family of about 50 species. Eight are common off the coast of Borneo, though they are rarely met with. Probably a good thing: their venom is among the deadliest known. Containing up to 40 nerve and muscle toxins, it is considered four times deadlier than cobra venom.

Fortunately, sea snake are not aggressive. The estuarine Beaked sea snake, though, will approach swimmers and has been known to climb up anchor lines. Offshore fishermen deal daily with sea snakes tangled in their nets, but generally this is no problem. Most species lack the strong musculature of terrestrial snakes and cannot bend their heads up to bite if you hold them by the tail. Their fangs are tiny and their mouths so small they can only bite the webbing between your fingers. This is little consolation to the occasional fisherman who does manage to get bitten, mostly by the Beaked sea snake. Victims who do not die within three hours usually survive, but can take months to recover.

Tiny Kalampunian Damit Island (in Tiga National Park, 30 miles southwest of Kota Kinabalu) is home to 600 or more Amphibious sea snakes, which slither up onto the rocks during the day to sleep in crevices or in piles of beach litter. Rob Stuebing of the National University in Kota Kinabalu reports that at night during mating season, males "drape themselves over rocks or float at the water's edge then slowly but persistently pursue any passing females. By morning there are piles of entangled snakes—up to 50 males for every two or three females." Though most other sea snakes bear live young that can immediately swim, these lay eggs on land. The adults feed on eels, including young morays. Other sea snake species specialize in fish eggs or fish, especially sea catfish. The snakes, in turn, are preyed on by sharks and seabirds, and their eggs are eaten by rats, mice and monitor lizards.

COASTAL BIRDS

The sea snake's principal avian predator, the beautiful White-bellied sea eagle, nests on Tiga and other coastal islands. B. E. Smythies, author of *The Birds of Borneo*, calls it "one of the world's finest eagles." Its "clanging cry of many notes" is unusually loud for an eagle and can be heard from a long distance as it soars over the coastline searching for sea snakes and cuttlefish. Like most eagles it is not above scavenging on the beach, a habit shared by Borneo's commonest raptor, the Brahminy kite.

Resembling a small eagle, the Brahminy kite, like the larger White-bellied sea eagle, has a white breast; its black-and-white underwing pattern, though, is a reversal of the eagle's. It also scavenges, but it fishes more skillfully—in a manner similar to that cosmopolitan, highly specialized fisher, the Osprey. When fishing, both the Brahminy kite and the Osprey swoop above the water, pausing with legs held rigid, then plunge talon-first into the water; both can seize fish much heavier than themselves. But unlike the similar-sized Osprey, which fishes from an exposed perch over the water, the Brahminy kite soars buoyantly for long periods before plunging.

Opposite:
The attractive Brahminy kite, Borneo's commonest raptor, is a sacred bird to traditional Iban.

The prize for soaring, though, must surely go the frigate birds that visit Borneo during the latter half of the year, especially in September and October. Though the Lesser frigate bird's body is only 32 inches (80 cm) long, the span of its bent, pointed wings is double the body length, allowing it to soar for hours without a wingbeat. So aerial is its design that a frigate bird cannot lift off directly from sea or land, and it rarely perches on trees except awkwardly during breeding season. Snake Island is a favorite roosting place: Smythies reports seeing 200 frigates there at one time—an awe-inspiring sight when a large group of them take up soaring stations at various altitudes, filling the sky with huge, seemingly prehistoric wings.

Frigate birds feed by swooping down to delicately pluck flying fish and squid from the sea surface but their name derives from their habit of robbing boobies and other seabirds on the wing. They act the role of pirate mainly around their breeding areas (the southern Philippines and beyond) when their fast-growing chicks demand extra food. Two local species of boobies, the Brown and the Masked, visit Tiga Island at the same time as the frigates, evidently without being harassed.

Though awkward on land when they breed—thus nicknamed "gooney birds" by American servicemen stationed on Pacific atolls during World War II— boobies (closely related to gannets of temperate seas) are consummate fishers; they dive like sleek missiles, straight down, headfirst onto their prey. The boobies are also common in eastern Sabah's Darvel Bay and at Santubong near Bako National Park.

One type of seaside bird is unexpectedly absent from Borneo's coast. "Those accustomed to the vast numbers of gulls along the coasts of temperate regions," says Smythies, "will be disappointed . . . Of all the 44 species of gull in the world, only one [the Black-headed gull, similar to the temperate Laughing gull] is found on the coast of Borneo, and then only as a rare winter visitor."

Of the gulls' smaller, more buoyant relatives, the terns, only the graceful Black-naped tern is resident and locally common. Small numbers of Bridled terns nest off Sarawak, though, and four other species can be found wintering on the mangrove islands of Brunei Bay. Beccari wrote of the Black-naped terns at Cape Datu: "I shot a few terns, which were abundant here, and found many of their eggs, which were deposited on the bare rock without any attempt at a nest."

At the other extreme of nest building is the strange Megapode. Called the "incubator bird," it is the region's lone representative of a family otherwise found on the other side of the Wallace Line in New Guinea and Australia. In Borneo the Megapode is native only to Sabah, where it inhabits forested islands such as Gaya and Tiga, scratching through litter and rotten wood for worms, grubs, termites, seeds and fruits.

An otherwise undistinguished, partridgelike bird, the Megapode has a unique method of breeding. At the onset of the rainy season (around October), the male constructs a large mound of sand and debris on the beach. In the mound are chambers for the eggs. Instead of brooding the eggs, the parent birds are free to leave them in the nest—the mound insulates them from the midday sun, and fermentation of the nest material keeps them properly warm at night. The nest also hides them from prowling Water monitors.

Monitor lizards are the world's largest lizards—the very largest being the Komodo dragon, a monitor species found on a few Indonesian islands east of Borneo. The Water monitor of Borneo can grow to almost 8 feet (2.5 m) and to 110 pounds (50 kg). Despite its dinosaur looks and muted gray-green color as an adult, one herpetologist writes: "young monitors are among the most attractive of lizards, showing intricate patterns of spots and bands on a skin whose texture resembles fine beadwork."

Opposite:
A Rufous-backed kingfisher, one of the smallest of Borneo's dozen kingfisher species.

The monitor's tongue is snakelike—long, protruding and deeply forked—and like a snake, it possesses a Jacobson organ to "taste" the chemicals it picks up on its tongue. On the other hand, its habit of lashing with its tail ("a propeller when in water and a weapon on land") is croc-like and, like the Estuarine crocodile, the monitor ranges from inland rivers, where it is eaten by the Dayaks, to far out at sea. It is catholic in its carnivorous tastes: insects, fish, crabs, rats, carrion and especially the eggs of ground-nesting birds such as the Megapode.

Unfortunately, except on these few national park islands, nothing protects Megapode eggs from being collected by people for food, and so the bird is elsewhere almost extinct.

The dominant tree on Borneo's sandy beaches, other than the ubiquitous coconut, is *Casuarina equisetifolia*. Found on beaches throughout the Pacific, casuarina is called *rhu laut* locally, "she-oak" in Australia, "ironwood" in Hawaii. Useful as a wind and salt screen, it was spread by early Spanish colonists to Florida and the Caribbean. At first glance the casuarina tree looks like a shaggy conifer but is not. Its grayish green "needles" are thin chlorophyll-bearing twigs that function like leaves and are shed periodically. Helping it survive the infertile sand, its roots support clusters of small nodules filled with symbiotic bacteria that can fix nitrogen from the air. Since its seedlings cannot grow in their parent's shade or among their fallen needles, casuarina thrives only where the beach is widening, offering unlittered open space for the seedlings.

Mornings and towards evening casuarina groves are filled with some of Borneo's prettiest birds. Ruby-cheeked sunbirds hover briefly, like novice hummingbirds, to feed on the pollen. Brightly-colored Fiery minivets (red-and-black males and orange-and-black females) flit through the foliage like tiny flames, while the Velvet-fronted nuthatch busily works its way up and down the trunk. Handsome Golden-backed woodpeckers pick ants off the gray, fissured bark. The small, shimmering Ruddy kingfisher dives down on crabs and insects. The beautiful Blue-throated bee-eater and dour White-breasted wood-swallow hawk insects from the vantage of the casuarina's branches. Now and then, a Brahminy kite swoops down from the sky to pick off a lizard or large green locust.

The graceful coconut palm is found in scattered clumps throughout Borneo's coastline. Like all palms, it cannot widen as it grows, and so the slender trunk depends on a tough, fibrous structure to keep it upright—though in windy situations, the trunk may grow almost level with the ground. Coconuts are not overly resistant to seawater and so cannot float very far. People, in fact, are the most common dispersal agent. As the mainstay of many tropical island cultures, all parts of the nut are useful: the fibrous husk for mats and rope; the dense, woody shell for bowls and medicinal charcoal. The ripe flesh yields milk, the dried flesh (copra) is pressed for cooking oil, and its residue feeds the chickens and pigs. Unripe nuts are filled with one of the world's most refreshing hot-weather drinks.

The coconut trees on the beach attract Copper- and Brown-throated sunbirds, which feed on coconut nectar and on the small insects drawn to the nectar. Although sunbirds visit many flowering trees and shrubs, the coconut is critical because it is almost always in flower. In return, sunbirds and their long-billed relatives, the spider hunters, help pollinate the coconut. Sunbirds "perch on the twigs and stems," writes Smythies, "flitting actively with shrill call-notes from flower to flower and often hovering on rapidly vibrating wings in front of a blossom, but only for a short time. When perched on a branch they have a curious habit, which they share with the spiderhunters, of rhythmically swinging, stretching and contracting their necks and at the same time swaying the body from side to side."

Opposite:
Rocky headland at Bako National Park, Sarawak.

The most conspicuous bird along all of Borneo's beaches, though, is the Collared kingfisher, whose handsome iridescent blue-and-green back and thin, black bill contrast sharply with its bright white breast and neck-collar. While hunting, the White- collared kingfisher acts much like its temperate relatives— sitting hunched over on its perch and diving down to catch prey; but like some other Bornean kingfishers, which are predominantly forest birds, it is often found far from water. Its prey is less apt to be fish than herptiles such as agama lizards, tree frogs and small snakes; or large insects and earthworms.

COASTAL GEOLOGY

Much of Borneo's coastline consists of swampy coastal plains fronted on the sea by impenetrable mangrove forests. Inland, the land's structure is draped in layers of thick vegetation. But here and there its underlying rock formations are exposed—in the limestone mountains of Sarawak's Gunung Mulu National Park, for example, or the sandstone cliffs of Bako.

On the sandy beaches at Bako National Park, just an hour from Kuching, Borneo's rock base reveals itself in the most attractive way possible: The exposed layers of sandstone have been sculpted into free-form sea stacks and archways, sensual boulders, wave-cut terraces and surf-splashed caverns. Framed by spidery pandanus trees, hundred-foot (30-m) cliffs tower above the white beaches like larger-than-art murals: stained ochre by iron, crusted white by sea spray, etched and filigreed by the wind. Globular nests of House swifts cluster under overhangs as clouds of the small, dark aerialists hawk insects for their young. High above the cliff, White-bellied sea eagles glide on the updraft, scanning the calm, green shallows of the South China Sea.

According to geologists, Bako was once a delta at the mouth of a huge river. Sandy sediments washed down from the inland mountains over millions of years were covered for long periods by overlying seas, compressing and cementing the particles into hard, porous sandstone.

As the Australian and Asian tectonic plates collided, deforming Borneo, the coast here was uplifted far above the sea. At various times (such as during the past 5,000 years) relative sea level has been constant for long enough periods for the waves to cut broad, horizontal plateaus or terraces: the ancient one above the cliffs, for example, or the present beach at the base of the cliff. When major storms drive waves against the base of the cliff, sea caves are gouged, and eventually large blocks of the cliff above collapse onto the beach to be slowly reduced to sand again.

The attractive rust and ochre patterns that paint the cliff faces are also formed by water. As rainwater filters down through the porous layers of sandstone it dissolves iron from the mineral particles. When the water oozes out onto the surface of the cliff, the change in environment causes some of the iron to be precipitated out of solution. The oxidized iron turns reddish and mixes with other minerals to form varied colors. These spread along the cliff face to create patterns of colored lines and concentric rings.

With time, layers of iron oxide can form a thick skin or crust that is harder than the sandstone itself and more resistant to erosion. When water breaks through the skin, it quickly eats away the sandstone below, etching honeycomb patterns in the cliff. Ridges are formed by resistant bands of iron oxide. Together, the colored skin and ridges and the honeycomb of circular, tan pits create a visual masterpiece as the setting sun accentuates the cliffs' textures and colors.

KERANGAS FOREST

On the wavecut, sandstone terraces above Bako's beaches and on ancient deposits of beach sand (now sometimes found far inland) is an unusual forest that is more common to Borneo than anywhere else: the kerangas, or heath, forest.

Heath is the British term for flat, open "wasteland" underlain by coarse, sandy soils or peat, with poor drainage. The analogous *kerangas* is an Iban word referring to land incapable of supporting a rice crop. Kerangas ranges from rather tall pole forest through scrub to (under the harshest conditions) a rocky, open formation called "padang," with sparse vegetation rooting only in crevices in the bare rock. Kerangas soils are sandy or clayey, thin and generally poor in nutrients. If thin soils are underlain by flat rock, drainage is poor, yet on deeper sand it can be excessive. Both waterlogging and drought are common problems.

Ant plant tubers contain smooth-walled chambers, in which ants raise their broods; they eat and excrete in the rough-walled chambers, from which the plant extracts nutrients.

Kerangas forest tree covered with the epi-phytic ant plant Hydnophytum.

These beautiful aerial pitchers of Nepenthes gracilis *are actually death-traps for insects attracted by false nectar glands within the pitcher and under its lid. The plant absorbs the insects to supplement nutrient-poor soils.*

Nepenthes albomarginata, *a pitcher plant with a narrow white band around the top of the pitcher. The vinelike plants climb trees; the pitchers themselves are greatly modified leaves.*

Unlike the dark green, fluffy, multilayered canopy of the rainforest, the kerangas canopy is flat, and its leaves are pale. The pole-like trees are slender and stunted due to poor nutrition. Streams draining these forests appear tea-colored by transmitted light and look black in reflected light owing to the presence of organic colloids; the water is generally acidic and low in oxygen.

Because of the poor soils and harsh conditions, a majority of kerangas trees are unique to the formation or to beach conditions: *Tristania*, with its characteristic flaky gray bark peeling to expose the orange trunk, is a relative of *Eucalyptus*; tough little *Baekia*, the conifers *Dancrydium* and *Agathis*, along with some sedges and lilies are also Australian in origin. In fact kerangas resembles dryland Australia more than it does the nearby rainforest. *Casuarina nobilis*, a common beach species that is equally common in kerangas, fixes nitrogen in bacteria-laden root nodules. On the forest floor, small carnivorous plants supplement their diets with animal protein: Sundews trap ants with drops of sticky fluid; bladderworts trap microscopic animals in tiny traps with valvelike doors; pitcher plants digest drowned insects.

Within the low, open growth, kerangas is bright and sunny—a real change from the shadowed rainforest. Orange-bellied and Scarlet-backed flowerpeckers are common, along with spider hunters, all of which feed on flower nectar and nectar insects. In the harsh sunlight there is no need for large leaves packed with chlorophyll, and since water loss is critical, the leaves tend to be tough, waxy and brownish. Thorny palms are common, as are ferns. Epiphytic orchids are common on the lichen-covered trunks and branches. Big, woody vines are rare, but small, wiry types are abundant, mainly pitcher plants and "ant plants."

Ant plants (myrmecophytes) are one of the most interesting features of kerangas forest. All four species here are epiphytes (plants growing on other plants); three are clinging vines and one a creeping fern. Two vines in the madder family, *Hydnophytum* and *Myrmecodia*, are the most abundant. Both offer living space to ants, primarily to *Iridomyrmex myrmecodiae*, which has coevolved with the plants. The aerial tubers of both species contain two types of chambers. In the smooth-walled ones, the ants raise their broods; in the rough-walled chambers, the ants eat and excrete. The rough-walled chambers are lined with highly absorbant tissue and fine rootlets with which the plant absorbs the ant's nitrogenous wastes.

That the ants actually help nourish these epiphytes is indicated by the fact that ant plants thrive in the meager kerangas soils but are rarely found on the more fertile soils of the nearby rainforest. The ants may also protect the plants from herbivorous insects and in some cases may help in seed dispersal. Kerangas trees may be laden with ant plants: Often, two or more species will grow on a single tree, and these may be used as a base for even smaller epiphytic orchids.

Pitcher plants (genus *Nepenthes*) are vines with climbing tendrils whose large leaves have been modified into ornate pitchers, complete with lids. The Ibans call them *puo 'yok kera* (monkey's rice pot). Often the aerial pitchers growing up the host's trunk are shaped differently than those growing along the ground: Aerial pitchers tend to be slender, while ground pitchers tend to be fuller in shape. Ground pitchers of the largest species can hold up to a quart of water and were reputedly used to cook rice in.

Pitchers are dotted with two types of glands. Those around the lid and "peristome" (the ornate, overhanging collar around the pitcher) secrete nectar to attract insects, which then slide down the glassy walls into the pitcher. Other glands, near the bottom of the pitcher, secrete juices that help to drown and digest the insects. One secretion lowers the surface tension of the fluid so that the almost-weightless insects will sink. A secreted enzyme breaks the insect nitrogen into peptides, which cannot be taken up by the plant; a second enzyme—manufactured not by the plant directly but by bacteria living in the fluid—converts the peptides into amino acids that the plant can absorb.

Aside from drowned insects, the pitcher's fluid may contain a whole microcosm of aquatic life, from mosquito larvae to frog spawn, adapted to live in pitcher fluid without being digested.

Eighteen pitcher plant species are found in Sarawak alone: six in Bako's kerangas forests. *Nepenthes rafflesiana* is strikingly handsome: The body is light green with maroon to red blotches, the peristome light green with maroon stripes. Aerial pitchers may be 12 inches (30 cm) tall, but are usually half that size. The ground pitchers have two distinct fringed wings down the front—a feature generally absent from aerial pitchers. *N. gracilis* Bako's most abundant species, is found in scrub, often festooning trees in great numbers. It reaches 4 to 6 inches (10–15 cm), but in some habitats may be as small as 1 centimeter. Its small ground pitchers thrive in sunny, open areas. *N. albomarginata*, a

Mangrove-lined estuary of a small stream flowing into the South China Sea.

uniform green, has a characteristic bright white band circling the pitcher just below the peristome. *N. ampullaria* produces mainly small, pot-shaped ground pitchers growing in clusters surrounding a small rosette of leaves and partly embedded in moss of leaf litter, never in sunny, open areas. The lid is very reduced and turned back like a pot handle. Pitcher plants' ingenious design allows them to store water for dry times, as well as using it both as an attractant fluid and as a deathtrap.

Borneo's beach forests, especially when framed by magnificent sandstone cliffs at sunset, can be aesthetically overwhelming; yet as a naturalist, the humble forest growing in the mud at the end of the beach draws me away, and I walk along the sea's edge to the mangroves.

FIDDLERS
IN THE MUD

The deserted tide flat fronting Gaya's mangroves is pitted with holes as if recently visited by clam diggers or a herd of water buffalo. A muted, irritated *krra krraa!* issues from the edge of the forest as the troop of Long-tailed macaques takes off noisily into the trees. I have disturbed the monkeys as they sort through the soft mud for a breakfast of fiddler crabs and peanut worms.

Long-tailed (Crab-eating) macaques, and their cousins the Pig-tailed macaques found inland, resemble small baboons, often walking with straight limbs on all fours. Unlike Borneo's other monkeys, which subsist on leaves and occasional fruit, macaques eat mostly small animals, along with ripe fruit. They are not normally shy: The large troops of Long-tails that populate the woods and lawns around Bako National Park headquarters fight brazenly like urban teen gangs over turf, and the dominant males delight in intimidating visitors by displaying their formidable canines with an angry screech. The larger Pig-tailed macaques are often pests in plantations and gardens, and even local villagers fear the more aggressive males. But this troop of Crab-eaters on Gaya, evidently not used to humans invading this unpopulated stretch of muddy beach, decided to vacate peacefully.

At first glance, the coastal mangrove forest hardly looks like an exciting place. The trees lack stature; the muddy sands and black muds are rather ugly next to the glistening sand beach with its graceful casuarinas, pandans and coconut palms. But the mangrove ecosystem is actually much richer than the rather sterile sand beach. In fact, it ranks with the coral reef and tropical rainforest as one of the most productive biosystems on earth. And once you start to look closely, it is one of the most intriguing. Bright, colorful crabs, their eyes atop tall stalks, wave their swollen claws in ritual semaphore. Fish "walk" on land, and some even climb up the barnacle-covered prop-roots of strangely shaped trees. Snail shells zip over the mud as if they've had too many cups of coffee. Clouds of birds rise from the water's edge, then settle back down, probing the mud with long bills. Stately storks and egrets pose like statues in the shallows.

There are good reasons why this unspectacular habitat is so spectacularly rich. Three major ecosystems intermingle here: the salt sea, freshwater rivers and the land.

The land itself has been brought here by the rivers. As the current slows when river meets the sea, it drops the suspended sand and mud carried from interior mountains and forests. The meeting of fresh water and seawater also tends to clump ("flocculate") tiny organic particles into larger ones, causing them to sink. The riverborne sediments are mixed with crushed coral sand from

Following page:
White mangrove (Avicennia). *Its aspara-gus-like pneumatophores ("breathing" roots) rise from the dense mud.*

offshore and with sand moved along the shore by coastal currents. Together, these form broad deltas extending out into the shallow sea.

Tides cover and expose this flat landscape, bringing plankton, organic nutrients and salt from the sea, while rivers flood it with thin layers of fresh mud. The firmer areas of mud offer refuge to burrowing animals such as clams, fiddler crabs, mud lobsters and worms, and these provide food for macaques, otters, herons and shorebirds.

Leafy mangrove trees not only shade the mud from the hot tropical sun but provide another dimension of living space. Their trunks and prop roots offer solid attachment for barnacles, snails and mussels, and provide refuge from the incoming tides for air- breathing snails and crabs. The upper branches create perches and nesting sites for raptors and songbirds. The leaves, nectar and fruit of mangrove trees provide food for monkeys, birds, bats and insects.

Even the dead mangrove leaves, dropping like manna onto the mud, contribute greatly to the flow of energy. Shredded by crabs and snails, the leaf particles are colonized and further degraded by bacteria and fungi. The tiny leaf particle "crackers" spread thickly with a nutritive "peanut butter" of microbes and feces, become detritus snacks for a complex community of detritivores: worms and clams and crabs and tiny shrimps. These, in turn, are eaten by larger shrimp and fishes—some of them highly prized by humans—which as adults are caught far out at sea. As fuel for migratory shorebirds, these small tropical mangrove creatures are eventually transported, in the form of fats, as far as the birds' Arctic breeding grounds.

Despite this richness, the mangrove swamp is not any easy environment. The soil is saturated with salt. The surface of the mud can change within hours from seawater to almost pure river water or, even more extreme, from evaporated saltpan to cool, pure rainwater. Muds range from soft and unstable at the

The familiar prop roots of red mangroves (Rhizophora) *support the tree above the tides and dense, saline mud. The smaller rootlets below the mud actively exclude salts.*

Red mangrove prop roots offer solid anchorage for oysters, mussels and barnacles.

water's edge to dense and clayey farther back. In either case the muds lack oxygen and are often high in sulfides. Only a few trees have been able to solve these problems, and they have done so in a limited number of ways.

Borneo's 13 species of mangrove trees come from three unrelated families found throughout the tropics: Rhizophoraceae, Avicenniaceae and Sonneratiaceae. Each family has overcome the difficulties of unstable, salty, waterlogged, anaerobic soils in different ways. The most familiar of these, two species in the genus *Rhizophora*, or red mangroves, have long slender prop roots that arch from the trunk down to the mud. The roots stabilize the tree and, by being partly out of the anaerobic soil, allow the root to "breathe." A good supply of oxygen is necessary because *Rhizophora*'s underground roots work hard to actively exclude salt as they take up water from the salty soil.

The trees have also had to solve the problem of their seeds falling into inhospitable soil or being washed away by the sea. *Rhizophora* seeds remain

Blossoms of a red mangrove.

Opposite:
Tangle of red mangrove prop roots.

connected to the branches until they become mature seedlings, called pro-pagules, complete with long, pointed, well-developed taproot. When the heavy propagule falls, either the root end sticks into the mud like a spear or it floats until becoming stranded, point down, in the mud. Held high above the mud by the propagule's long shaft, the plant's shoot tip can grow upwards and prop roots grow out from the shaft to support it.

The family's other genus, *Bruguiera*, also has propagules, but the roots of mature trees differ from *Rhizophora*'s. The majority of roots spread out hori-zontally from a taproot bent in waves that are partly below the surface of the mud and partly above. The "knees," which curve above the mud, have gas-ex-change openings and are able to breathe. Borneo's four species of *Brugiera* are found at various distances back from the sea's edge in the firmer, drier muds—sometimes in pure stands. One species prefers to grow on mounds constructed by large crustaceans called mud lobsters.

In place of prop roots or knees, the three species of *Avicennia* have spreading "cable" roots growing off a taproot. The horizontal cable roots sprout hundreds of slender, green, vertical pneumatophores (breathing roots) that stick aspara-gus-like a few inches above the mud. Instead of excluding salt as *Rhizophora* does, *Avicennias* excrete it from pores in the tough, waxy leaves. One species—*Avicennia alba*, or white mangrove—is a successful pioneer, growing in the softest, saltiest muds.

The four species of *Sonneratia* also have pneumatophores, but these are brown instead of green and are much stouter than those of *Avicennia*. The trees prefer rich, organic muds and can grow in thick stands to 60 feet (18 m) in height. Because they are succulent and have fairly thin surfaces, *Sonneratia* leaves are enjoyed by leaf-eating langurs and their cousin, the bizarre, endemic Proboscis monkey. The trees also are favorites of two species of bats. Long-tongued nectar bats feed on the nectar and pollen, pollinating the white, tubular night-blooming flowers, while the fruit is eaten and the seeds dispersed by flying foxes, the world's largest bat. Back in the 1860s, when there were more mangroves and more bats, Beccari wrote: "In this rainy season . . . immense numbers of flying foxes passed over Kuching every evening . . . When night closed in they congregated in search of food on the fruit-bearing trees, especially *Sonneratia acida*, the fruit of which they devoured with avidity."

HORSESHOE AND FIDDLER CRABS

Some of the more interesting mangrove animals are found out on the mudflats where only the most adventurous pioneering trees have gained a roothold. Near large rivers, the mud is so soft that it is almost impossible to walk on. But where small streams disgorge between sandy beaches, the mud is firmer, and one can wade in the shallows from the sea side. At Gaya Island and Bako National Park wooden walkways have been built over the tide channels, allowing the visitor to walk comfortably among the mangrove trees, looking down into the shallows or, better yet, to explore the edge of the stream channel during low tides.

At full moon, when the tide is high, a strange animal of even more ancient lineage than marine turtles crawls up on the mud to lay her eggs. The horseshoe crab is actually not a crab but is more closely related to the great sea scorpions that inhabited the seas some 200 million years ago. Of that group only the horseshoes have survived, but they continue to do quite well throughout the world's oceans. The two species found here can be told apart by the shape of the sharp tail that extends from under the carapace. The smooth, brown,

A male fiddler crab displays its colorful, oversized claw to attract females.

dome-shaped carapace covers many sets of leaflike appendages used for feeding and swimming. At breeding time, the male clings tightly onto the back of the much larger female as she searches for a proper beach on which to lay her eggs. The process may last six to seven weeks. Attached to her legs, the female carries thousands of eggs; eventually, at the highest tide of the month, she digs a shallow depression in the mud and deposits the eggs. After the male releases his sperm over them, the pair return to the sea. A month later, at the next spring tide, the horseshoe crab hatchlings are washed out to sea as zooplankton.

The most noticeable of the mangrove animals are the colorful little fiddler crabs, which look rather extraterrestrial with their tall, slender eyestalks. Their name comes from the male's enlarged pincer—an inch or two (2–5 cm) long, often as large and heavy as the rest of the crab's body. This colorful claw is bright red, orange, yellow, blue or white, depending on species, and may contrast with the carapace color for maximum effect.

The male fiddler waves or rotates this appendage continuously to advertise his territory and to attract females. The females don't seem to be overly impressed by this show of hands. They just keep feeding busily on algae and detritus on the surface of the mud with both their thin, dextrous pincers, while the males are limited to a single effective one. But as one biologist notes: "It would serve a mutant male fiddler crab little if its larger pincer was reduced in size and could be used for feeding, if it could not then attract females for mating."

As the tide ebbs, the fiddlers emerge from their burrows in the mud, the males waving their bright claws like flags even before they fully emerge. While the females feed purposefully, the males spend half their time in macho displays. They also seem to delight in crawling down the holes of smaller individuals after claw-to-claw contests. When threatened by herons or monkeys, they zip down into their own burrows.

They are less successful at evading the unusual Crab-eating frog, the only frog capable of living and breeding in salt water. The large, mud-colored amphibian waits patiently for a crab to approach—usually a male whose attention is elsewhere—then with a flick of its long, sticky tongue the crab disappears.

A fiddler also retreats into its burrow at high tide, first cutting a circular trap door of mud that precisely fits the opening to the burrow, to seal it and trap air within. Of the two common species, *Uca dussumieri* is a larger; *Uca mani* is smaller and more numerous. Together, their populations are enormous: There may be 50 fiddlers for every square yard of mud, providing a feast for a variety of snakes, spiders and wading birds. Also feeding on the fiddlers are the larger species of one of the world's most unusual group of fishes—the mudskippers.

MUDSKIPPERS

Mudskippers have bug-eyed, swollen-cheeked heads tapering into eel-like tails; they are small, 3–6 inches (7–15 cm) and rather drab, but their behavior compensates for this lack of size or flashy color. In the water they swim like other fishes; but to avoid an underwater predator, or wading naturalist, they can also skip rapidly across the surface of the water. Even more unusual for a fish, mudskippers spend much of their time completely out of the water, on the mudflats, on prop roots or on rocks. The smaller species graze on algae growing on the mud surface; larger ones prey on small fiddler crabs.

In order to leave the sea, a mudskipper takes a bit of the sea with it. By dipping or rolling in puddles of water on the mud it refills its gill chambers with water; as long as the gills remain wet, it can breathe, and it can also absorb oxygen through its tail. It also periodically draws its stalked eyes down into internal pockets of seawater.

Mudskippers "walk" on the mud, using their stiff pectoral fins, leaving characteristic tracks on the mud. "A broad, fleshy base on each fin and elbowlike bend," writes S. Dillon Ripley in *The Land and Wildlife of Tropical Asia*, "add to the illusion of forearms. The pelvic fins act in somewhat the same manner to help this walking motion; the tail at this point is merely dragged along. But if the mudskipper wants to accelerate, the tail comes powerfully into play: The whole body arches, the tail pushes against the ground, and the fish flips rapidly over the ground or water."

One species, the large (to 6 in/15 cm) Golden-spotted mudskipper, can climb far up the prop root of a red mangrove or wriggle up the splash zone of a smooth boulder on a rocky shore; its pelvic fins are fused to form a ventral sucker that can cling even to vertical surfaces, and its well-sealed gill covers allow it to spend long periods out of water.

Mud-dwelling species live in deep burrows, evenly spaced due to territorial conflict. During the breeding season the male displays near his burrow by jumping and by erecting his dorsal fin. When erect, the fin has tall, curving spines connected by a sail-like webbing. Conflicting males may face each other, eyeball to eyeball, trying to "psyche each other out" with ritualized body gestures until one makes a sudden jump at the other, often knocking his antagonist over. After mating, the female lays her eggs on the sides of the burrow, which is guarded diligently by the male.

The mudskipper lives in two worlds. By filling its gill chamber with seawater it can remain out of water for extended periods of time.

MUD LOBSTER

Mudskippers and fiddler crabs are not the only animals that burrow; the mud of mangrove forests is riddled with holes. Some are from sedentary clams but others are tunnels used by active creatures for refuge, feeding and access to the water table at low tide. Most burrow straight down, some with double entrances or complex chambers; others burrow horizontally into the mud bank from below the low-tide mark. The most complex is engineered by a creature that is almost fully adapted to life beneath the mud—the mud lobster.

The mud lobster grows up to about 20 inches (50 cm) including a swollen carapace and a long, segmented abdomen. Not actually a lobster, it is placed in a family of its own, more closely related to the hermit crabs zipping around on the surface of the mud. But instead of housing its soft, vulnerable body in a borrowed snail shell as hermits do, the mud lobster protects itself by staying within its burrow, coming out only at night or on very cloudy days to find a new site. It digs by scraping with the small, hooked, fixed lower "thumbs" of its claws, then excavates with the large, flat, movable upper "palm." The burrow may be three yards long, while the characteristic "volcanoes" created at the beginning of the dig may rise up to a yard (meter) above the mud. The aptly named mud lobster even feeds on the mud it digs, extracting algae, protozoa and organic detritus as the mud passes through its gut, and it is remarkably tolerant of the dense sulfuric layers of mud through which it must dig.

The mounds themselves, lifted above the wet mud, are an important structural component of the mangrove forest and of muddy riverbanks. One of the *Bruguiera* mangrove trees, as well as the nipa palm and the large Mangrove fern, take advantage of the well-drained mud for an elevated perch. Many creatures, such as the smaller mud shrimp, the square-shelled sesarmid crabs and the edible brown mussel known as *tua tow*, burrow into the sides of the mounds.

The secretive mud lobster has played an important role in mangrove ecology for millions of years but has gained notoriety only recently—as a pest to aquaculturists when it bores holes in the laboriously constructed mud walls of shrimp or fish ponds.

WADING BIRDS

The small crustaceans, worms and clams living in the mud provide a critical source of food for migrating shorebirds, or waders. Small, short-billed plovers and turnstones pick small animals off mangrove roots and the mud surface. Sandpipers, dowitchers, curlews and godwits probe into the mud and open burrows with their long, forceps-like bills. Phalaropes and avocets skim the surface of the mud and water for tiny crustaceans.

From October to May, Borneo's mangrove shores are important wintering grounds or "fueling" stopovers for dozens of species of shorebirds. These extraordinary long-distance travelers breed in Siberia in June and July and migrate to Southeast Asia or Australia in the fall; a few even travel to the southern tip of New Zealand, an annual round trip of 26,000 miles! For this they depend almost exclusively on protein-rich crustaceans from the mud.

Pulau Bruit, a low, 150-square-mile (400-sq-km) deltaic island surrounded by mudflats and mangrove forest at the mouth of Sarawak's Rajang River, is particularly important. A single 10-day survey in late November 1986 sponsored by the World Wildlife Fund counted 16,000 shorebirds of 25 species. Aside from shorebirds it found 4,000 terns of six species, including the rare Caspian tern, 500 herons of 12 species, and a resident population of Lesser adjutant storks.

The most populous shorebirds include the crab-eating Greater sand plover; the Common redshank and Common greenshank; Terek, Curlew, and Broad-billed sandpipers; and the Rufous-necked stint. Biologists conducting the survey estimate that 50,000 to 80,000 shorebirds use this single island each year. They rate coastal Sarawak of "international importance, especially for rare birds such as the endangered Asian dowitcher." A survey of Brunei Bay also found large numbers of shorebirds, herons and terns. Muddy deltas along the entire coast of Borneo are probably of similar importance to migrant and resident waders.

A number of larger wading birds also hunt along the mangrove shores, in the shallows of the sea or along the tidal channels: four species of Egret,

Opposite:
A mangrove-lined tidal channel.

The silky ball covered with leaves is a Weaver ant nest. The leaves are woven together by silky threads exuded by larvae held in the adults' jaws.

including the graceful, white Great egret; five heron species; and the massive-billed Adjutant stork. Most stand statue-like until a fish, prawn, crab or snake comes within range of their long, stabbing bill. The Little green heron, however, actively stalks crabs and fishes. The most attractive of all is Storm's stork—a small, rare stork (sometimes considered a race of the Woolly-necked stork) found on the mudflats and far up Borneo's rivers. The crown of its head is black, glossed with iridescent green; its slender bill and facial skin are bright red, especially during breeding season, as are its long legs, its fluffy neck and lower belly are a contrasting bright white. It hunts invertebrates and small vertebrates in the mud and is hunted in turn by humans for food.

In this world of mud and brackish water, the trunks and prop roots of the mangrove trees provide the only solid attachment for intertidal animals. Lower portions of the trees are often covered by individuals of two barnacle genera; *Balanus*, the larger of the two tends to live below the tiny *Chthamalus*. A mussel, *Brachydontes*, clings by means of strong byssal threads onto the shells or bare spots between the barnacles. Carnivorous snails, *Thais* and *Murex*, prey on both barnacles and mussels. One survey of a single white mangrove tree counted more than 15,000 animals, two-thirds of which were mussels.

The leafy branches of the mangrove trees provide a shaded structure for a number of canopy birds. Five species of warblers are among the many birds that pick insects off the trunks and branches. Others include five species of cuckoo, especially the Banded bay cuckoo; two cuckooshrikes; the Mangrove whistler, the Yellow-vented bulbul, and the Common iora. Four kinds of flycatchers, including the Mangrove blue, hunt flying as well as crawling insects.

Flowerpeckers eat the small mangrove fruits as well as canopy insects, while four pigeon and three parrot species specialize in mangrove fruits. Iridescent sunbirds hover around the flowers, feeding on nectar and on the insects drawn to it. The beautiful Blue-tailed bee eater intercepts large insects flying above the crown, leaving the smaller ones to the swifts and swallows.

INSECTS AND SNAKES

Two of the many insects living in the mangroves are especially interesting. One—the large, red Weaver ant—is better known than liked. Found throughout the lowlands, it is commonest among the mangroves. Its name comes from its curious method of "sewing" leaves together to construct a nest to house its greenish queens. The worker ants form living chains to bridge the gap between adjacent leaves, gradually shortening the chains to pull the leaves into contact. They then take their own offspring in their jaws, causing the larvae to exude a fine, sticky thread. Passing the larvae back and forth like shuttlecocks, they bind the leaves together with the quick-drying, gluey threads.

Beccari wrote of them: "There is the red ant found everywhere in the jungle of secondary growth, where it makes huge nests, binding together dead leaves by filaments like strong spider's web. These are found at about a man's height from the ground on shrubs and bushes. It is one of the greatest pests one meets with in the forest, for its bite causes a burning pain on account of the formic acid it instills into the wound . . . so that to free myself from them I have been obliged to strip entirely." He adds: "The Dyaks eat this ant, or rather they mix it with their rice as a condiment."

Having brushed my head through a nest of Weaver ants I can strongly confirm the first observation. Their use as a condiment, though, seems rare these days—or at least not mentioned to foreign dinner guests.

The other insect is less of an engineer and more of an artiste—a light-show specialist to be exact. The males of a species of firefly beetle called *kelip-kelip*, gather in huge numbers of *Sonneratia* trees. During the night they begin to blink, soon in unison, lighting up the whole tree like a Christmas decoration. The show is to attract females rather than to please human observers, but it does both impressively well.

Also in the canopy, feeding on the lizards and on the eggs of breeding birds, are at least three species of snake. Two are called cat snakes because their pupils are vertical slits, as in cat's eyes. Beccari wrote of the Yellow-ringed cat snake: "This species frequents trees by the riverside, or the mangroves, and it is not uncommon for specimens to drop into a passing sampan, for it has a habit of resting half-twisted on overhanging branches, easily shaken by a passing boat. The natives assert that it is poisonous." The Yellow-ringed cat snake could be confused with the poisonous Banded krait, except its yellow bars do not form complete rings. The Dog-toothed cat snake, a tree-dweller with bright yellow bands on its tail, is considered mildly venomous.

The most interesting species is the Paradise tree snake—a "flying snake." By spreading out its flexible ribs, this slender snake can glide from a high branch of one tree to the trunk of another, a skill useful for avoiding the mud (and predatory herons) of the mangrove floor.

MONKEYS

The most abundant monkeys in the mangroves are macaques and the langurs (formerly called leaf-eating monkeys). Langurs are good-size monkeys with fashionably pointed "hairdos" but sometimes with unfashionable "beer-bellies." Their sacculated guts can ferment and digest cellulose, allowing them to eat leaves as well as fruits.

The Banded langur, the rarer of the two coastal species, is found on Borneo only along the island's west coast. One subspecies is mostly charcoal gray with white under the long tail and a darker band across its face; the other differs radically—reddish brown with darker bands, white underparts and punkish gold-red "do." The infants of both races are light gray with dark bands.

The more common Silvered langur is often seen in the trees around Bako's hostel. The adult's fur is silvery gray, but its energetic infant is a brilliant golden orange. Silvered langurs are found throughout the lowlands in swamp forests and far upriver. Troops of five to 15 individuals, led by a male, move slowly through the trees, feeding on leaves and shoots and the nectar-rich flowers of the *Sonneratia* tree. Considered the quietest of the leaf monkeys, Silvereds nevertheless are territorial and have a shrill alarm call.

The rarest of the leaf-eating monkeys is one of the world's strangest primates. The bizarre Proboscis monkey (placed in the same subfamily as the langurs) is found only in the lowlands of Borneo. It is actually more of a riverine creature, returning to the riverbank trees every evening, but it spends much of its time feeding in the mangroves, which supply a steady source of leaves and fruits. Elizabeth Bennett, who has been studying Proboscis monkeys for a decade, found it feeding largely on *Rhizophora*, while Beccari wrote: "I had often met with this curious creature on the big trees along the river near the town, feeding on the fruits of the . . . *Sonneratia* . . . for which they have a special predilection."

A mature male Proboscis weights more than 50 pounds (20 kg), with a huge belly, its sacculated stomach full of bacteria capable of processing masses of the tough, low-grade mangrove leaves. His trademark huge nose hangs on his

reddish, bare face like a pendulous fruit. Natives of Borneo called the monkey "Dutchman," in honor of Kalimantan's former colonial rulers.

The male's coat is a quite handsome, two-tone rust and gray; it has a red crown with whitish beard, shaggy rust coat with fluffy white collar, gray forearms and legs. The whitish rump leads to a long, thick gray tail, which usually hangs downward from the branch on which he sits. Bennett aptly describes his red-brown torso as "resembling a tight bomber jacket which was acquired in his youth and into which he is now trying to cram his middle-aged spread."

The normally placid male is highly territorial at his family's sleeping site. To rival males he displays his large canines as well as his large nose, and delivers a variety of grunts, groans and honks; he "stands on all fours, leans forward, staring at his rival with jaw jutting and mouth open; he leaps through trees, roaring & breaking branches . . ." A successful mature male may guard a shifting harem of up to eight females with their young.

The much smaller female weights only half as much. Her snubbed nose, like her stomach, is much smaller, her coat duller. The young have sparse black fur, a dark blue face and a cute upturned nose.

Proboscis monkeys mostly stick to the canopy but are quite capable of swimming rivers or crossing mud or shallow water on two legs, walking upright with arms raised as if grasping branches above. They can be seen at Bako and at Samunsam Wildlife Sanctuary on the western edge of Sarawak but more easily along rivers, where they retreat each night to sleep.

Opposite:
Male Proboscis monkey, a leaf-eating primate found only on Borneo. It lives among mangroves or along riverbanks.

A dense school of small fishes resembles a large, dark stain in the shallows. Mangroves form invaluable nursery areas for many species of commercial fishes and shrimp caught far offshore.

FOREST MANAGEMENT

On the Malay Peninsula, mangrove forests were the first to be brought under intensive management: for house poles, firewood, charcoal and as "crutch" (tannin) for tanning leather. In Borneo, the uses have been the same, but "intensive management" consists mostly of cutting them down. Formerly, this was for firewood and charcoal; lately, it has been woodchips, exported mostly to Taiwan for chipboard manufacture. In Sarawak in 1950, 30 tons of mangrove trees were harvested for firewood, and lesser amounts for poles and charcoal. By the mid-1980s harvesting for firewood and charcoal was minimal, but cutting for poles was up by a factor of six, and woodchips had jumped to more than 200 tons/year (a maximum 300 tons in 1976).

Properly managed, fast-growing mangrove forests can actually produce much more wood than an equivalent area of rainforest. But if cut thoughtlessly,

Red mangroves fronting a hillside dipterocarp forest.

the mangroves may fail to regenerate, and the high-sulfur soils can release sulfuric acid into the surrounding waters. Aside from the loss of wildlife habitat, destruction of the mangrove forest can result in increased flooding and storm damage, eroded coastlines and the muddying of nearby sand beaches, and salt water intrusion into coastal farms. Conversion of mangrove forest to wet-rice fields often fails because of acidic soils.

When mangrove trees are felled, leaf-fall ceases, and the whole food web based on leaf detritus breaks down. Tree roots no longer provide shelter for small fishes avoiding larger predators. In areas where mangroves are being felled to provide room for prawn or fish ponds, one recent study showed that an average fish pond may produce about 300 pounds of fish per acre per year (287 kg/ha/year). At the same time, the loss of the mangroves as nursery and feeding area for commercial offshore prawns and fishes more than offsets this gain, causing a net loss of almost 500 pounds per acre per year (480 kg/ha/yr).

Mangroves are also being cleared to "reclaim" coastal land for construction and industrial parks. On the Malay Peninsula, the Malaysian cabinet recently gave approval for a mammoth 30-year project to reclaim for "economic growth areas" a 2-mile (3.2-km) wide strip along the entire length of the peninsula's west coast. On Borneo, mangrove "reclamation" will probably take place without any grand master plan or cabinet approval. But either planned or not, the mangrove forest and its unique wildlife are at risk, in Borneo and throughout the tropics. A lofty mountain, picturesque canyon or towering forest is easy to defend on aesthetic and recreational grounds. It is far less easy, no matter how rich the habitat, to promote a sprawling, mosquito- and snake-infested forest growing on a gray mudflat, even if it be a thousand times more productive than the nearby beautiful, white sandy beach or clear tropical sea. We can only hope that politicians with a regard for the future will set aside large areas of mangrove forest for preservation or renewable harvest.

Meanwhile, a thousand fiddler crabs wave their festive claws and bug-eyed mudskippers walk the mud, under a Great white egret's patient eye.

ROADS OF RAIN

L ike bears and cobras to the jungle trekker and sharks to the snorkeler, crocodiles have a way of slithering into the imagination of anyone swimming or boating on Borneo's rivers. One friend of mine always refers to the Niah River in Sarawak's Niah Caves National Park as "crocodile-infested." When pressed, he admitted that he had seen one there once. Yet the Estuarine crocodile, growing up to 22 feet long, *is* the largest reptile on earth, and fierce enough that just one can be called an infestation. Normally torpid as it lurks among the mangroves or sculls slowly through the water at night—with only a broad snout, piercing eyes and dragonlike ridges along the back and tail showing—it can, when hunting or when annoyed, thrash through the water in a sprint or rush on land at 20 mph (32 kph) for short bursts.

Given this speed, its brute power and toothy jaws, our fear of crocodiles is not entirely irrational. The Estuarine crocodile figures in the sacred art and bad dreams of peoples from India to northern Australia. And, in fact, Borneo's crocs do occasionally eat people.

Most of the recent attacks in Sarawak have taken place along the broad, shallow lower Batang Lupar (main stem of the Lupar River). Many local residents believe the attacks are by a single crocodile of immense size and extreme age, but a study led by biologist Robert Steubing of the National University suggests otherwise. The researchers found that the normally solitary crocs concentrate along the banks of the estuarine tide channels during breeding season. There, the males become highly territorial, and females jealously guard their nests of mud and vegetation in which they lay 20–50 leathery eggs. Crocodiles tend to breed in the spring and in the fall, coincident with high populations of prawns in the lower river.

Unfortunately, both the crocs and the native fishermen frequent the estuary at the same time. Both are drawn here by concentrations of three types of prawn, which themselves come to the estuary to breed. Ten-inch-long (25 cm) Tiger prawns move down from upriver, while two smaller species—the medium-size *Caridina* and the smaller *Penaeus*—move in from the sea. As the tide drops, local fishermen trap the prawns against the channel banks by throwing nets from shallow-draft, 6- to 10-foot sampans. From the croc's underwater view, the scientists theorize, the sampan resembles an intruding crocodile. A sudden, thrashing charge by an outraged 14–20 foot (4–6 m) male defending his territory knocks the hapless fisherman overboard, to be dragged under, and perhaps later eaten.

More usual crocodile prey consists of fish and prawns, and whatever land animal—pig, monkey or deer—that might pass too close to the motionless crocodile's huge jaws or thrashing tail. Large animals are usually taken underwater and stashed in the mud, to be fed on later as they rot and are more easily torn apart.

Opposite:
Small estuary on the South China Sea.

An Estuarine crocodile, the world's largest reptile, lurks at the water surface, patiently awaiting dinner.

A crocodile is able to eat underwater because of a fold that presses against its palate, separating the air passage from the mouth; its ear openings have a special flap that also closes underwater. Below the surface, the croc's already slow heart rate drops to three or four beats per minute. Nostrils are located at the tip of its snout, raised to the same height as ear and eye openings, so that it can make use of all senses while barely breaking the surface.

Crocs are at home in both fresh and salt water. They have been seen swimming in the South China Sea 60 miles (100 km) offshore, and at a similar distance upriver above the tidal zone. But they prefer the brackish, turbid water at the mouths of Borneo's larger rivers.

According to Beccari, crocodiles were more numerous and even less timid in the 1860s: "In the Sarawak River the crocodile is abundant, even in the vicinity of Kuching; and there have been instances of persons carried off by these voracious reptiles, even from the bazaar quay. A premium of one rupee was given per foot (in length) for every crocodile caught."

From 1881 a bounty was also offered in Sibu on the Rajang River, and in the 1930s commercial exploitation for hides began in earnest. Croc hunters hung large hooks baited with monkey, flying fox or chicken on the end of rattan lines tied to branches overhanging the river. By the mid-1950s 6 tons per year of crocodile skins were exported from Sarawak. After a peak of 8 tons in 1961, exports began a steep decline due to overhunting, and by the 1980s were down to half a ton a year. During the peak decade 1954–64, an estimated 80,000 crocs were exported from Sarawak alone.

Despite the notoriety of attacks on humans, a 1986 study (Cox and Gombek) called crocodile populations in Sarawak "so seriously depleted that its continued existence in some river systems is in grave doubt." A similar study in Sabah's remote Klias Peninsula (Stuebing, Ghazally Ismail and Ling) found that though potential populations were high, at least 50 medium-sized crocs had been poached during just the one month of the study. Human greed may doom the Estuarine crocodile despite its hundreds of millions of successful years on earth—and despite the fact that the danger of being eaten by one, even for a shrimp fisherman, is very much less than being killed on a motorbike while heading into town.

DOLPHINS, PORPOISES AND FISHES

Two other large estuarine animals more easily elicit our affection. Or would if they were noticed. The Snubfin (Irrawady) dolphin is quiet and inconspicuous, rarely leaping out of the water. It prefers inshore estuarine waters, including very murky water, but probably ranges far up Borneo's meandering lowland rivers. It has been sighted in Sandakan Bay in eastern Sabah, up the Mahakam River in East Kalimantan and in most of the estuaries of Sarawak and Brunei. Dark above and pale below, the Snubfin has broad, rounded flippers inserted well forward, almost beneath the eye. It grows to about 8 feet (2.5 m) and is shaped like a pilot whale, but with a smaller, rounded dorsal fin and a less swollen "melon" on its blunt forehead. The melon is an organ for directing its sonar, allowing it to catch fish at night or in water too murky for sight.

Once common in Borneo, the Snubfin dolphin is now rare for reasons unknown. Perhaps the rivers have become too laden with silt or its food supply depleted. Two large estuarine fishes sought by Borneans, and probably also by the dolphin—clupeids called *ikan terubok* and *ikan bakawal*—have lately become scarce. Both species are prized for their flesh and even more so for the eggs, which, preserved and salted, are sold at a premium. The two are caught in the shallow sea or are gill-netted in Sarawak's estuaries during the summer. Recent overfishing has led to a sharp decline, and the Batang Lupar is now the only rich source remaining. Sarawak's entire inshore fishery, in fact, declined

The archer fish can spit a stream of water accurately enough to bring down a terrestrial insect 2 feet above it.

by almost 50 percent just between 1978 and 1983, probably due to overfishing by large trawlers, but perhaps also from excessive sediment from heavily logged watersheds.

Another cetacean found here, the Finless porpoise, is smaller (to 6 ft/1.9 m) than the Snubfin. Similar in shape, it lacks a dorsal fin and is paler in color. The Finless swims singly or in small groups along the coast or up into estuaries—probably not up into the rivers themselves—feeding on squid, prawns and small fishes. It was once common in Sarawak's estuaries, but now is seen only in the north end of the state.

Though more than 20 economically valuable fish species live in the Batang Lupar alone, plus juveniles of many others, an estuarine fish of no economic importance whatever is one of Borneo's most interesting. Of the archerfish, Beccari writes "I saw here [on the upper Batang Lupar] for the first time that singular fish which has received from the natives the name of 'blowpipe-fish.' The size of one of our domestic goldfish, it is neither remarkable in shape or coloration, but has the strange power, on coming to the surface, of being able to squirt a jet of water from its mouth. This it uses with unerring aim against insects, such as grasshoppers and flies, and even spiders, resting on plants near the water's edge, causing them to fall into the water, where they become easy prey to the clever marksman."

The archerfish's water dart is accurate to 20 inches (50 cm), three to five times its body length. Not surprisingly, it has large eyes, and its silvery, striped body is almost invisible as it lurks near the surface of the brackish water.

The sea reaches into Borneo with long arms: Travelers by paddle-powered longboats once scheduled their trips to take advantage of the tidal currents, and every boater feared the so-called tidal bore, a sometimes immense wave that can race upriver like a locomotive. Beccari noted, "Normally strong tidal effects reach to 14 miles north of Kuching, except when the river is swollen during the rainy season; then the tide reaches only to Kuching [itself 15 mi/25 km from the sea]."

The incoming wedge of dense, saline seawater that pushes upriver, allows many fishes that are normally marine or estuarine to be found deep into Borneo. A major survey done by American icthyologist Tyson Roberts along West Kalimantan's Kapuas River drainage found normally marine Whiptailed stingrays "hundreds of kilometers" upriver, along with many members of marine catfishes. Some members of other marine families have adapted to river life in the Kapuas: Roberts found four freshwater pipefish species, four freshwater halfbeaks, and two species each of herring, anchovy and bony tongue.

Freshwater animals try to avoid the saline water either by moving up and down the river with the tides or by moving off the main stern into smaller streams. Two large aquatic turtles, the Painted river terrapin and the Asiatic softshell, move upstream or into side streams until the tide ebbs. On Sarawak's Baram River and elsewhere, the Painted terrapin is heavily harvested for its meat, while other species are prized for their eggs, believed to be "good for the libido." In peninsular Malaysia the eggs of one terrapin are so sought after that it has received royal protection, and a large hatchery has been set up in the state of Perak.

PALMS

The intrusion of seawater into Borneo's rivers depends on two factors: the monthly pattern of tidal heights and the opposing pulse of fresh water being discharged at any moment by the rapidly fluctuating rivers. When river levels are low, high tides may influence large, low-elevation rivers for a hundred miles from the sea. Brackish-water mangroves, for example, grow 150 miles (240 km) up the Kapuas River, which drains the vast West Kalimantan swamplands.

A rather monotonous, solid wall of arching, feathery fronds fronts the tidal portion of Borneo's rivers—the large, stemless nipa palm. The sole species in the *Nypa* genus, nipa is an advanced palm that has existed since the Cretaceous period with so little variation that only one species has ever been recorded. And, despite its vast range and the changes in climate during its 100 million or so years, it has barely changed structurally.

So successful is the nipa that it dominates the tidal reaches of rivers through-out Southeast Asia and Australia, forming pure stands to the exclusion of all other palms. Only the mangrove *Sonneratia* can compete with it, and then only when they share the elevated mounds created by mud lobsters. The secret of nipa's success are its unique roots, which contain large air cavities. As the tide rises, air is pumped up through the roots to the fronds, overcoming the dense, anaerobic riverbank muds.

Like the coconut palm, nipa is utilized by local villagers in dozens of ways. Leaves are cut for roofing thatch. The surface tissue stripped from the leaflets is cut to make cigarette papers. The trimmed leaves are also used for basketry, matting and hats. The adult leaves, cut at the very base, are tied in bundles and used as floats in the sea to attract fish; the stout leaf-bases, containing many air spaces, act as the floats for the submerged leaves.

Dawn along the Melinau River near Mulu National Park.

Wrote Beccari: "The Nipa fruits grow close together, forming a great ball a foot across, and each fruit, when immature, contains, like the coconut, a watery liquid and the soft edible albumen of the seed . . . Even the pollen, which as the aspect of violet-colored meal, is utilized, being eaten as a condiment both with rice and sago." Brown, treacly, nipa sugar and white, aromatic, coconut milk poured on sago pudding make the "three-palm pudding" that terminates every proper coastal Malay curry meal.

The juice of the unripe nipa fruit is tapped for sugar, wine and vinegar. As the cluster of fruits begin to form, the stalk is beaten for several days with a stick. The bruised part is cut across and a collecting vessel attached below the cut end. A thin slice of the stalk is removed daily to open a clean unfermented surface for the flow, which is then kept in a large jar for two to three months. The sugary juice ferments into nipa wine, which later turns to vinegar. The juice is also either evaporated to produce the brown molasses-like nipa sugar, sold in thick discs, or is distilled, after fermentation, to produce alcoholic arrack.

Since one acre of palms can produce 3,000 gallons of alcohol, nipa is an obvious candidate for fuel. As early as 1924, the colonial government of North Borneo erected an experimental plant to manufacture alcohol-based fuel—an idea reportedly nixed by the petroleum industry.

The only other trees breaking the monotony of the nipas are the tall, graceful nibong palm and a species of *Pandanus*, of which Beccari was considerably less fond than those along the coastal beaches. "There are tracts of rivers where the pandans prevail over palms in serried & impenetrable ranks . . . Unlike palm trunks, they are commonly branched and the branches curve upward in the manner of rosette trees . . . The long leaves are horribly barbed. The edges and underside of the midrib have curved spines. In the upper or distal part of the leaf the thorns point upward & catch the hands moving on. In the lower or proximal part, the thorns point backwards and catch the hands as they withdraw . . ."

FRESHWATER SWAMPS

Along the lower reaches of many large rivers, inland from the mangroves and nipa palms, lie huge areas of peat swamp forest—covering an eighth of Sarawak and much of the vast coastal plains of West and Central Kalimantan. Due to the dissolved humic acids in the soil, the slow, sluggish streams issuing from these swamps are darkly colored. Where these highly acidic "blackwater" streams flow into the main rivers, the Tapah come to breed.

A tasty catfish with a prominent head and a tapering body, the Tapah is easily the largest freshwater fish in Sarawak. One caught in the Baram River weighed 180 pounds (82 kg). Its upward-pointing mouth with protruding lower lip is so huge that a human head can easily fit inside the mouth of a 110-pound (50-kg) specimen. A long pair of barbels hang from the side of its mouth, helping it feel its way along the muddy bed of the river and to hunt at night, when it is a ferocious predator on other fishes.

The Tapah inhabits the lower stretches of rivers, above the tides but below the first sets of rapids. In September or October, during the first big water rise after the dry season, it makes its annual spawning runs up certain blackwater streams. Gravid (egg-bearing) females congregate in shallow water. The spawning run lasts only one day. The eggs must develop quickly (within two to three days) because of the rapid rise and fall of local rivers.

Unfortunately for the Tapah, local fishermen have discovered these spawning streams and now block them with gill-nets from stream mouth to spawning site. Few individuals escape, and many of those are netted on their way back

downstream. The fish fetches up to $5 per pound ($12/kg), and so a single large one can equal a day's catch of less valuable fish. As a result, Tapah populations in Sarawak are declining. Fisheries experts are calling for regulations to protect the spawning streams, gravid females and a sufficient number of sexually immature fish.

Also inhabiting freshwater swamps and the rivers draining them is a toothy reptile closely related to the crocodile. The False gharial (or gavial) grows to 17 feet (5 m) but is extremely shy and is considered harmless to humans. It is lethal to fishes, though, and to small mammals, birds and Monitor lizards, which it kills by slashing its long, slender snout back and forth like a parang (Dayak machete) in the water. The False gharial is even more aquatic than the croc, often sleeping underwater on the bed of a deep river pool.

Though they are rarely seen, Cox and Gombek's crocodile survey found False gharials "not infrequent" in Sarawak, especially on the Sadong River, which lies between Kuching and the Batang Lupar. They are thought to be present in most lowland freshwater rivers and swamps in Sarawak, and sometimes in deep, clear pools upriver. Females lay their 30 to 40 hard-shelled eggs in the riverbank mud and guard the eggs. Though the False gharial's hide is not valuable, the eggs are frequently robbed from the nest by people for food. Whether populations are effected is hard to tell at this point, since few naturalists ever encounter this low-profile reptile outside of an occasional one kept at the Sarawak Museum aquarium or the excellent exhibit at the Singapore Zoo.

But, as I was to find, there are other large reptiles upriver—one of them not as shy as the gharial.

A modern, high-powered express boat on the lower Baram River, Sarawak.

A JOURNEY UPRIVER

Pulling out from Kuala Baram near Miri, the 60-foot-long express boat begins its three-hour, 80-mile (130-km) trip up Sarawak's meandering Baram River

Rafts of dipterocarp logs, formerly rainforest trees, await export to Japan.

to Marudi. The wide, brown lower Baram consists of endless vistas of clear sky and a muddy riverbank lined with monotonous nipa palm. Beyond the influence of tides, the river is bordered by thin rows of tall, broad-leaved riparian trees, behind which lie hidden fields and pastures cultivated by unseen villagers.

Otherwise, the banks are piled high with huge logs that once were rainforest trees. Most were cut hastily, rejected by Japanese buyers and stored here for years, barkless and hollow within, slowly disintegrating in the rain. At the active logging camps, wide dirt ramps slope down from temporary wooden buildings to the riverbank, for rolling the logs to the water and for moving machinery up from the barges. The only traffic, aside from other express boats, are tugs pulling huge herringbone rafts of logs, or tall, squared boats with cranes—floating cradles for stacks of giant logs. Sarawak has become the world's largest exporter of tropical hardwoods—6.7 billion board-feet (15 million cubic meters) each year. This is about 50 percent above what even the International Tropical Timber Organization believes is sustainable—a pace that the ITTO believes will deplete the state's forest reserves within a decade.

Now and then the express boat angles to the side of the river and noses up to a platform of floating logs, or to a small floating washhouse fronting a longhouse. We do not actually stop but merely touch the platform for just enough time to allow an old man carrying a new bicycle from town to step off, or a lithe young couple to jump aboard, the wife cradling a small baby, the husband with long bundles of rattan for the market at Marudi.

Until recently, rivers were Borneo's only highways and narrow longboats its only form of long-distance transportation. Paved roads now connect most of Borneo's coastal cities, and a network of dirt logging roads has opened up much of the forested interior. But most settlements have been built on rivers, and rivers remain the most convenient way to haul goods and people. Off the mainstems served by transport boats, everyone utilizes the nearest stream whenever water levels are high enough yet not in flood—even Dayak groups not born with a paddle in their hands (highlanders, for instance, living far above the rapids, who routinely perform amazing feats of travel and transport via paths through the upland forests or over mountain passes on their sturdy legs alone).

Before the advent of diesel engines and outboard motors, river travel was physically limited by tidal currents in the downriver reaches and by water levels upriver—and was further inhibited by the warning signs of certain omen-birds along the way. These days, bird omens and other messages from the forest gods have largely been replaced by more explicit prohibitions introduced by Catholic missionaries who cast for souls along the lower Baram and by airborne Borneo Evangelical Missionaries who proselytized the uplands. Outboards have overpowered the tidal currents of the lower river and airplanes have opened up remote villages above the rapids. Yet the rains still dominate the pulse of travel. Air schedules to the Kelabit Uplands, for example, are determined by the amount of water covering the Bario airfield. Highland trails that are a pleasure to walk when dry become canals or muddy slides during rainy periods. During drought, low water upriver still blocks boats whose draft exceeds a few inches.

At Marudi, we disembark for lunch. We are greeted by a small but incredibly ornate Chinese temple, covered with writhing dragons and goddesses of prosperity, costumed in lipstick red and bright gold, the gilt and lacquer peeling a bit but meticulously cared for. From it, the center of Marudi stretches upriver for three or four blocks, a bustle of crowded shops and open-air restaurants to

A Dayak woman with elongated earlobes.

landward, a cluster of awned stalls selling fruit, biscuits and canned soda along the riverside.

A goodly percentage of those filling the short cement sidewalk wear strange hats and sport silver or hornbill ornaments embedded in loops of earlobes stretched down to their shoulders—spry Kenyah and Kayan elders from upriver longhouses and Kelabits from the upland valleys on the far side of the Tama Abu Mountains. It is the leisurely period following the rice harvest, a time of downriver trips and relaxed socializing. A time to bring some goods to the market and pick a few tools, or to stop here on the way down to Miri to visit the son or daughter working for Shell, or a grandchild in boarding school. Everyone seems to know everyone, though they may live far away and have not met for a year.

We order a meal, but before we can eat, we are hustled up to the District Officer's offices. We did not have time in Miri to pick up our permits to travel upriver—a custom initiated by Sir James Brooke to protect the inland Dayaks; at present the reason seems more to keep the district from suffering any more Bruno Mansers.

Manser, a young Swiss national, took this same trip upriver in 1984 and did not return home until 1990. In the meantime he lived in the rainforest with the semi-nomadic Penan, encouraging them to resist the logging companies encroaching into the upper Baram watershed. Though the ensuing blockades by the Penan and some dissident Kenyah and Kayan have done little to stop the furious pace of the logging, they proved an embarrassment to the state government and rallied world opinion against government policies that the Penan claim will force them to abandon the forest and their way of life. Manser and others, such as the Marudi-based Sahabat Alam Malaysia (Friends of the Earth), also claim that excessive concessions and poorly regulated logging practices will, within a generation, destroy Sarawak's rainforest entirely.

After an hour of explanations and assurances, and another half hour of permits and signatures, we gratefully return to the restaurant for a quick bowl of *mee* (noodles), pick up some fruit from the market, and jump aboard the upriver express.

Like the range of the terrapin, which moves up- and downriver according to the tide levels and river flow, the progress of any long upriver trip depends on the level of the river. It has been relatively dry this past week, and so the express boat's destination is vague. If water levels permit, it will take us up the Tutoh River as far as the town of Long Terawan (*Long* signifying "at the

Dock sign reads "Welcome to the village of Linei Hill."

junction of " in this case, the Terawan River). If not, we will shift to a smaller, slower longboat somewhere downriver of the town.

We continue up the muddy Baram for another two hours, sluicing around the bends like waterskiers; then turn east at a grassy junction onto the Tutoh. The Baram continues southward past extensive Kenyah and Kayan longhouses and a series of serious rapids before collecting the rivers that drain the Kelabit Uplands. The Tutoh, one of the larger tributaries of the Baram, swings around Brunei before turning southeast into the interior, where it branches into a network of headwaters draining the western foothills of the Tama Abus.

As the river narrows, the scenery is reduced to a more human scale. Every few miles there is a village on the banks, with brightly colored clothes hanging on lines between coconut palms, or a woman in a huge, conical rattan sunhat washing clothes, and children on stairs leading down into the water. We touch in briefly at a boarding school, and since it is Saturday, a half-day, the children are out to wave and shout at the boat; two older boys hop on board, returning to their upriver longhouse for the weekend.

The afternoon clouds have been building up quickly, muting the bright day. As the sky begins to seriously darken and the winds heralding the approach of rain begin to whip the loose ends of the baggage, the boatmen appear from below with huge tarps and manilla ropes, with which we secure the tons of gear on deck as the first drops fall. Raindrops the size of hail fall hard at first, and soon slash harder. The straw hat under my rainjacket hood protects my head, but my arms actually hurt from the pounding. The tempo increases into a furious drumming; it is quickly too dark to take photos. The sky is falling. The Baram River watershed has rains as intense as any in the world. A rain gauge in Marudi once recorded more than 3 feet (1 m) in 24 hours. In this climate river levels can rise and fall with lightning speed. Biologists Robert Inger and P. K. Chin, authors of *The Freshwater Fishes of North Borneo*, write that "a river as large as the Kinabatangan [Sabah's largest] exhibits startling changes, rising two to five meters [6-16 ft] overnight even during the months

The river provides bathing and laundry water, waste and sewage disposal—and often even drinking water—to riverside kampongs.

A boarding school along the Baram River. The students are primarily Kenyah and Kayan.

of minimal rainfall." During one month it rose 8–13 feet (2.5–4 m) within 12 hours on three separate days. During such deluges, huge mudslides occur on the sides of steep hills—some natural, some exacerbated by logging or clearing for agriculture.

Much of Borneo is formed of sandstone and of even more easily eroded mudstone, causing the rivers of eastern Sabah to run naturally muddy during rainy spells. But Beccari, who spent months traveling the rivers of Sarawak in the 1860s, wrote: "Although rains are torrential and continuous, the waters of the rivers in Borneo rarely get turbid, because the amount of soil not covered with vegetation is of small extent. Rain, however violent, is, in a country covered by forest, obliged to filter through great masses of vegetation, and comes gently to the ground, where, again, it meets a thick layer of dead leaves. The water, therefore, has been filtered through this vast stratum of vegetable matter."

These intense but brief afternoon rains notwithstanding, it has been fairly dry here lately. Yet the Tutoh is running muddy. Logging certainly appears to have had an effect, as confirmed by the clarity of the Melinau River flowing out of unlogged Gunung Mulu National Park, or the clear rivers of nearby Brunei.

The rain ends as quickly as it began. The sun immediately transforms the river surface and the glistening pools of water on the riverside foliage into clouds of rising steam. A fifth of all the rainfall that falls on the Baram's vast watershed is reevaporated directly back to the atmosphere. Another two-fifths seeps into the ground to be sucked back up and transpired into the air by the jungle plants. Most of the remaining two-fifths will seep out of the riverbanks from the groundwater to join the river on its twisting course back to the sea. But some—the amount depending on the ground cover and the condition of the soil—now flows directly overland to the streams. This is the source of much of the river mud.

At Long Terawan, we are given about half a minute to grab our gear and transfer to the waiting longboats. People and packs and boxes of supplies are hustled into the boats tied on one side as new passengers jump aboard the express from dockside. The river was high enough to get us here; the captain wants to make sure he gets back past the shallows before the water level and the curtain of tropical darkness both fall.

For a half hour, a 50-horse outboard pushes our longboat up the winding Tutoh. The riverbank trees are larger now, clothed with woody lianas (large, ropy vines) and dripping epiphytes. Finally, just after the river veers southeast, we turn northeast onto the Melinau. Immediately the water is much clearer. The Melinau and its tributary the Melinau Paku drain the limestone hills and caves of Gunung (Mount) Mulu National Park; the eroded limestone dissolves back into the calcium carbonate of its marine-shell components rather than the mud and sand of Borneo's extensive mudstone and sandstone. And there is little logging here to exacerbate erosion.

After a half hour of smooth travel past tall riparian forest and superb views of Mount Mulu, we reach the Kenyah lodge below the boundary of the park in time for a cold shower and delicious meal. The trip that has taken us just eight fairly comfortable hours once would have taken days of hard paddling. The next day we can see why...

The first few miles up through the park to the Melinau Gorge run smoothly enough, as in our outboard longboat we pass scenic cliffs and rugged entrances to limestone caves. Kingfishers perch on overhanging branches, and striking Black-and-red broadbills with sky-blue upper bills whip across the river into the trees, where their shaggy, pendulous nests hang out over the river. A Grey-headed fish eagle circles above, its eye out for river catfish. Then the river begins to bottom out, and we are forced to jump in and out of the boat, pushing

it with great difficulty over the shallow gravel. Finally, barely, we reach the end of the line, where the boat can go no further but where the path along the river begins.

We lunch near a patch of sand that has drawn a dense crowd of a dozen species of spectacular butterflies—a mineral lick where some animal has urinated—then head off for a four-hour hike through the woods. It begins to rain, and long before we reach the wooden shelter, the path has turned to a leech-infested river of mud.

The next morning—while photographers Terry Domico and others hike up the steep, slippery trail through Mulu's unique, razor-sharp limestone pinnacles—a companion and I hike farther upstream, to where the river has cut a spectacular gorge between two 5,600-foot (1,700-m) limestone spires—mounts Benarat and Api. The cliffs, covered with pandans and palms and huge ferns, rise straight above us for a thousand feet (300 m) as we cross and recross the knee-deep river. Finally we reach a spot that is too beautiful to leave.

I take a cool swim and explore the riverbed rocks for aquatic insects and tiny fishes. I have not seen water this transparent in over a month—since my last visit to the Danum Valley Research Station in eastern Sabah. There, I hiked one day a few miles down along the upper Segama River . . .

Stripping off my sweat-soaked clothes I donned mask and snorkel for a peek into the delightfully cool tree-shadowed pool formed by a small creek just above its confluence with the river. I was pleasantly surprised to find many tiny fishes swimming in the tannin-stained water: most seemed to be small carps and minnows.

Swimming near the surface were a small group of scissortails, popular aquarium fish with black-tipped tails that snap together like scissors, and upturned mouths ready to catch any ant or spider that might fall onto the surface. In tropical streams, many fish feed on aquatic insects, just as in

Mount Mulu stands above the Melinau River in Sarawak, close to the Brunei border. The large national park surrounding it includes one of the world's largest cave systems.

temperate streams, and Borneo's support dozens of species of insects with predominantly aquatic larvae: dragonflies, aquatic beetles and mayflies (though relatively few stoneflies). But the size and numbers of the larvae do not compare with those of temperate streams, and so insect-eating tropical fishes such as the scissortails depend more on the hoards of terrestrial insects that forage on the leaves above. When an ant or caterpillar loses its footing or is blown off by the wind, hungry fishes are waiting below.

Two-spot barbs, perhaps the most widespread species in all of Southeast Asia, also swam near the surface. They, too, lunge at material hitting the pool's surface; but they are after seeds or flowers, and especially fleshy fruit from the poolside trees. Terrestrial plant debris is a much more important food source here than in temperate streams; many river fishes depend on fallen fruit as the mainstay of their diet. Conversely, many riparian (streamside) plants have evolved to depend on fishes to distribute their seeds.

One of Borneo's dozen species of *Osteochilus*—silvery fishes with a characteristic dark spot in front of the tail fin—vacuumed the grayish film of diatoms and algae from the stony sides of the basin. (Its much larger close relative called *mata merah* is caught commercially on the Rajang and other major rivers.) Also cleaning algae from the rocks was a tongue-twisting *Epalzeorhynchus*, hardly longer than its name. Silvery, with a yellow stripe along its side, it is a close relative of the aquarium fish called the flying fox.

A member of the widespread genus *Hampala*, with large, silver scales and characteristic large black saddle over its back and dark lines edging its tail, was also common in the pool. It will be a voracious feeder on the other species when mature, but here in this nursery pool it is no bigger than its future prey, and probably concentrates on fallen insects.

The only other fish in the pool—a tiny, slender, greenish eel called *Anguilla*—repeatedly slithered under my net or into small cracks in the rock near the bottom of the pool. Feeding on insects, crabs and freshwater shrimp, it will grow considerably bigger as it moves into larger rivers. One caught in the Padas River in western Sabah was more than 5 feet (1.5 m) long and weighed over 25 pounds (12 kg). The Chinese consider it a delicacy.

After an hour or so of trying to catch the quick little fishes in my clumsy scoop-net, I carried my gear down to the stream's confluence with the open, sunny, mainstem Segama. There, a month-long drought had lowered the level in the river's riffles to knee depth and had left the water unusually free of silt. It was a rare opportunity to observe life in a major Bornean river.

Flowing through the Sabah Foundation's forest preserve, the picturesque Segama is still lined with giant trees, all dripping with liana vines and epiphytic ferns, the banks decorated with an unusual number of flowering bushes. Three different dragonfly species, arrayed in various combinations of brick red, crimson and Day-Glow orange, patrolled small pools left by the receding river. Along the water's edge, sand beaches alternated with car- to house-size boulders that gave some indication of the power of the river at flood stage.

Face down in the middle of the river, my fingers gripping the bedrocks, I soon lost track of time, oblivious to everything but the turbulent water humming past my ears, the silvery fishes vacuuming the rocks for algae and the larger, carnivorous ones lurking in the calm spots between the shifting eddies. Most species are larger versions of the same ones I'd seen in the stream pool. I could easily see why they would first need to grow stronger and more skillful in the nursery of the quiet pool before braving the current and predators of the river.

Despite stories of crocodiles, poisonous snakes and thread leeches that entered one's nose to lay eggs in one's brain, the wilds of Borneo were turning out to be rather benevolent, certainly more so than Sabah's death-defying minibus drivers on narrow mountain roads. Yet not ten minutes after leaving the water, I looked up from my lunch to see what appeared to be a crocodile swimming sinuously down the middle of the river, directly over the spot I'd been snorkeling.

Heart thumping, I ran a few meters downstream to a huge boulder that jutted out over the water. Down at the tail end of a long pool, I saw an enormous snake swimming steadily back upstream: a 13-foot (4-m)-long King cobra—the world's largest poisonous snake.

I watched in fascination as the cobra nosed, or rather tongued, its way along the water's edge. I retreated to the top of the boulder, pumped up with adrenaline and ready for a battle that I would probably have lost. In India, King cobras kill up to 2,000 people each year, mostly villagers stumbling over the female's egg nest. (The King cobra is the only snake known to build a nest—usually a pile of bamboo litter up to 3 feet [1 m] in diameter and 20 inches [50 cm] high—of which it is notoriously protective.) The Bornean variety is considered less aggressive than its Indian counterpart but its venom is just as lethal.

The serpent appeared on the upstream side of the boulder and continued its investigations of the near bank. When its forked tongue flicked over my bare footprints in the sand at the water's edge yet declined to follow them up onto land, I relaxed a bit. The cobra was, in fact, one of the most magnificent animals I had ever seen. Its massive, triangular head was tinged red; its slender, muscular body a dark greenish black. About 8 feet of body length wriggled at the surface, while another 5 or 6 feet of narrowing tail dragged below.

The huge serpent continued up the water's edge, searching for signs of other snakes or lizards (its scientific name, *Hannah ophiophagus*, means snake-eater). The King cobra is not considered aquatic, but this one was a skillful swimmer and obviously at home in the water. It fought its way through the cascade at the confluence of the stream (where, in profile, I could see for the first time its yellow throat with black splotches) and up to the same dark, peaceful pool in which I had earlier been snorkeling! The snake had been mellow enough, but I now understood why Dayaks always carry a parang (machete) in the forest and vowed to carry one myself in the future.

The fishes I'd been observing through my mask before being so rudely interrupted by the snake all seemed to be from the same Cyprinid family of carps and minnows. As the premier freshwater fish family of Southeast Asia, Cyprinids make up a third of Borneo's 600 species of river fishes and a much larger percentage of those in small streams. Cyprinids are not all tiny. In fact,

The Golden gourami, a popular aquarium fish from Borneo.

Swamp barbs and Tee barbs, two species of a widespread genus of popular aquarium fishes inhabiting Borneo's rivers.

seven of the 10 most important commercial river fishes in Sarawak are from this family: *Semah*, Sarawak's state fish, grows to at least 92 pounds (42 kg). *Tenggadek* fetches $5/lb ($11/kg) in the market at Sibu on the Rajang River. *Mengalan*, growing to 22 pounds (10 kg), is a favorite food fish in western Sabah and Sarawak.

These latter two are members of the genus *Puntius* (or *Barbus*), of which 10 or so smaller species—called barbs—are more valued in aquariums than in the pot. Their colorful names, such as Golden barb, Clown barb, Tiger barb, Zebra barb, Tinfoil barb and so forth, are suggestive of their varied beauty. Two others, the Tee barb and the widespread Glass barb, are from different genera but the same family.

Borneo's streams are home to another family of well-known aquarium fishes: the "labyrinth fishes"—gouramies (genus *Gouramy*) and bettas (*Betta*). These members of the unique Anabantid family have evolved an auxiliary breathing apparatus on top of the head called the labyrinth. A modification of the first gill arch, it consists of two bony cavities filled with wrinkled tissue covered with many tiny blood vessels. The labyrinth allows the fish to breathe oxygen directly from the air; some species are even obligated to come to the surface to breathe. They then release the spent air as bubbles from their mouths. The unusual organ allows labyrinth fishes to live in warm, slow-moving rivers or shallow pools that may be almost devoid of oxygen.

Bettas are attractive little labyrinth fishes. (One *Betta* species not native to Borneo but introduced into some ditches is the spectacular Siamese fighting fish.) The long, sharp pelvic fin precedes an elongated anal fin and a large, flame-shaped tailfin. One betta found by Tyson Roberts in the Kapuas River broods the hatchlings in the male's mouth. (Notes Roberts: "Western Borneo has the most diverse assemblage of oral-brooding fishes anywhere on earth, involving at least 11 species in six families. This is truly remarkable when it is recalled that the total number of fish families known to practice oral breeding is only 11." One *Channid* male was seen with nearly 100 young of two different age classes in his mouth!)

Another Betta species found only in Borneo lives at the uppermost headwaters of forest streams, in small pools that are sometimes fed only by intermittent trickles. Though growing only to a maximum of 4 inches (10 cm), it can jump more than a foot (30 cm) high. This ability, along with its air-breathing labyrinth, allows it to reinvade headwater pools after flash floods have washed it out. It can surmount—or even get around by flipping up the streamside rocks—waterfalls up to 17 ft (5 m) high.

The other main group of labyrinth fishes, the gouramis, includes some of the world's most popular aquarium fishes. A gourami male turns brilliant colors during mating periods, becoming highly pugnacious and territorial. He builds a frothy nest of long-lasting bubbles to which he lures the female by energetic, colorful displays. After coiling around and embracing her to squeeze out the eggs, he gathers the fertilized eggs up into his mouth and forcefully spits them into the nest. He then guards them until they hatch.

The Giant gourami grows to 24 inches (60 cm). It has a big head with bug-eyes, huge lips and, at maturity, a fatty protuberance on the forehead. The wide, flat body has bluish stripes on large, pink to silvery gray scales; the pelvic fins are long sensory filaments; the long, bright blue anal fin is edged with red. The Giant gourami normally lives near the surface in pools and side channels of turbid rivers, where it feeds on fallen fruit and insects; but it is also an important aquaculture fish, grown in farm ponds throughout Borneo, where it feeds quite happily on insects and taro leaves.

Three smaller species are aquarist favorites. The beautiful Pearl gourami's color varies greatly, but often has a body pattern of white dots on a golden background, overlaid with a shimmering mother-of-pearl iridescence, and yellow dots on the large fins. The male's pectoral fins and the front of the anal fin turn a brilliant orange, red or violet during courtship.

The Three-spot gourami grows to 6 inches (15 cm); a mutant variety (Blue gourami) has been bred for aquaria. The pelvic fins have evolved into long, trailing sensory filaments. The base of the Three-spot's fins are yellow and the

Tee barbs.

dorsal and tail fins have white spots against a dark background. The Blue variety is gray, with a beautiful electric blue along the base of the long anal fin. When mating, the male becomes a marbled bluish black and gray.

The third aquarium favorite—the Kissing gourami— is bred less for its beauty than for its unique behavior: It can roll back its prominent lips while feeding on algae, and does the same to "kiss" others of the species. Yet cute as it may seem, the habit of lip-to-lip contact is actually an aggressive display between competing males rather than a sign of affection. The Kissing gourami is not native to Borneo, having been introduced as a pond fish in the mid-1950s; but growing to 12 inches (30 cm) and being so aggressive, it has now invaded many oxbow lakes and small streams of the lower Baram and Tinjar rivers.

Borneo's most attractive large river fish, the dragonfish, or arawana, is the latest aquarist craze. The green, silver or golden varieties grow up to 3 feet (1 m) but are usually displayed at about half that size. The arawana's large scales form a quilt- like pattern of iridescent pink, sky blue, light green and silver-gray. White dots further decorate the lateral line and along the dorsal and anal fins. Rays of green and yellow spread outward from its large, mobile eyes, and a pair of short, stiff horizontal barbels protrude from the lower lip. There is hardly a Chinese restaurant in Southeast Asia that does not feature a tank graced with a few of these large, shimmering fishes (far too expensive for all but the most sumptuous of feasts, it is nevertheless eaten), putting wild populations under heavy pressure.

The only group inhabiting Borneo's rivers that comes close to the Crypinids in diversity and commercial importance are the catfishes, with almost a hundred species, but these include seven separate families. Members of the larger catfish families, the Siluridae (which includes the huge Tapah mentioned earlier) and Bagriidae, are more apt to be found as bottom-dwellers in the estuaries and main stems of Borneo's large, turbid rivers than in its small headwater streams. But the Pangsilidae are large, mid-water fishes; the Sisoridae are bottom-dwellers in fast streams; the Akysidae are small, camouflaged stream fishes.

Certainly the strangest-looking of all the strange catfishes is the Angler-catfish, or chaca, small specimens of which are exported worldwide to aquarists. Adapted to slow-moving lowland rainforest streams, the chaca is a master of camouflage. The flattened, tadpole-shaped body looks just like a fallen leaf, down to the tapered, veined, rot-stained back that leads to a tail resembling a long leaf stem. In the wild, it ambushes small fishes and prawns by lunging sideways to suck prey into its huge mouth. When lying in wait, the chaca barely

Arawana or "Dragon fish" native to Borneo's rivers. Though this large individual may be worth a small fortune as an aquarium fish, it may eventually be center-piece of a sumptuous Chinese meal.

breathes, and in order to keep movement to a minimum, its gill covers have pores that allow water to escape without moving the gill covers.

Most members of three Bornean fish families have largely escaped the aquarium despite their unusual looks because most of their species are adapted to fast-moving streams: loaches (Cobitidae), the largest and most versatile family, has more than 30 Bornean species, more than any single family other than the Cyprinids. Most loaches are small, slender, odd-looking fishes with warty (sensory papillae), underslung mouths for vacuuming up nematodes, copepods and other tiny creatures. Some are found in slow-moving streams, a few of these introduced as aquarium fishes; but many are found only in riffles.

Torrent loaches (family Homalopteridae) are found throughout Borneo in fast-flowing mountain streams or in riffles of lowland rivers. All are long, smooth, streamlined fishes with very broad pectoral and pelvic fins. Together, these four fins and the smooth, flat belly between act as a large suction pad to hold the fish against smooth rocks in the rapids as the fish feeds on the film of diatoms and algae, occasionally supplementing its diet with aquatic insects and worms.

Just as the gouramis are unique in their ability to breathe in oxygen-poor pools and sluggish streams, another Bornean fish may be the world's most highly specialized for fast-water streams. *Gyrinocheilus*—the sole genus in Southeast Asian family that contains only a few scattered species—has developed a unique way of breathing with its mouth closed. Almost all other fishes breathe by taking water in through the mouth and expelling through the gills, where oxygen is extracted though the thin walls of blood vessels in the gill filaments. But since *Gyrinocheilus* has developed expanded, sucker-like lips on its underslung mouth, which it attaches for long periods directly to the rock for holding on in the current and for rasping algae, it cannot take water through the mouth. Instead, it has evolved a spiracle-like opening at the upper end of the gill cover that takes in the water, allowing it to breathe while feeding, and to feed in currents that would wash away any other fish.

A Pig-tailed macaque chews on a piece of sugarcane. The ground-dwelling macaques adapt well to rural farm areas and plantations, where they are considered pests.

RIVER MONKEYS

As clear as the Melinau is, and as beautiful as its gorge is this sunny day, there are few large animals along the river or in the forest behind it. The gorge is a thoroughfare for Penan hunting parties heading east or west to or from their longhouse downstream, and few monkeys, hornbills or Monitor lizards would survive along this stretch, where silent men with sharp ears and lethal blowpipes walk each day. But other rivers are still rich in wildlife.

I had met a man in Sandakan who transported small groups of visitors to the Kinabatangan River in eastern Sabah, mainly to see Borneo's endemic Proboscis monkeys. By late afternoon—after a rough boat ride across the bay and a bone-jarring jeep drive across a huge area being cleared for oil palm plantations—we finally reached the river.

Turning off the muddy, well-logged mainstem into a narrow, slow-flowing tributary, we had a quick glimpse of a pair of huge Rhinoceros hornbills. A small flock of large Green imperial pigeons perched on the tops of the riparian trees that walled the tributary. Then in quick succession we spotted a Broad-billed roller, or Dollarbird, a large-billed Frogmouth waiting for dusk and, far in the distance, a Storm's stork perched majestically on the branch of a lone, dead tree.

Rounding a bend, we saw the monkeys. A female Proboscis grabbed her baby and leapt noisily over to an adjacent tree where three other females and their babies were feeding. A large male turned toward us and, crouching on the limb, directed a string of invectives—an expressive series of growls, grunts and screeches. We cut the engines and began to drift. The male moved to a nearer tree and continued his threats, though in a mellower tone. His large face, with huge, fleshy nose, along with his puffed-up chest and massive forearms, gave him a certain intimidating grandeur, though the ponderous beer-belly under-cut his image somewhat.

Gradually, the monkeys returned to their evening toilette, settling in for the night. The huge male turned his back to us disdainfully, and a female came over to groom him with her long fingers. There were a dozen or so in the troop. We also saw a few Silvered langurs in the trees just upriver from the Proboscis troop. One of the langur juveniles still had a head of orange hair, the only remnant of its once-golden infant coat. The dark gray langur adults looked like skinny adolescents even next to the Proboscis females, and childlike compared to the Proboscis males, which can weigh four times as much as a male langur.

Proboscis monkeys return to the rivers each evening. It is believed that the riparian zone is their primary home and that they go out to the mangroves or swamp forest only for supplemental food. The river helps delineate territories between troops, and the view from the tall riparian trees gives them security both along the open river and perhaps also inland from the built-up levee.

The Proboscis monkey's habitual use of the trees, though, is becoming a danger to it. Increasingly, lowland forests are being cut for plantations, isolating the ribbon of riparian trees from the coastal and swamp forests behind. The riparian forest here was now only a thin strip between the river and the huge new plantation clearings that we had seen from the road as we drove the rough logging roads to the Kinabatangan. That would explain why the Silvered langurs had joined the Proboscis on this last bastion of riverside forest.

The other problem is that the unobstructed view the river offers the monkeys also gives a clear view of the monkeys to boaters. Coastal Malays have always disdained hunting monkeys for food, but the Dayaks and Chinese of fast-growing urban areas have no such dietary inhibitions. And greater prosperity has resulted in a growing number of recreational boaters who drive their speed-boats down the rivers to the estuaries. In Sarawak, according to Elizabeth

Opposite:
Eastern Sabah's Segama River flows through Danum Valley Conservation Area. The water is clear and the level particularly low during a drought, but within hours it could become a raging, muddy torrent.

Langanan Falls, Sabah.

Bennett, some of the boaters hunt or take evening target practice on Proboscis monkeys in the trees.

Here on the Kinabatangan, the dependable habits of the Proboscis and the ease of observation is becoming a valuable resource in itself. It is unclear what long-term effects "eco-tourism"—such as the trip we were on—will have. It may disturb the monkeys, yet may also provide the only convincing economic argument to preserve a bit of their riverside habitat.

The silence was broken by a shrill cry, sounding increasingly annoyed, as a pair of Pied hornbills took off from a tree behind us. The broad black wings contrasted with the white belly and tail. Both birds had large, yellow hornlike casques arching over the huge, curved bill. Though the Pied is one of the smaller of the hornbills, the pair still left us breathless as they flew with powerful wingbeats across the pastel sky. Later, we would see other, even larger hornbills when we followed the rivers up into Borneo's most complex world—its magnificent lowland rainforest.

JUNGLE IN THE SKY

A male Rhinoceros hornbill lands in the crown of a huge rainforest tree. Hopping through the vegetation with a practiced eye, it spots a cluster of sour wild figs on a vine that has snaked its way upward from the crotch of a branch in the dim light a hundred feet below to flower and fruit under the open sky. The hornbill snatches one of the globular yellowish fruits. Tossing it into the air, he catches it deftly in his long, swollen scimitar of a bill. A squirrel scolds him with a birdlike *chewit-chewit* but the hornbill makes only a half-hearted lunge at it. A lizard on a lower branch is not so lucky; its freeze posture fails to keep it from being snatched up by the surprisingly deft tip of the bird's massively-horned forceps.

The hornbill launches out over the canopy with loud swishes of 50-inch (125-cm) wings to land in an enormous Tapang tree that spreads its leafless limbs high above the other trees. Clinging to the smooth bark of the trunk, the male regurgitates the lizard into the tip of a similar bill protruding from a narrow horizontal slit in the trunk. After his mate's bill disappears back into her, he lifts off from the tree with a hoarse *grok*. Beating his huge wings against the wind, he begins again to search for ripe fruit or unwary animals on the billowy surface of the rainforest canopy, far above the jungle floor.

CANOPY PLANT LIFE

The hornbill's domain is a lofty one. Many of Borneo's forest trees rise straight up from the jungle floor for 150 feet (45 m) or more before spreading out into the leafy crowns that support the rolling green surface of the canopy. The top of the main canopy often stands more than 200 feet (60 m) above the ground, with some trees rising 50 feet (15 m) above this. "Tropical rainforest of this stature and with this density of top-of-canopy trees," writes one scientist, "is unique in all the world."

The imposing height of the forest is largely due to a single family of broad-leaved evergreens—the dipterocarps, so named because the two (sometimes three or five) carpels remain attached to the fruits like long wings.

Dipterocarp species contribute most of Southeast Asia's taller trees, and Borneo, as center of the family's diversity, hosts its very tallest members. Of 150 dipterocarp species studied in Brunei, 42 reached 200 feet (60 m). The rainforests of Amazonia and central Africa, on the other hand, can boast just one species that grows so tall. A few giant trees, called emergents, even rise above this imposing layer. Two dipterocarp genera, *Shorea* and *Dryobalanops*, include emergent species that often reach 250 feet (75 m).

Dipterocarps, not surprisingly, are the mainstay of Borneo's timber industry. There are so many species that for timber purposes they are simply grouped into categories: red meranti, white meranti, white seraya and keruing. Red marantis, which include about 70 species in the genus *Shorea*, have a fascinating pollination story.

Despite their enormous height, most *Shorea* are pollinated by thrips—minute insects that can barely fly. A large *Shorea* tree may have 4 million flowers, but a fifth of these never open; instead, they serve as breeding sites for thrips. The tiny insects crawl into the fertile flowers as they open at dusk. By dawn the petals fall to the forest floor, along with the pollen-covered thrips. Drawn by the flower's strong, "sickly" odor, the thrips spiral slowly upward on weak air currents and manage to reach the next evening's offering of flowers. Since the only open blossoms are on trees not the ones the thrips fell from, the trees are cross-pollinated, if only over a short distance.

Opposite:
An "emergent" tree rises above the lofty rainforest canopy. Some emergents attain a height of more than 250 feet (75 m).

The epiphytic Bird's-nest fern grows to 10 feet (3 m) across, providing an aerial refuge for insects and for other epiphytes.

Following page:
The rainforest canopy of Mulu National Park as seen from Mount Api.

The tallest forest tree of all, however, the Tapang or Mengaris (*Koompassia excelsa*), is not a dipterocarp. It is not even an evergreen, but a deciduous legume. One found growing in Sarawak measured 277 feet (84 m) in height. *Koompassia* is sometimes called the "bee tree" because wild honeybees hang their huge, teardrop nests from its upper branches—perhaps because the tree's smooth bark makes it difficult for Sun bears to climb. Humans, however, are more resourceful. By pounding bamboo pegs into the trunk and connecting the pegs with rattan to a series of bamboo poles, Dayaks have for centuries braved the heights and the stinging bees to bring down the combs—not just for the sweet honey but also for the wax. When beeswax was the best source for candles and candles were a major source of lighting, the world market was enormous. In 1812 an estimated 80,000 pounds (35,000 kg) of beeswax were exported from eastern Sabah alone.

By intercepting most sunlight, the upper canopy shades the layers below; only 2 to 5 percent of the sunlight striking the top of the canopy reaches the forest floor. Few annual flowering plants can survive this little light, which is why so few flowers grace the rainforest understory. The top of the canopy, though, is sprinkled with brightly colored or sweet-smelling blossoms, put there, say Christianized Dayaks, "for the eyes and nose of God alone." And since many of the long-lived forest trees flower only rarely—often simultaneously during years of favorable rainfall—most of the flowers and fruit come from the vines and epiphytes that reach the top of the canopy.

Most rainforest plants reach the sunlight by taking structural advantage of the huge trees. The seeds of epiphytic plants are dispersed by fruit-eating birds or bats—deposited in droppings onto rough bark of trunks or upper branches. Fastgrowing, woody lianas start on the forest floor but quickly spiral up the trunks of the trees to flower in the canopy. Thinner clinging vines climb the trunks, then sprawl over the tree tops.

Strangler figs start as epiphytes from seeds deposited in a mid-level crotch. They then send cordlike roots down to the ground and vinelike shoots up above the canopy. The network of roots and shoots encircle the host tree, "strangling" it by not allowing its cambium layer (the new cells beneath the bark which transport water and nutrients) to expand. Eventually, the host tree rots away, leaving in its place a huge, hollow fig tree.

Both Wallace and Beccari noted the importance of figs and were especially impressed by the stranglers. Beccari, who collected 55 species of fig, 16 of them endemic to Borneo, noted:

> *The topmost leaf-mass in the forests is largely composed of the foliage of trees of the genus Ficus [figs], whether springing from a separate unsupported trunk rising straight from the ground, or from some gigantic epiphyte which has later become arborescent . . . Some species are diminutive epiphytes. Others climb first on tree trunks and on rocks and mount to the tops of the most lofty trees . . . Some enclose their hosts in meshes of colossal size and become themselves gigantic trees. Others develop numerous roots from their branches, which either become secondary trees or else remain cord-like.*

Wallace, co-developer of the theory of evolution, saw the stranglers as perfect examples of "an actual struggle for life in the vegetable kingdom, not less fatal to the vanquished than the struggles among animals which we can so much more easily observe and understand. The advantages of quicker access to light which is gained in one way by climbing plants, is here obtained by a forest-tree, which has the means of starting life at an elevation which others can only attain after many years of growth, and then only when the fall of some other tree has made room for them."

BIRDS AND BATS

Contemporary ecologists corroborate the value of the forest fig. Mark Leighton, who studied dispersal of rainforest fruits and now directs the research station at West Kalimantan's Gunung Palung National Park, writes: "In the rain forests of Malesia [Malaysia, Indonesia, the Philippines and New Guinea] no genus is more important than the figs, especially the giant trees, which are mostly stranglers or banyans. In every forest studied it has been found that the figs collectively are in fruit the whole year round. Big fig trees fruit copiously and great congregations of animals assemble in their crowns at these times. Cranbrook observed large aggregations of hornbills in fruiting fig trees in Sarawak, with as many as 50 birds of up to four of Borneo's eight species present simultaneously."

Hornbills are critical to the dispersal of the figs because they eat the entire fruit, including the seed, and then fly long distances, dispersing the seeds widely. Fruit bats, pigeons and Fairy bluebirds, which also relish figs, often simply nibble at the flesh, dropping the seeds below the parent plants.

Sarawak is known as the "Land of the Hornbills," but these remarkable birds are found throughout Borneo. They have close relatives in mainland Asia and Africa but are not related to the large-billed Amazonian toucans.

Growing from the base of the upper bill is a horny excrescence called a casque. It is usually hollow or filled with spongy tissue, but the Helmeted hornbill's large, square gold-and-crimson casque is solid—ideal for carving into earrings, snuff bottles, belt buckles or statuettes. Hornbill "ivory" was for centuries shipped to China as *ho-ting* (golden jade), fetching higher prices than elephant ivory or even jade itself. The carving was originated, however, by Bornean Dayaks. Some of the most spectacular examples can be seen in Kuching's

Secondary rainforest canopy seen from the primary canopy.

A male Wreathed hornbill. Hornbills feed on fruit and small animals in the rainforest canopy; females and nestlings are enclosed in hollow tree trunks and fed by the male.

Sarawak Museum, and elderly Kelabits in Sarawak's uplands still carve the casques into pendants for their shoulder-length earlobes.

During mating season, the male hornbills themselves reportedly use their casqued bills for spectacular head-on collisions in mid-air, and as a tool during the hornbills' unique mating and incubation.

A month or more before mating, the male begins courtship feeding of the female, who, when ready to lay, enters a nest hole high in a hollow tree. The pair then spend two or three days plastering up the hole with her clay-like droppings—she on the inside, he on the outside—using the sides of their bills as trowels.

The female is now imprisoned for the next three months, with only a finger-width slit between her and the outside world. The male delivers food, first to her, and then to her one or two chicks.

When the hornbill chick is partly reared, the female breaks down the nest wall and emerges. The obese chick (who has never observed the procedure) reseals the entrance by itself and, after another month or so of being fed by both parents, breaks out to join them.

Wallace discovered a hornbill nest, and asked two assistants to procure the contents: "In about an hour afterward, much to my surprise, a tremendous loud hoarse screaming was heard, and the bird was brought to me, together with a young one that had been found in the hole. This was a most curious object, as large as a pigeon, but without a particle of plumage on any part of it. It was exceedingly plump and soft, and with a semi-transparent skin, so that it looked more like a bag of jelly, with head and feet stuck on, than like a real bird."

The female must be able to reach from the floor of the hollow to the opening at the top, and so oftentimes the pair must fill the nest hollow to raise the floor. Proper nest trees are therefore rare, and whenever possible, hornbills use the same nest over and over. British ornithologist John Whitehead, an early explorer in Sabah, supposed that the female hornbill's seemingly torturous imprisonment protected the egg and nesting from bands of monkeys, lizards and snakes. This he considered the evolutionary force behind the design of most tropical bird nests, which otherwise hang from the tips of branches and are never the open cups typical of northern birds.

Collecting on Mount Kinabalu in 1888, Whitehead found a Black hornbill female and chick being fed by all five adults of the small colony. This would ensure the female's survival if anything happened to her mate.

The Rhinoceros hornbill, with its upswept phallic casque, represents one of the most powerful Dayak gods, Singalang Burong. It plays an important part in Iban religious festivals, especially Gawai Kenyalang, the most lavish and prolonged (usually five nights) of all the Iban religious festivals. An elaborately carved figure of the bird, which itself may have taken weeks to create and which may be kept for years before the opportunity to display it, is the ritual centerpiece.

The Rhinoceros hornbill represents a sacred messenger to traditional Iban. Its feathers are central to many Dayak rituals and dances.

This does not, however, protect living hornbills from being hunted, and in fact makes their casques and feathers (used in men's headpieces and as hand ornaments in the women's graceful "hornbill dance") all the more desirable. Though the Rhinoceros hornbill keeps to the tree tops and is very wary, Iban hunters often lure it down by imitating its remarkable call.

Many other birds and mammals depend on the figs and other canopy fruits, and most fruiting plants depend on these animals for seed dispersal. More than 30 bird species, including barbets, Pink-necked and Little green pigeons, the Green broadbill, and the handsome blue and black Fairy bluebird all follow the shifting, unpredictable pattern of fruiting. Others feed on the nectar of canopy flowers.

Small, brightly colored flowerpeckers, says Smythies "often congregate at the tops of very tall flowering trees and then through binoculars, the busy birds can be seen flitting like a swarm of bees about the blossoms on the exposed surface of the forest canopy. They eat small spiders, insects and small berries."

Fairy bluebirds are fond of figs in the rainforest canopy. They descend to streams at midday to drink and bathe.

Above the canopy, Crested serpent-eagles circle, searching for snakes and lizards; swifts and swallows hawk for insects drifting up from the trees. One large swift, the Brown needletail, is considered one of the fastest—if not *the* fastest—fliers on earth. Smythies reports: "Usually seen hurtling through the air in small parties with a loud swish of wings . . . at other times it hawks insects over some ridge-top, taking advantage of the rising currents of air to remain almost motionless in one spot or moving back and forth along the ridge in a wide circuit. I have seen a party of 20 circling high in the air above Ranau in a 30-knot wind."

At night the birds are replaced by bats. Half of Borneo's 140 mammal species are bats, and more than 50 of these feed primarily on insects. As night falls and birdsongs are replaced by choruses of crickets and frogs, hoards of bats emerge from caves, from overhanging rocks and hollow logs. Their weird-looking but highly evolved ears and noses function as sonar devices as they engage in blind attacks on moths—who have evolved similarly complex evasive techniques. The moths hover over the canopy in clouds as they seek nectar and pollen of night-blooming flowers.

Fruit and nectar bats, with large red eyes and doglike muzzles are much more conventionally handsome than insectivorous bats because they have no need for sophisticated sonar. They flit over the canopy or through the forest's middle layers following the scent of ripe fruit or nectar from coevolved, pale, tubular, night-blooming flowers, many of which smell faintly like the bats themselves.

Fruit bats and nectar bats are extremely important pollinators of wild fruit. The many species of wild banana are pollinated by the Long-tongued nectar bat, along with spider hunters and a few other birds. The fruit-eating flying fox, the world's largest bat, and the Cave nectar bat both pollinate durians and many other forest trees.

A large, colorful orb-weaver spider. The thread of its web, for its thickness, is the strongest tensile material known.

Tropical moths are often as colorful as temperate butterflies.

The Slow loris, a nocturnal primate that feeds on insects and soft fruits, has adapted to secondary forest and cocoa plantations.

Figs aside, the spiky, coconut-sized durian may be the most valuable of all rainforest fruits. Orangutans savor the wild varieties, while human inhabitants of Southeast Asia consider the cultivated varieties "the king of fruit."

When left open or stored in an enclosed space, a durian develops an overwhelming smell (perhaps to lure seed-dispersing mammals) that can induce nausea in the uninitiated. But the soft, yellow fruit itself, inside the bright, white inner rind, has a unique taste (avocado mixed with sourcream and chives?) that is as complex and hard to describe as a fine wine, and varieties have tastes that differ as much as a newly bottled Rhine wine does from a vintage Bordeaux. Wallace quickly became one of its most enthusiastic converts:

> *The five cells are satiny-white within, and are each filled with an oval mass of cream-colored pulp, embedded in which are two or three seeds about the size of*

A flying lizard being held to show its "wings," which are actually expanded ribs covered with a gliding membrane.

chestnuts. The pulp is the eatable part, and its consistence and flavor are indescribable. A rich butter-like custard highly flavored with almonds gives the best general idea of it, but intermingled with it come wafts of flavor that call to mind cream-cheese, onionsauce, brown-sherry, and other incongruities. Then there is a rich glutinous smoothness in the pulp which nothing else possesses, but which adds to its delicacy. It is neither acid, nor sweet, nor juicy, yet one feels the want of none of these qualities, for it is perfect as it is. It produces no nausea or other bad effect, and the more you eat of it the less you feel inclined to stop. In fact, to eat durions, is a new sensation worth a voyage to the East to experience.

Strong words from a veteran traveler in a land that also boasts the mangostene, the rambutan and a dozen other delicious tropical fruits.

The rainforest canopy has been described as an entire plant community above ground. Numerous animals found in this habitat are born and die without ever touching the ground. Under undisturbed conditions, many species, or even one sex, of butterfly live entirely in the aerial jungle. The female Raja Brooke's birdwing, for example, was a great mystery until finally found living happily in the canopy.

As Beccari noted, Borneo was "formerly one unbroken primeval forest from the sea coasts to the summits of its highest mountains. In Africa most of the Mammalia are adapted to move and live on extensive plains, and most of them are swift of foot. In Malaysia, on the other hand, arboreal animals far outnumber the others, and hence, when it comes to rapid movement, the suitable method of attaining it is by flight" (birds and bats), or by bracheation—swinging along branches by means of long arms with hooklike hands (gibbons), or by running along branches and jumping (squirrels, tarsier, monkeys). "We find a bare dozen of ungulates adapted to run and roam on plains," he concludes, "against over 150 species of mammals belonging to other Orders, of which two-thirds are strictly arboreal when not actually aerial."

OTHER "FLYING" ANIMALS

Wallace and Beccari considered a few of Borneo's canopy animals among the most unusual on earth (or more accurately, above earth); and they still fascinate naturalists lucky enough to see them. Of these "flying" animals, three herptiles

A flying lizard ("flying dragon") photographed in mid-glide.

especially caught their attention. Wrote Beccari: "Among the various small reptiles which we were able to collect in our neighborhood the most singular were the flying lizards (*Draco*) . . . These surprising little creatures can be seen at any moment during the hot hours of the day flying through the air from one palm tree to another by the aid of the membranous expansion with which the sides of their bodies are provided. When they take their spring they start with the head downwards; when they reach their destination they alight with the head upwards."

Beccari searched for the flying frog of Borneo described by Wallace, but never had the good fortune to meet with it. One of the few illustrations in Wallace's book (used on the cover of some editions) is of this unusual amphibian, of which he wrote:

> *One of the most curious and interesting animals which I met with in Borneo was a large tree-frog, which was brought to me by one of the Chinese workmen. He*

A tree frog silhouetted on a large rainforest leaf. Tree frogs make up more than a third of Borneo's more than 100 frog species.

*assured me that he had seen it come down, in a slanting direction, from a high
tree, as if it flew.*

*On examining it, I found the toes very long, and fully webbed to their very
extremity, so that when expanded they offered a surface much larger than the
body. The fore legs were also bordered by a membrane, and the body was capable
of considerable inflation . . . The body was about four inches long, while the webs
of each hind foot, when fully expanded, covered a surface of four square inches,
and the webs of all the feet together about twelve square inches [75 sq cm]. The
extremities of the toes have dilated discs for adhesion, showing the creature to be
a true tree-frog. It would appear to be a new species of the genus* Rhacophorus.

Two unusual Bornean snakes are also able to glide from tree to tree. The
Golden flying snake is the more common. Variable in color, it tends to be dark
above with greenish and red spots. Its gliding ability is gained by the hinged
scales along its ribs; when the snake is airborne the large side scales spread out
to greatly increase air resistance. Launching itself from high in one tree, the
snake seems to writhe through the air on its way to a lower position on a
neighboring tree.

Another animal highly adapted for life in the trees is a strange mammal
resembling a large flying squirrel. The colugo, or flying lemur, has a small head
with big eyes, tiny ears, a long, pointed muzzle and strange, comblike teeth. Its
slender body is draped in a loose, oversize cloak of reddish fur. There are only
two members of its family—one in the Philippines and the Southeast Asian
species that Wallace first described from Borneo:

*Another curious animal which I had met with in Borneo is the flying lemur.
This creature has a broad membrane extending all round its body to the
extremities of the toes, and to the point of the rather long tail. This enables it to
pass obliquely through the air from one tree to another. It is sluggish in its
motions, at least by day, going up a tree by short runs of a few feet, and then
stopping a moment as if the action was difficult. It rests during the day clinging
to the trunks of trees, where its olive or brown fur, mottled with irregular,
whitish spots and blotches, resembles closely the color of mottled bark, and no
doubt helps to protect it.*

*Once, in a bright twilight, I saw one of these animals run up a trunk in a
rather open place, and then glide obliquely through the air to another tree, on
which it alighted near its base, and immediately began to ascend. I paced the
distance from the one tree to the other, and found it to be seventy yards [65 m];
and the amount of descent I estimated at not more than thirty-five or forty feet
[12 m], or less than one in five.*

At night the colugo feeds on leaves, shoots, flowers and perhaps tree sap with
its unusual comblike teeth. During the day the nestless creature sleeps hanging
upside down, camouflaged by lichen growing in its fur. The voluminous gliding
membrane also serves as a handy cradle for the female's single baby. The tail
is enclosed by the membrane, rather than being free, as with flying squirrels.

Flying squirrels themselves make up the bulk of the canopy's community of
gliders. Just as nocturnal bats "partition" the rainforest feast with diurnal birds,
nocturnal flying squirrels divide up mammal-dispersed fruits and seeds with
diurnal squirrels. More slender than tree squirrels, flying squirrels are clumsier
climbers due to the bulky gliding membrane—the patagium—which hangs
from their sides in loose folds. Borneo's 14 species range in size from two rare,
mouselike pygmies—the Lesser pygmy flying squirrel measuring less than 5
inches (13 cm), half of which is tail—to the Red giant, which grows to 3 feet
(90 cm). The Red giant flying squirrel can easily make a single continuous glide
of 330 feet (100 m), longer than an American football field and equal to a soccer
pitch. Since they are all nocturnal and inhabit the inaccessible canopy, most

Opposite:
*The Binturong, or bearcat, is a large arbo-
real civet with prehensile tail. It searches the
canopy for ripe figs and small animals.*

flying squirrel species are considered rare, though they may in fact be rather common. Few specimens have been collected of even the large, widespread Red giant.

Most of Borneo's cat family—the beautiful Clouded leopard as well as four species of smallish jungle cats—tend to stick to the lower canopy and travel extensively on the ground. The same can be said for most of the civets.

Civets are slender, medium-sized omnivores that look like a cross between a mongoose and a cat. The largest species, however, the Binturong, or bearcat, is a full-fledged member of the canopy community. Its face resembles that of a black bear, but with long tufts of hair from small ears outlined in white. Its dark, thick, shaggy fur is also bearlike, though it stands and moves more like a long-bodied cat. The Binturong also can be found on the ground, but it tends to move slowly through the canopy, feeding on figs and small animals. It is so adapted to life in the trees that its long, shaggy tail has become prehensile, like that of New World monkeys, and much more so than Bornean leaf-eating monkeys, whose long tails are used primarily for balance rather than clinging.

MONKEYS AND APES

The ability to live on a diet of leaves and seeds is the one trait that unifies Borneo's subfamily of arboreal, leaf-eating monkeys. (The two macaques, a separate subfamily, spend much of their time on the ground and eat mostly invertebrate animals and fallen fruit.) The singular Proboscis monkey constitutes its own genus; the other five species are closely related, all in the genus *Presbytis*. Formerly called leaf-eating monkeys, they are now called langurs, as are their many relatives throughout South and Southeast Asia.

Like the Proboscis monkey, langurs have a sacculated stomach similar to, though less complex than, that of a deer or cow. It contains bacteria that ferment and break down the cellulose in the leaf's tough cell wall.

Four of the five Bornean langurs have dark faces, ranging from silvery gray to black, surrounded by a long, spiky hairdo, mutton-chop sideburns and short beards. Hose's langur (Gray leaf monkey), though, has a flesh-colored face with dark cheek markings, which in some subspecies is set off by a snowy white beard. The adults of four species range from silver to black. The only fully colored adult is the widely distributed Maroon langur (Red leaf monkey), whose shaggy coat is red-orange; but infant Silvered langurs, who as adults wear dull gray "flannel," are a striking golden orange.

Langurs live in small troops of up to a dozen members, usually consisting of a single adult male with a few females and their young. The troop travels slowly through the canopy, stopping to feed for long periods. But they are capable of moving quickly, and noisily, through the canopy by running along branches and making prodigious leaps to nearby trees. When annoyed, the male sometimes comes forward and scolds the intruder until the other members have fled.

Langurs feed at all levels of the canopy, and so can often be heard moving through the trees, or, if lucky, one may see them feeding and grooming on lower branches. Bako National Park in Sarawak and Sepilok Wildlife Reserve in Sabah are two of the better places to see them in the wild.

Another monkey-like creature is more often heard than seen. The Bornean (Mueller's) gibbon is similar in size to a Silvered langur and looks much like one. But gibbons are actually the smallest and slenderest of the lesser apes (family Hylobatidae); and can be differentiated easily from monkeys by the lack of a tail.

The gibbon's way of moving through the trees is also different—it swings from branch to branch, a method called "brachiation." Its arms are very long

and slender; its elongated hands act as hanging hooks; and its long feet function almost as hands for landing on the slenderest of branches. To watch one swinging effortlessly through the canopy, or even around the artificial branches of a zoo display, is almost dizzying, making even the greatest human trapeze artist look stiff in comparison. Though they feed mostly on ripe fruits, gibbons are capable of catching an occasional small bird or large insect on the wing as they themselves "fly" through the air.

Gibbons are not easy to see. John MacKinnon considers them "very shy and difficult to approach. Whenever they caught sight of me they rushed off to the topmost crowns . . . with a deafening riot of derisive hoots." The best spot to observe them in the wild is at a large fig tree whose fruit has just ripened. Because they move so quickly and can cover so much territory, gibbons are quick to find figs. But because they prefer their fruit ripe, they often arrive after the hornbills, orangutans and other less finicky animals that have been feasting on the tree for days.

Gibbons live in small family units—a monogamous pair with two to four young. The families are highly territorial over an area of about 40–125 acres (15–50 ha); and so, though hard to see, gibbons are easy to hear as they advertise their territorial presence with loud calls (hence the local name *wa-wa*). In the early morning (6:30–8:30 A.M.) the adults sit high in the treetops and call, a sound that, along with the ringing song of cicadas and the monotonous *took-took- took* of barbets, is the quintessential sound of the dipterocarp rainforest.

Beccari wrote: "In the mornings the adjoining forest echoed with its singular and characteristic call. It is so strange a sound that for a long while I could not believe that it came from a monkey; it was to me more like the loud harmonious cry of some large bird. It consists of the syllables 'wa-wa' many times repeated with great force, dropping in tone and increasing in rapidity."

A pair of Bornean (Mueller's) gibbons spend much time grooming each other. The long, slender hands act as hooks as gibbons swing from branch to branch.

The female's call is louder than the male's, and she has a "great-call" that is far more impressive than anything in the male repertoire—a prolonged wail, which rises by irregular swoops through about two octaves. The alternating high trills and low notes accelerate through the call, the low notes resonating from an inflated pouch. The calls can be heard for over a mile.

Mueller's gibbon, endemic to Borneo, lives throughout lowland and hills in primary rainforest. Its shaggy fur is silvery gray and in some varieties darker below. Its hands and feet are black, as is its small face, which may be outlined by a thin band of white hair. Borneo's other species—the Agile gibbon—is also found on peninsular Malaysia and Sumatra, but only in the south-central part of Borneo. Though the two species are similar in appearance and habits (and are known to hybridize along Central Kalimantan's Barito River), experts can tell the two apart by their calls.

Gibbons are hunted by Dayaks for food; coastal Malays, whose Islamic religion discourages consumption of animals "with sharp teeth or claws," shun them. But both groups keep young gibbons for pets. Despite the fact that they make endearing pets (I know of one young gibbon who was practically a member of the family), the practice is illegal. However, no way has been found to successfully release captive or orphaned gibbons back into the wild. Troops consist of nuclear families that are so fiercely territorial that they even chase off their maturing adolescents (seven or eight years old), who must then fight to carve a territory from the edges of established troops. A released gibbon, especially a young, inexperienced male, has little chance of establishing itself. Studies of gibbons released at Semengol Forest Reserve near Kuching showed a mortality greater than 90 percent—from starvation, disease and hunting. Researchers were forced to conclude that confiscated gibbons might just as well be put away immediately as released into a hostile environment.

The title "King of the Canopy" goes to Borneo's only great ape. So humanlike that it is called orangutan ("man of the forest"), it is otherwise known as the red ape, or, in Wallace's time, the *mias* or *mawas.*

A mature male orangutan is an imposing figure. A large individual reaches only 4.5 feet (1.4 m) in height but may weigh up to 220 pounds (100 kg). The female is shorter and half the male's weight. The male's bulk is emphasized by a shaggy reddish coat, a face enlarged by dark jowly cheek flaps and a bulky chest covered by large flaps of black skin. Though generally retiring and not easily angered, his strength is legendary. A Dayak chief told Wallace: "The *mias* has no enemies; no animals dare attack it but the crocodile and the python. He always kills the crocodile by main strength, standing upon it, pulling open its jaws, and ripping up its throat. If a python attacks a mias, he seizes it with his hands, and then bites it, and soon kills it. The mias is very strong; there is no animal in the jungle so strong as he."

Nor is any more intelligent. A young orangutan looks rather like a person in a shaggy coat—albeit one with a very protruding lower face—and its behavior and attitudes would seem familiar to a human parent. Wallace, whose chapter on orangutans in *The Malay Archipelago* is mostly a dreary account of collection by shotgun, was charmed by an infant orang whose mother he had shot. He kept the infant for a month and found it a young macaque monkey for a playmate.

It was curious to observe the different actions of these two animals, which could not have differed much in age. The mias like a very young baby, lying on its back quite helpless, rolling lazily from side to side, stretching out all four hands into the air, wishing to grasp something, but hardly able to guide its fingers to any definite object, and when dissatisfied, opening its almost toothless mouth and expressing its wants with a scream; the little monkey, on the other hand, in

Opposite:
A large male Bornean orangutan ("man of the forest"). The mostly solitary red ape—one of our closest relatives—is the least known of the three great apes.

constant motion, running and jumping about wherever it pleased, examining everything around it, seizing hold of the smallest objects with the greatest precision, balancing itself on the edge of the box or running up a post, and helping itself to anything eatable that came in its way. There could hardly be a greater contrast, and the baby mias looked more baby-like by the comparison.

Although orangutan infants are helpless, a two-year-old is remarkably agile, moving through the trees or on the ground equally well in any direction, and is as comfortable upside down as upright. As it grows heavier the orang becomes more conservative, sticking to larger branches and traveling closer to or on the ground, but still with an agility belying its bulk. Wallace observed:

It is a singular and very interesting sight to watch a mias making his way leisurely through the forest. He walks deliberately along some of the larger branches, in the semi-erect attitude which the great length of his arms and the shortness of his legs cause him naturally to assume; and the disproportion between these limbs is increased by his walking on his knuckles, not on the palm of the hand, as we should do. He seems always to choose those branches which intermingle with an adjoining tree; on approaching which he stretches out his long arms and, seizing the opposing boughs, grasps them together with both hands, seems to try their strength, and then deliberately swings himself across to the next branch on which he walks along as before.

He never jumps or springs, or even appears to hurry himself, and yet manages to get along almost as quickly as a person can run through the forest beneath. The long and powerful arms are of the greatest use to the animal, enabling it to climb easily up the loftiest trees, to seize fruits and young leaves from slender boughs which will not bear its weight, and to gather leaves and branches with which to form its nest.

One renegade scientist, Jeffrey Schwartz of Harvard, feels that the orangutan is our closest relative, though much of the argument is abstruse and perhaps meaningless. We have both come a long way over the past 15 million years or so (as estimated by the latest genetic analysis) since we diverged from a common ancestor. But had our ancestral primate line been more successful in competing with monkeys in the trees, argues John MacKinnon, we, like the orangutan, might never have abandoned the deep forest.

While we have been forced to adapt to increasingly dense populations, orangutans have become the most solitary of primates. Like humans, they have evolved remarkable intelligence—more, in fact, that they would seem to need as rather solitary vegetarians whose social interactions are minimal. MacKinnon believes orangutan intelligence has evolved for reasons more connected to food than to communication.

The orangutan diet consists largely of figs and other fruit, and as the world's largest frugivore (fruit-eater), the orangutan faces a critical problem: To sustain its immense body, it has to find enough low-protein fruit within its territory, with a minimum expenditure of energy. This is the primary reason why adult males lead fairly solitary lives and why females and juveniles, according to Birute Galdikas's long-term study in Kalimantan, interact only about 20 percent of the time. (The main interactions are between mother and offspring; between 10- to 18-year-old sub-adults, who often hang out in pairs during the period between independence and mating; and between mothers, who may themselves be siblings.) After the infant is weaned, mother and offspring, or siblings, or adolescent "friends" keep in contact by continuous calling.

While the gibbon strategy is to skim its territory quickly and often, the orangutan survives by sheer efficiency. Although it relies somewhat on flights of hornbills to point out trees in fruit, the orangutan seems to possess a mental map of all the fruit trees—at least the figs and durians—within its area of accustomed travel.

It must also keep track and remember the state of ripeness of each tree. It prefers sour, or even bitter, unripe fruit—often of species that are wild ancestors of commonly cultivated orchard trees—and strips the tree's crown over a period of two or three days. But if it arrives at the tree too early, the fruit or seed has little nourishment. If it arrives when the fruit has ripened, the quicker and more numerous gibbons (who prefer ripe fruit), monkeys, squirrels and birds may already have plundered it. MacKinnon believes that the mental agility needed to keep track of this larder and visit the widely scattered trees in the most efficient possible manner has given the evolutionary edge to the most intelligent orangutan.

Orangutans were once found from southern China to Java and Sulawesi. But in historical times the two remaining subspecies have been limited: one to northern Sumatra the other to Borneo. A recent genetic study has shown the two to be as dissimilar as are some closely related pairs of full species.

The Bornean orangutan is found throughout the island below 5,000 feet (1,500 m) but is absent from certain large patches of seemingly good habitat. It is believed to have been extirpated from these areas by hunting. Butchered orangutan remains have been excavated from Sarawak's Niah Cave in soil layers that date back more than 30,000 years, indicating that they have been hunted for food for at least that long.

Orangutans make nightly "nests"—rough platforms of vegetation pulled over the crotch of a branch high in the crown of trees—wherever they happen to end up at the end of the day. They also sometimes make the shelters during afternoon rains. (Young orangutans instinctively like to pull branches or blankets over their heads when they want to sleep or escape notice.) Recently, scientists have discovered that they can get a fair idea of orangutan populations in surveyed areas by flying over the canopy and counting the nests.

MacKinnon estimates that there are about 100,000 Bornean orangutans left in the wild; Kalimantan researcher Birute Galdikas believes that there are no more than 30,0000—the population of a single human town, and not a very large one at that. In either case, we will need to preserve the red ape's remaining habitat and protect it from hunting or capture for the pet trade if we are not to lose one of our closest relatives.

BELOW THE CANOPY

I have arrived long after scheduled feeding time at Platform B, hoping for a quiet glimpse of Sepilok Wildlife Reserve's orangutans. But except for a handsome black Prevost's squirrel nibbling at one of the few remaining bananas, the small platform attached about 10 feet up the trunk of a huge forest tree is deserted. A bevy of colorful butterflies, drawn by the smell of bruised fruit, hover around the tree, as do clouds of tiny fruit flies. Off to my left, a noisy flock of small birds sweep through the trees, too well hidden among the saplings and lianas for me to get a good look. But as I try to focus my binoculars on them, I realize that I am the one being watched.

A large female orangutan has been sitting in the crotch of a sapling all the while, her baby hanging around upside down just above her. Gathering it in, she rocks the sapling back and forth, just enough for her to reach the branch of a larger tree. The baby, perhaps two years old, clings to her with one hand as she transfers effortlessly to the larger tree.

Just then another red ape appears, leading another, larger, youngster. The first mother pauses indifferently as the second passes by. It's a different story with the juveniles. They begin to chase each other up and down a sapling and swing on lianas, using both feet and hands to hang in seemingly impossible positions.

After a while the older one begins to grab at the younger, teasing it by pulling it down to the ground every time it almost escapes up the tree. The younger soon seems to tire of the game, but the elder might have continued forever had the first mother not rescued her baby. They move without haste up into the canopy and out of sight.

An orphaned baby orangutan. Many are illegally held as pets or smuggled to Hong Kong, Taiwan and other countries.

Opposite:
A feeding platform in the rainforest at Sepilok Orangutan Rehabilitation Center, eastern Sabah.

As youngsters, both these orangutan mothers were either orphaned by hunters or were illegal pets seized by wildlife officials who brought them to Sepilok for eventual release back into the wild. They, like the present crop of young orangs kept at the holding cages at the rehabilitation center, had gone through a slow process of education and exploration, before finally weaning themselves of the center's care.

After a period of quarantine, young orangutans are led out into the forest daily to feed at Platform A, a similar platform much nearer the center. After being released into the forest, they return at first to more distant Platform B for supplemental feeding. Eventually, they find sour forest fruits tastier than the bland fruit offered at the platforms, and jungle life spicier. The females mate with wild males, but they often return with their babies for extra food. What happens to the released "rehab" males is less well known, and it is rarely known whether they have been successfully rehabilitated or simply perished.

Orangutan rehabilitation was originally the concept of Barbara and Tom Harrisson, who set up an area in Bako National Park. Unfortunately the preserve proved too small to accommodate the released animals. Later, Birute Galdikas and her husband, Rod Brindamour, founded the Orangutan Research and Conservation Project at Tanjung Puting in the swamp forest of Central Kalimantan. Galdikas was one of the original "Leakey Girls"—along with Dian Fossey and Jane Goodall—chosen by famed anthropologist Louis Leakey and sponsored by the National Geographic Society to carry out long-term studies of our three great ape cousins. Galdikas later founded the Los Angeles–based Orangutan Foundation, a group working to preserve the orangutan from extinction.

During the past two decades, logging roads have opened up orangutan habitat to hunting; orangs, being the largest target, are often killed. Sometimes mothers are shot just to capture the babies.

The demand for orangutan babies as exotic pets is very great—especially in Hong Kong, where Galdikas claims there are dozens, perhaps hundreds, of pet orangutans that were smuggled in from Borneo. Recently, one was even confiscated at an airport near Paris. Early on, Galdikas convinced the Indonesian authorities to ban the keeping of baby orangs as pets, and wildlife officers began bringing the confiscated primates to the center. Twenty years later, Galdikas is still caring for orphaned orangutans. She sometimes regrets the time taken from her research on wild orangs, but not the joys and hassles of mothering such a highly entertaining brood.

Here in Sabah, the Forestry Department, faced with a similar problem of what to do with growing numbers of confiscated orangutans, set up a rehabilitation center at their Forest Research Center at Sepilok (now managed by the department's Wildlife Division). It remains to be seen, however, whether the nearby forest can support many more released orangutans. Or, indeed, whether it is actually supporting those already released. As a way of educating the public, though, Sepilok is a definite success.

At Platform B, the second pair continues to feed on the last bananas, even the youngster content with the slow midday place. A few years earlier, the mother might have been curious about me, even pesteringly so. But now, mature and oriented to the forest, she assumes the solitary indifference of wild orangs. Her child is more actively curious, and would probably approach if not for its mother's example. I could see in its earlier play behavior flashes of mischievous but good-natured cunning, though little of the frenetic, aggressive energy of chimpanzees. And there is something about older Bornean orangutans that seems not only intelligent but meditative.

The youngster, a male, will eventually develop hugely inflated black cheeks that will flatten his puckish flesh-colored face, and a wild mane of reddish hair; he will walk carefully balanced on huge, callused knuckles. But at this age he

Opposite:
Confiscated orangutans being rehabilitated at Sepilok Forest Reserve.

stands upright, if rather swaybacked, hands above head as if reaching for a branch. He looks remarkably human, especially his varied expressions and sly, playful attitudes.

INSECTS

Sepilok's protected rainforest on this sunny day in March is buzzing with life. Even the shadows are dappled with dancing patches of light—hardly the gloomy, silent world depicted so often in travelogues. If, however, it were middle of monsoon season, with constant cloud cover or soaking rain, and the incessant rumblings of distant thunder, no birds breeding and butterflies too cold and damp to fly. . .

Beneath the dense canopy, the midday temperature is a constant 85°F (30°C) or so year round, rarely falling below 75°F (24°C) at night. The sticky equatorial humidity hovers around 90 percent, except during the driest months, when it may fall to 80 percent. Light, too, is fairly constant—about 5 percent of that

Stag beetle (unidentified species). Some species grow to more than 4 inches (10 cm).

reaching the top of the canopy. Some visitors find this gloomy, but on a sunny day, even 5 percent of the tropical sun is plenty for me, and there are enough dazzlingly bright spots here and there to lighten the mood.

The most visible animals by far are butterflies, termites and ants. The ubiquitous ants forage ceaselessly over the forest floor and tree trunks, some types searching for fallen fruit, others ready to pounce on a corpse of a spider, bird or insect. Still others seek out termite nests or nests of smaller ants on which to feast or to carry away the occupants as slaves.

Beccari noted: "One kind [of ant], a very large one, which I found on the ground when touched covered itself with a white froth which issued in quantities from its sharp-pointed abdomen. Another, which lived on the leaves of an oak, gave off a very strong odour of pepper. Yet another species . . . is possessed of powerful defence in the shape of a sting like that of a wasp . . . But the most ferocious of all is the 'ant that leaves its head,' so called on account of the ferocity with which it bites, leaving its head attached to the object it has seized with its jaws rather than let it go . . ." Occasionally huge solitary black ants cross the trail. They look ferocious but really are not, which cannot be said about many of the smaller red varieties.

Providing much of the jungle's visual glory are the bright butterflies. Against the lichen-covered tree trunks, the endless muted hues of shadowed greenery and the dull browns of vine and fallen leaves, the colorful, dancing butterflies are pure delight. They draw attention to the rare understory flowers, so often shrouded by dense leaves, on which they perch to feed. And, alighted on some bush or vine, they themselves resemble flowers.

Most Bornean butterflies stay hidden in the upper canopy, where nectar-bearing flowers are more easily found. Others prefer the more open secondary forest. But there are more than enough kinds here in the forest understory to keep a curious visitor alert.

Like most tropical life-forms, the butterflies are low in individuals of any given species but infinite in variety. To further the variety, males and females of many species have different patterns. And while the undersides of the wings of temperate butterflies tend to be drab, the underwings of tropical butterflies are often as brightly colored or as fantastically patterned as the upper wing surface. The names say all: Painted jezebel, Orange albatross, Black-veined tiger, Royal Assyrian, Malay lacewing, Autumn leaf, Straight-lined mapwing, Tawny rajah, Branded imperial, Malay red harlequin. Others with duller names, such as the Wanderer, Red Helen and Common birdwing, are no less spectacular.

Of Borneo's most famous species, the Rajah Brooke's birdwing, Wallace wrote:

> My collection of butterflies was not large; but I obtained some rare and very handsome insects, the most remarkable being [Trigonopters brookiana], one of the most elegant species known. This beautiful creature has very long and pointed wings, almost resembling a sphinx moth in shape. It is deep velvety black, with a curved band of spots of a brilliant metallic-green color extending across the wings from tip to tip, each spot being shaped exactly like a small triangular feather, and having very much the effect of a row of wing coverts of the Mexican trogon laid upon black velvet. The only other marks are a broad neck-collar of vivid crimson, and a few delicate white touches on the outer margins of the hind wings. This species, which was then quite new . . . I named after Sir James Brooke.

Many of the more conspicuous butterflies are colorful for a purpose. They are able not only to tolerate the toxic chemicals that some plants manufacture to defend against browsers, but can convert these poisons into an anti-predator defense of their own, similar to the temperate Monarch butterfly's use of

Caterpillars of the Malay lacewing butterfly. The bright color advertises their toxicity to predatory birds.

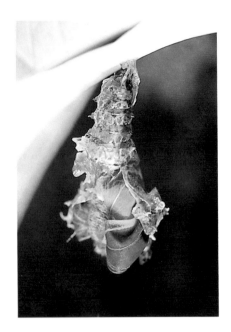

A Malay lacewing butterfly emerging from its chrysalis.

Adult Malay lacewing butterfly.

Malay lacewing emerging from chrysalis.

alkaloids in the milkweed latex on which it feeds. And for every ill-tasting species there seems to be at least one mimic. The Common rose is mimicked by one of the two forms of female Common Mormon, not only in appearance but in manner of flight. Often the mimics are of a totally different family from the distasteful one being copied: The Blue glassy tiger (a Daneid) is mimicked by the Common mime (swallowtail family); the Yellow glassy tiger by the female Wanderer (a Pierid). The smaller Wood nymph is even mimicked by a day-flying moth.

Adult butterflies, their eggs and especially their larval caterpillars are vulnerable to birds and lizards as well as to parasitic flies and wasps. For defense, camouflage is even more common than chemistry or mimicry: "A caterpillar," writes R. Morrell in *Common Malayan Butterflies*, "may resemble a curled leaf, a leaf vein, a bird-dropping, a bud, a stalk end, even the head and neck of a snake; a live pupa may be disguised as a leaf, growing or withered, an unripe berry, a broken-off twig, or a pupa case already empty. Many larvae habitually rest crookedly, so that their symmetry is broken and they are unrecognizable; some build themselves hides or barriers or backgrounds against which their camouflage is more effective; others construct decoys—inedible dummy caterpillars to distract attention from themselves . . ."

A bat-winged moth. Many tropical moths are as colorful as temperate butterflies.

The attractive Tailed jay butterfly is common in forest clearings.

There is rarely a time when some butterfly or another is not within sight, and it is only willpower or weariness that keeps a camera-toting trekker from flittering in all directions as one so tantalizingly alights.

THE SOUNDS OF THE RAINFOREST

As usual in the rainforest, no mammals are visible save an occasional squirrel scurrying along a low branch, and there are only quick flashes of birds in the canopy. Yet the sounds of unseen creatures surround us.

The famed male Rajah Brooke's birdwing butterfly.

The graceful Wood nymph butterfly.

A well-camouflaged praying mantis.

This feathery caterpillar of the Archduke butterfly is almost invisible against a forest leaf.

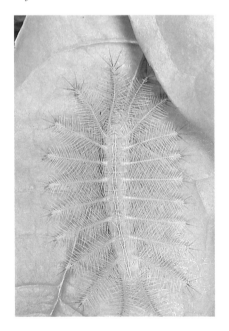

Opposite:
An Autumn leaf butterfly perfectly mimics a dried leaf, complete with false midrib. It prefers the jungle to shade.

The Bornean rainforest is rarely silent, and often downright noisy. The wash of forest sounds—like an Indian raga or Kenyah *sape* session—seem random at first but soon becomes hypnotic, eventually assuming a kind of aural logic.

The background drone is an incessant, almost irritating whine of cicadas—large, sap-sucking bugs, which here in the tropics are often decorated with bright blazes of Day-Glo color. The most common afternoon cicada song warms from a dry buzz to a musical trill rising higher and higher in pitch and finally to a grating metallic screech before fading away, to be taken up a moment later by another a few meters away. And this is set against the endless *took-toook-tarook took-took-took-took* of barbets in the canopy.

Superimposed on these are countless chirps, whistles and trills: the chatter of babblers in the underbrush, the rich voice of the leafbirds, and the long, unbelievably complex melodies of White-rumped shama and Magpie-robin. As I approach, no matter how silently, the songs are replaced by sharp, nervous alarm calls—and the equally telling silence of cicadas—signaling my location to the forest community as effectively as any bush telegraph.

Punctuating the birdsongs are mysterious guttural grunts, roars and barks: monkeys? orangutan? Barking deer? Sun bear? hornbill? These come always from just around the bend, or up in the canopy—it is never easy to tell exactly from where, or what is calling. It is sometimes difficult to tell Sun bear from orangutan, or even a Paradise flycatcher from a large frog.

In the muted light beneath the jungle canopy, with vision blocked by tree trunks and patches of shrub, visual communication over any distance is limited at best, and at night is useless. Sound is the most efficient way for flocks or mates to keep in touch, for territorial neighbors to keep their distance, or for yearning males to advertise. But the rainforest's rich species diversity creates the same problems as in a metropolis with limited radio bands. The birds and insects have overcome this with an amazing array of tones, harmonic patterns and rhythms.

To us who are used to orienting with our eyes not ears, this limit on vision and reliance on sound is a large part of the jungle's mystery. As soon as you learn to identify the call of one animal, you hear another that may be the same species, or another that merely sounds similar—perhaps purposefully—at least to the dulled human ear. To modern urbanites, a forest-dwelling Penan, or even a master birder, seems like a modern shaman, tuned in to conversations far more ancient than human speech.

Reddish "baby leaves" are common to many rainforest species. Red compounds (anthocyanins) may act as antifungal agents. The absence of green chlorophyll minimizes the plant's investment in new leaves before they are tough enough to resist insects.

THE TREES

Almost all rainforest trees are broad-leaved but evergreen. Their leaves fall continuously and are immediately replaced. Many are shaken loose by the gusts of wind that precede afternoon rains, but a constant rain of dead leaves falls throughout even the most windless of days. Some flutter down weightlessly like butterflies; some twirl like tops; others sluice from side to side like a saucer in water. The largest ones, true giants of the leaf world, crash through the layers of lower branches like a monkey racing through the canopy. Occasionally an entire branch falls or is torn off by an angry primate. One can never be sure if a falling leaf or branch is simply that, or if it signals a rare glimpse of a gibbon, a langur or even a wild orangutan.

Almost half the large forest trees, especially the dipterocarps, are expanded from ground level to a height of 4–10 feet (1–3 m) by ridgelike extensions called buttresses. Basically triangular but often sculpted into graceful, sinuous curves, they connect at ground level to a network of ropy roots that writhe snakelike through the leaf litter, intertwined with those of neighboring trees.

A buttressed rainforest tree.

Buttresses appear to prop up the trunk like a Christmas tree tripod, but they are actually more important as tension members—like steel cables guying up a radio tower. This is indicated by the fact that they are usually found on the uphill side of the tree or on the side of prevailing winds. The combination of buttresses and the wide mat of roots serves the same stabilizing function as would a deep tap root, if a tap root could penetrate the rock lying just beneath the thin forest soils.

Despite the poverty of the soils, huge trees can grow because their roots are assisted by other life forms. Termites, beetles and springtails quickly break down the fallen leaves and branches; fungi not only break down the thick leaf litter but may even directly bridge the gap between a root and a rotting leaf or termite nest, allowing the nutrients within to be recycled immediately.

Odoardo Beccari was one of the first to realize that the tropical rainforest's invisible world of bacterial rot and fungal decay are critical to recycle forest nutrients:

> *Who will ever be able to form an adequate conception of the amount of organic labour silently performed in the depths of the forest under such [wet] conditions? Who can even in imagination realise the untold myriads of living, palpitating cells that are struggling for existence in the tranquil gloom of a primeval tropical forest?*
>
> *. . . What numberless obscure vital phenomena run their course, motionless and in silence, under the shadow of these ancient trees and to what an infinity of microscopic beings does not the death of one of these giants give birth? How can one picture the vast hosts of these creatures peopling the soil and air, the roots, trunks, flowers, and fruits, and realise their metamorphoses, their habits, and*

Many rainforest leaves have a spout-like "drip-tip" designed to spill water off the upper surface.

Leaf litter on jungle floor, rapidly broken down by fungi and insects, is the main source of recycled nutrients for rainforest trees.

the relations in which they stand towards the plants amongst which, or on which, they live? In short, how can we ever come to know the biology of this vast living world, which even the philosopher fails to grasp as a whole . . . ?

These invisible workers do quite a job of compensating for thin, leached soils: The biomass, or total amount of vegetation growing at any moment, in Borneo's forests may be greater than anywhere else on earth. One recent study estimated that lowland rainforest in Brunei contains almost 400 tons per acre (880 tonnes/ha) of vegetation, 98 percent contained in the trees, most of the rest in woody vines—lianas, climbers and stranglers. No other region produces more than two-thirds that biomass.

BIODIVERSITY

Many of the trees along Sepilok's trails have been given aluminum name tags; but my attempt to memorize the species names is constantly frustrated. No two

Fruiting body of a fungus in the forest duff. Hidden hyphal threads of fungi weave the rainforest into a seamless web of nutrient exchange and recycling.

trees are of the same species, and with the crowns so far above and a random mix of leaves on the forest floor, there is only the bark to identify them. Foresters have the advantage of their parangs to slash through the bark into the wood, where color, grain and sap give useful clues.

The biological diversity of Borneo's forests is truly staggering, especially to someone from the relatively impoverished temperate zones. And it is truly daunting to anyone trying to distinguish the actors in this ecological extravaganza, with its cast of thousands—dozens of them co-domiants—and none of them extras.

One study on a 4-acre plot here in Sepilok counted 200 tree species of a hundred different genera, 20 of them dipterocarps. On a plot only half that size in Kalimantan, researchers counted 240 tree species, not including palms. Vines, herbs and epiphytic ferns and mosses might have pushed the total toward a thousand. Tropical forestry expert T. C. Whitmore asserts, "Even the incomplete data available clearly suggests that on small areas of a few hectares these hyper-rich rain forests are in fact the most species-rich communities known from anywhere in the world."

Malesia (the bioregion consisting of Malaysia, Indonesia, the Philippines and New Guinea) has at least 25,000 species of flowering plants, perhaps half of them endemic to the region. By contrast, the British Isles are home to fewer than 1,500 types of flowering plants—about half the total of just the trees in the state of Sarawak alone.

The region is similarly rich in animals. More than 633 bird species breed in Malesia, which is about the same number as in all of North America. In one 20-square-mile (50-sq-km) patch of Sarawak forest, 135 species of herptiles (frogs and toads, lizards and snakes) were found, compared to just over 40 species in similar-size areas of the southern United States or southern China. More than 4,000 species of moths have already been recorded in Borneo.

Wallace provides a spectacular example of insect diversity: "When I arrived at the mines [east of Kuching, Sarawak] on the 14th of March, I had collected in the four preceding months 320 different kinds of beetles. In less than a fortnight I had doubled this number, an average of about 24 new species every day. On one day I collected 76 different kinds, of which 34 were new to me. By the end of April I had more than a thousand species, and they then went on increasing at a slower rate; so that I obtained altogether in Borneo about two thousand distinct kinds, of which all but about a hundred were collected at this place, and on scarcely more than a square mile of ground."

There are a number of reasons for this astounding diversity of plants and animals. One is the Bornean rainforest's massive architecture: Since the canopy and emergent trees are so huge, there is more space within and beneath the canopy, and more complexity. There are simply more physical niches available for epiphytes and for arboreal animals that in a simpler forest of smaller trees.

A second reason for such diversity is the forest's ancient lineage and relative stability: Portions of Southeast Asia's tropical rainforest have existed for perhaps 100 million years, under optimum conditions of light and moisture. And though the climate has varied, there have always been areas of warm, damp forest.

During glacial maxima, temperatures on mountain tops dropped 18°F (10°C). Land temperatures near sea level dropped far less, just a few degrees; but the climate probably became more seasonal, turning much of Sarawak and West Kalimantan into seasonal forest much like present-day Thailand. Yet large areas of surrounding rainforest remained essentially unchanged, a pool of jungle species to repopulate the rainforest when the climate heated up again.

Meanwhile, the drops in sea level exposed much of the Sunda region, connecting Borneo by land to Sumatra and to the Southeast Asian mainland.

Tree trunks offer a place in the sun to epiphytic plants such as these ferns.

During these millennia, waves of plants and animals (and, later, human settlers) moved southward and eastward into Borneo.

Wave upon wave of invaders competed with the native species, replacing them, mingling genes with them or (as seems to be the case with the Asian tiger) failing to gain a foothold.

Then for similar millennia the rising sea separated Borneo from the rest of Sundaland. Cut off from parental stocks, and isolated by mountain ranges, plants and animals evolved into new species—some of them now found only on Borneo, or even on just parts of the island.

Diversity feeds diversity. In a climate so amiable to bacteria and fungi, and one so stocked with immense varieties of insects, few densely packed groups of plants or animals could withstand the exploding populations of pathogens and predators that evolved to feed on them. Despite an array of defensive chemicals and thorns, tropical plants can survive only at low densities, scattered among hundreds of dissimilar species. Animals that feed selectively on scattered plants must also live at low densities. And they, too, survive their predators only by spreading themselves thin, or by clever camouflage, or by becoming secretive or nocturnal.

SNAKES

Animals, I knew, must be all around—in or above the canopy, in hollow trees, in chambers underground. Others slept on branches or under boulders waiting the night, or crept through streamside thickets or skulked along silently, out of view. They were not about to endanger themselves just for the sake of my curiosity. And in some cases, such as poisonous snakes, this reticence is appreciated.

Despite my encounter with the aquatic King cobra, I have not felt great anxiety at the possibility of meeting poisonous snakes in Borneo's jungles. Although Borneo boasts the richest snake fauna in Southeast Asia—about 175 species of snakes in eight families—only about 50 are poisonous to their prey (mostly small animals), and few of these are dangerous to humans. Most, wisely enough, avoid us like the plague. The only worrisome snakes include two species of cobra, six pit vipers and a couple of kraits.

The fixed-fang snakes (family Elapidae: cobras, kraits and coral snakes) are considered the most dangerous. The King cobra has little reason to strike if not attacked; its very confidence makes it less aggressive. Its cousin the Black,

This shield bug (undescribed species) is probably not tasty to birds.

or Spitting, cobra is dark brown with yellowish scales under the hood, without the King cobra's reddish head and spotted hood. It is much smaller than the King (reaching a mere 6 ft/2 m) but does, unfortunately, have the ability to rear up and spit poison into one's eye from a distance of up to 8 feet (2.5 m). Like the King it is generally a retiring creature. As with distasteful butterflies, there is a fairly harmless but aggressive snake (*Coluber*), in another family entirely, that imitates the Black cobra to enhance its own image.

One Sabah jungle guide has given me detailed instructions for defending against a Black cobra: Use a long, slender branch to push the snake's head from side to side, giving it no chance to set up for an accurate spit (never use a thick stick because the snake will grab onto it and crawl along it to bite your hand). While distracting the snake with the branch, carefully reach down with your other hand and deftly grab the snake by the tip of the tail. It will instinctively try to escape. Drop the branch and take out your parang. Lop off the snake's head. This method sounds great, but I'd prefer to see an actual demonstration before trying it.

Kraits are fairly small, attractive snakes. Their bite can be fatal to humans, but they tend to be unaggressive and they go to great lengths to avoid conflict. The Banded krait has broad cream-and-black bands; when irritated or threatened it warns off intruders by thumping its tail loudly on the ground. The Red-headed krait, with its brilliant scarlet head and tail, outperforms its cousin by twisting and coiling with a rapid, jerky motion designed to startle the intruder. Both the other local kraits are brightly colored with relatively huge poison glands.

The brilliantly patterned coral snakes are highly poisonous but very small, and their mouths, like those of sea snakes, are tiny. The most noticeable species—the Banded coral snake—has a long red-to-orange stripe, flanked by black along its back. Its head and tail have black and red bands. Outdoing even the Red-headed krait with its showmanship, the Banded coral twists and writhes, raising its tail or rolling over to display its gaudy underparts.

The final group of poisonous snakes consists of six species of pit vipers. Vipers (which include the North American rattlesnakes and water moccasins) comprise the most highly evolved snake family; the pit viper subfamily possess unique heat-sensitive organs in pits between eye and nostril that help them locate and track warm-blooded prey with deadly efficiency. Borneo's pit vipers are medium-size snakes with narrow bodies, but their heads are broad and rather triangular due to the large poison glands alongside the jaw. Wagler's pit viper, a handsome snake with black edging on its bright green scales, is probably the most common, found from lowland forests to the peaks of Borneo's taller mountains.

Pit vipers often rest by day fully exposed on the ground or among low branches. Though potentially dangerous, they are sluggish and, according to one expert, will remain still "unless actively molested."

The only other snake that can cause the Bornean rainforest trekker much anxiety is non-poisonous but otherwise quite formidable—the Reticulated python. Found throughout Borneo's lowland rainforest, this largest of the world's snakes can reach 30 feet (9 m) in length and is all muscle. It lies patiently in wait near game trails, on the ground or in low branches. Grabbing onto its prey with its jaws, it quickly coils around the chest, contracting slightly with every panicky outbreath. The lower jaw can unhinge to open amazingly wide, and its many ribs are greatly expandable, allowing the Reticulated python to swallow game as large as a deer or pig, and even an occasional small human.

There are local stories of pythons found trapped in bamboo cages in the morning after dining on a caged pig or monkey during the night; the pet, too large to squeeze through the bars when alive, is no smaller in the belly of the snake, whose digestive system might take a week to digest its meal. Pythons

are occasionally caught entering homes as well, and stories of children carried off or rescued at the last moment are rife. One 23-footer (7 m) captured within Kuching's city limits now hangs in the Sarawak Museum.

People attacked by pythons in Borneo are even fewer than those bitten by poisonous snakes. Moreover, the python deserves at least a few words in praise, not just for its ecological role and its awesome size and power but for its beauty. Those who have kept a python as a pet or have viewed one dispassionately in a zoo can attest to the brilliance of its handsome, iridescent patterns, especially just after it has shed its skin.

Borneo's other constrictor, the Short python, is rarely seen. It resembles a Reticulated python that has been chopped in third by a parang and then regenerated a short, pointed tail. But though its proportions and patterns are less pleasing than that of its reticulated cousin, it is handsome enough—a marbled brown and gray, with a brown-and-white band along its sides. It also has the admirable quality of being too small to swallow a person whole.

The attractive Wagler's pit viper is quite poisonous but is harmless unless actively harassed.

THE FOREST SHADE

Along the trail is an opening where a huge dipterocarp has fallen. Roped to neighboring trees by tangled webs of strong, woody lianas, the buttressed giant pulled down a half dozen smaller trees as it fell. A dozen saplings that had languished in the patriarch's shadow now race toward the sky; the first to reach a critical height will spread its umbrella-like crown to fill in the canopy gap, preempting all the precious sunlight.

Suddenly, a wraithlike apparition floats at eye-level across the gap. Alighting, the male Asian paradise flycatcher perches out of sight behind a tree, only the tip of its 18-inch (45-cm)-long white tailfeathers coyly showing. Then it glides back across the glade, its wraithlike trailing plume undulating weightlessly behind—surely one of the loveliest of jungle sights.

Another forest bird with unusual tailfeathers puts on an even more spectacular display. The all-black Greater racket-tailed drongo has 2-foot (60-cm)-long tailfeathers; the shaft is bare for most of its length, but at the tip is a short, curved thickening called a racket. As the bird flies, the rackets flutter prettily in the wind. Parties of the drongos sometimes gather in similar forest gaps or clearings, and there, according to one birder quoted by Smythies, "engage in counter-singing and aerial chases and acrobatics about the trees."

The most famous of Borneo's forest-gap birds is one that I have heard, and seen the dancing grounds of, but never managed to observe. It has been sought by almost every naturalist who has ever visited the island; Smythies collates the following notes:

The loud cry of the Argus pheasant is one of the ornithological features of the Bornean jungle, and as soon as you get away from the flat steamy swamps of the coastal districts into the foothills you can count upon hearing it. In the deep silence one is startled by the thrice-repeated tu-wau *in a clear sonorous tone." (St. John)*

His performance is striking, starting off as a number of clear, loud, single hoots like a Tawny owl or a Gibbon, repeated in succession from 15–17 times, the last few notes rising in pitch and increasing in pace to become almost syllabic and continuing in this higher pitch and increasing pace for a further 10–13 calls. He does not hurry, so the whole song may last up to 30 seconds . . . (Wayre)

They live quite solitarily, both males & females; every male has his own dancing room, of which he is excessively proud . . . Each male chooses some open, level spot—sometimes in a dark gloomy ravine, entirely surrounded and shut in by dense canebrakes and rank vegetation—sometimes on the top of a hill where the jungle is comparatively open—from which he clears all the dead leaves and weeds, for a space of six or eight yards square until nothing but the bare clean earth remains, and thereafter he keeps this place scrupulously clean, removing carefully every dead leaf or twig that may happen to fall on it from the trees above. (Davison)

"The display," adds Smythies, "consists of three phases: first, a period of excitement during which the tail sweeps the ground while the pheasant fidgets with twigs and pebbles about the hen; then, when she stands still, he erects his

Opposite:
Fan palms catch a beam of sunlight in the forest shade.

A male Great argus pheasant. Its courtship calls and dances have fascinated ornithologists for a century.

Tail feathers of the Great argus pheasant.

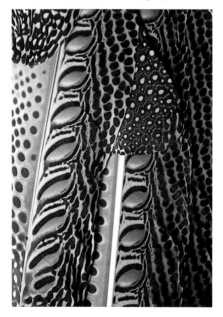

Opposite:
A column of termites forages along the forest floor and tree trunks.

ocellated plumes and confronts her with a great vertical, concave fan. In the third phase he bows rhythmically to her." Though his display is spectacular, the Argus disappears like magic into the underbrush when one approaches. Found feeding on fallen fruit, and on ants, leaves, nuts and seeds throughout the lowland dipterocarp forest, the Argus vies with the orangutan and hornbills for the title Mascot of Borneo.

Yet there is another Bornean pheasant, the Bulwer's, whose appearance is as striking as the Argus'. Though its large, white tail is less spectacular, it certainly stands out better against the dark forest; its red-and-blue body feathers are showier; and its head ornamentation is outrageous. Says Smythies: "This wonderful species was discovered in 1874, and has been much sought after by zoos and aviculturists. It is a bird of primary forest, and like the Argus pheasant it comes down to water twice daily to drink. It skulks along through the jungle, carrying its tail in a curve like a fowl. In display, the sky-blue lobes [on its head] are inflated by the injection of blood; the beak is then invisible, the blue being relieved only by the ruby-red of the eye, which is particularly noticeable owing to the red ring surrounding it."

Three other Bornean forest fowls—the Crested fireback, the Crested wood partridge and the Malaysian peacock-pheasant—are also stunning, and, like the others, are snared for the clandestine "prestige bird market."

TERMITES

Farther down the trail is a long, sinuous line of what appear to be ants. The narrow ribbon of black insects flows down from a tree trunk a few meters off

the trail, streams along a fallen log, crosses the trail on an exposed tree root, runs up a near buttress and down on the other side of the tree. It finally disappears into a low mound at the base of the tree.

The "ants" prove to be termites—probably of the genus *Hospitalitermes* (so named because members invariably share nests with another termite, genus *Termes*). *Hospitalitermes* is one of the "nasute" termites, whose defense against predatory ants is as effective as it is unusual. Instead of formidable jaws the soldier caste (all termites have one or more type of specialized soldiers, whose job it is to protect the workers, the larvae and the queen) has a frontal gland on its snout that produces sticky, irritating chemicals. The soldiers seem not only to be guarding the column but also keeping it neatly within narrow boundaries.

Close up, one can see little balls of pale green lichens held aloft in the mandibles of the scurrying workers. Some nasutes feed on dead wood, some on humus and others on rotten leaves; *Hospitalitermes*, though, feeds on tree lichens, which the workers bite off in small chunks. The termites forage both day and night in columns that may reach 130 feet (40 m) from the nest. Nasutes are the largest and most specialized subfamily of the "higher termites" (Termitidae) and are one of the major decomposers of rainforest wood, with more than 120 species in Borneo.

Another subfamily of higher termites, the Macroterminae, travels equal distances, but mostly underground. To reach new sources of food, they may tunnel more than 160 feet (50 m) from the nest. Within the network of tunnels they husband fungi of the genus *Termitomyces*, but not on "leaf gardens" (cultivated by many Amazonian and African termites). Instead, they build cardboardlike combs from their feces. The fungi feed on the otherwise undigestible material, breaking it down into sugars and concentrated nutrients. The termites then re-ingest the partly digested comb. Because they can handle large quantities of difficult materials, macrotermites are important members of the decomposer community.

The so-called lower termite families, though less numerous than the higher termites—composing perhaps 20–30 percent of the termite community—play an equally important role in recycling the organic material. Called "damp-wood" termites, they are often found off the ground in treetrunks and branches. By working on unhealthy and newly dead wood, they quicken the fall of branches and trees and speed up the process of decay by opening the tough plant cells to smaller insects in the leaf litter and to a host of bacteria and fungi.

Termites are one of the rainforest's "keystone" animals. They alone can feed on poor-quality woody plant material. They translocate and break down organic soil humus (many tree roots tap directly into abandoned termite nests). Some species even contain gut bacteria that can fix atmospheric nitrogen into forms usable by plants.

Termites themselves support a host of predators: from carnivorous ants and insectivorous birds to the Giant toad, the pangolin and the Sun bear. It has been estimated that the average termite biomass on each hectare (2.5 ac) of jungle is equivalent to that of one whole cow—three times the average combined weight of all mammals and birds.

ANIMALS OF THE FOREST FLOOR

Along the trail is an area of disturbed soil and devastated logs. It could be the work of a Sun bear, but more likely a pangolin. The pangolin, or scaly anteater, is a bizarre mammal. Toothless and covered with scales instead of hair or fur,

it curls up in a protective ball, like an armadillo, when threatened, wrapping its prehensile tail around its unscaled underparts. During the day, the pangolin sleeps in an underground burrow. At night it comes out to feed on termites and ants, ripping apart termite nests with its powerful forelegs armed with sharp claws, and licking up the inhabitants with its long, sticky tongue. Pangolins are slow-moving and evidently make good eating; their scaly skins are common wall decorations in longhouses from the lowlands to the Kelabit Uplands.

The Sun bear, or honey bear, whose claw marks can also be seen on hollow trees or among the ruins of fallen logs, also enjoys termites, along with bee larvae and other insect grubs, and it dotes on honey; but it eats just about any small animal or insect it chances on as it explores the understory and scoots along the forest floor. Its name reflects the golden crescent-shaped marking on its upper chest. Like an orangutan, the Sun bear builds a sleeping platform, though usually lower down in the canopy.

One of the smallest of the bear family, the Sun bear is powerfully built and has the reputation for being short-tempered; accounts of longhouse life by Harrisson and others mention men disfigured by bears. Just before John MacKinnon began his study on the Segama River, he met a party of geologists

A young Sun bear crosses a forest stream.

and Iban paddlers who had visited the area. "The men had had to shoot three honey bears, however, and the Iban considered these bad-tempered creatures as the most dangerous animals in the forest. A few years earlier honey bears had killed two men at a nearby timber camp, ripping open their bellies with sharp curved claws." Later, MacKinnon was forced to defend himself with a parang against an attacking mother and cub.

These days, of course, Sun bears usually come out the losers in such interactions, as logging roads and hunters in jeeps move deeper into the forest. There is presently a baby Sun bear living at the Sepilok Rehabilitation Center, along with a baby Asian elephant, a rare Clouded leopard and two even rarer Two-horned rhinos, all captured or orphaned by hunters. Because of these unusual animals, Sepilok has become a prime destination for tourists and photographers. Terry Domico, while doing research and photos for his *Bears of the World*, had the good fortune to help release a young Sun bear back into the wild and got the first shots of one "skimming" the forest floor in search of food.

The elusive Clouded leopard, the largest of Borneo's felines, is patterned with large black patches on its back, changing to spots on its legs and dark rings on its tail, all on a golden background. This handsome coat, long favored for ceremonial capes and hats by Dayak tribes, has been the cat's undoing.

The Clouded leopard hunts by day and night, capturing monkeys and small orangutans in the trees and deer and pigs on the ground. Like most large mammals, it is increasingly rare; but a Dutch visitor I met in Kuching had the luck to come upon one in daylight. As he rounded a huge tree, the leopard was climbing up along a buttress ridge. They stood eyeball to eyeball for an eternity before the cat bounded silently away into the forest shadows. He thought it the most graceful animal he'd ever seen.

For both the Asian elephant and the Asian two-horned rhinoceros, eastern Sabah and contiguous areas of northern East Kalimantan are the last refuges on Borneo—and one of the last anywhere. Perhaps the largest remaining population of wild Asian elephants—between 500 and 2,000—inhabits the forests of eastern Sabah. Although groups range from lone bulls to aggregations of more than 100 individuals, stable herd size is usually between three and 40, mostly mature females and their young. Along the more remote trails of the Danum Valley Conservation Area, deep, oval elephant footprints are common in the numerous mud wallows made by wild pigs. MacKinnon, who did his pioneering orangutan study in that area in the late 1960s, found elephants fairly common, and considered them one of the most dangerous animals in the forest because of their size, strength, intelligence and unpredictable nature. He writes of spending a sleepless night huddled within a tree buttress, harassed by a herd bull.

It has long been debated whether the Asian elephant is native to Borneo; the most popular theory is that some were donated as gifts by the Sultan of Sulu (now southern Philippines) back in the 16th or 17th century. In any case the elephants thrived in this area—neither hunted nor trained as logging beasts—until the recent conversion of large tracts of land to agriculture. Considered pests because of their taste for palm shoots and banana stems and their trampling of crops, elephants were exterminated from the Tawau-Semporna area (southeastern Sabah near the Kalimantan border) and from the Sandakan peninsula (including Sepilok) during the past two decades. They are now found mostly on the remote Dent peninsula at Sabah's easternmost tip and west of the peninsula in an area that is rapidly being converted to palm oil plantations. Elephant numbers in Borneo are uncertain, but probably declining rapidly.

The Asian two-horned (or Sumatran) rhino's story is even less sanguine. These small, woodland rhinos are surprisingly meek and endearing creatures which spend most of their waking moments wallowing in mud or eating. In the

The attractive coat of the Clouded leopard, largest of Borneo's cats, is used in Dayak ceremonial costumes.

wild they reportedly feed on mature leaves and twigs from a wide range of woody plants including saplings, lianas and small trees, which they may push over to obtain the leaves. There are presently two rhinos, one a young male, the other a mature female, in a stockade here in Sepilok. Their constant, plaintive, high-pitched moans seem more appropriate to a much smaller animal.

The stocky, short-legged rhino is hairy when young, but less so when older. The prominent horn at the tip of its long, rectangular snout may grow to a foot (30 cm) in males, but the second one, just above the eye, is barely visible.

The male Asian rhino has an unusual penis, which has figured prominently in Dayak culture. The rhino himself uses it for the usual purposes but also to mark his territory; it points conveniently backwards between the rhino's rear legs, obviating the need to raise a leg in the fashion of dogs. It sprays a great distance, as from a hose nozzle, and in fact is shaped like a nozzle, with an expanded flange around the base of the head. This flange inspired a Dayak sex-enhancement device called a palang. "The basic operation," writes Tom Harrison (who created the present palang display at the Sarawak Museum and implied that he himself had firsthand experience with one):

simply consists of driving a hole [crosswise] through the distal end of the penis; sometimes for the determined, two holes at right angles. In this hole a small tube of bamboo or other material can be kept, so that the hole does not grow over . . . The owner adds whatever he prefers to elaborate and accentuate its intention . . . The effect, of course, is to enlarge the diameter of the male organ inside the female and so to accentuate points of mobile friction . . .

The palang, which had not reached the isolated Kelabit Uplands until the 1930s, may have been centuries old among the Kenyah and other Bornean Dayaks. The custom has faded in areas that have embraced Christianity but has not died out completely among Ibans and others.

Thirty-thousand-year-old remains of the Two-horned rhinoceros have been unearthed in Niah Cave in Sarawak. Though never abundant on Borneo, the rhino was once widespread. Its only viable breeding population is now confined to the Tabin Wildlife Reserve on the Dent peninsula, with scattered populations in pockets on Sumatra and peninsular Malaysia. Its cousin, the Lesser one-horned (Javan) rhino, whose 10,000-year-old bones were unearthed from Madai Cave not far from here, was later extirpated from Borneo, perhaps by neolithic hunters, and is now confined to the westernmost tip of Java.

Both species have been hunted relentlessly for meat and for the horn, which, though merely a form of highly compacted hair, is claimed by traditional Chinese medicine to possess wondrous curative powers. China signed a recent international rhino protection treaty; but the demand for rhino-horn medicine is such that state-run pharmaceutical companies are reportedly grinding up even antique rhino-horn carvings for ingredients and continue to produce vast amounts of rhino-horn-based medicines. With such demand for its horn, the rhino will likely be extirpated from the wild in Borneo as elsewhere unless sufficient habitat is preserved and conservation measures are strictly enforced.

A rare Asian two-horned (Sumatran) rhinoceros; the species is on the verge of extinction.

THE HUNT

The Lesser mouse deer is not a true deer but is the world's smallest hoofed mammal.

Hunting has always been central to life in the interior of Borneo, as an important source of protein, a status symbol of manhood, and for many, an enduring passion. As Harrisson writes of the Kelabit:

> *The main attraction for the men is hunting. This is an abiding love in every male belly and chest . . . No man can not be a hunter. The idea of hunting is the idea of being a man. Only age or imbecility can excuse the inability to spend and enjoy long spells far out in the jungle, living without the every-night long-house comforts . . . These hunting trips, if successful, are as much devoted to giving the hunters an orgy of meat-eating for themselves as to bring back meat for the long-house. If the hunt goes on long, only the last few days of meat can be brought back. Beyond this, the point is to be out there, to move through the multiple interests of the wild; as men, without women . . .*

I once accompanied a group of Kelabits on a nighttime hunt in Sarawak's central highlands. The party's leader, a successful entrepreneur as well as one of Bario's most esteemed hunters, was one of the few who could afford unlimited shotgun shells (not just a matter of funds but of frequent business trips by plane to Marudi, where permits must be renewed and new shells bought). Three men had shotguns; three youths acted as bearers and retrievers.

The primary game was the flying fox—the world's largest bat, with a wingspan of up to 6.5 feet (2 m). By day, they roost en masse on tree branches (at which roosts they were traditionally netted). By night, they emerge to seek fruit and nectar from large trees.

The hunting of flying foxes is as widespread a custom as it is ancient. Wallace wrote from Batchian Island in the Moluccas: "These creatures are considered a great delicacy, and are much sought after. At about the beginning of the year they come in large flocks to eat fruit, and congregate during the day on some small islands in the bay, hanging by thousands on trees, especially dead ones. They can then be easily caught or knocked down with sticks, and are brought home by the basketfuls."

As the huge bats crossed in front of the bright full moon, on slow-beating wings as majestic as eagles, the hunters fired. Most shots hit the mark. Wounded bats were retrieved from bush or river and prodded unmercifully to elicit piglike squeals—distress calls that were believed to draw their comrades closer.

Between good bat sites, we followed invisible game trails—hunched over through dark, impenetrable thickets—and squished through swamps on sinking logs, like a night patrol through enemy lines, seeking, without luck, the shining eyes of mouse deer.

Mouse deer, or chevrotains, are tiny creatures (the Lesser, or pelanduk, weighs but 5 lbs/2.2kg; the Greater less than twice that). The Lesser mouse deer, in fact, is the world's smallest hoofed animal and smallest ruminant. Found throughout Southeast Asia, mouse deer belong not to the true deer family (Cervidae) but to the small tragulid family, which has just two other species, one in Africa, one in India. Mouse deer have ratlike faces with large eyes, slender legs and sharp, deerlike hoofs. They lack antlers, but males have curved upper canine teeth with which to fight rivals. Mostly nocturnal, mouse deer feed on fallen fruit, fungi and young leaves.

Borneo does have three true deer species, however. One, the Sambar deer, or rusa, is similar to North American deer. Its coat is grayish to reddish brown with a black tail. It is a favorite Dayak game animal, and its secretive, semi-nocturnal habits have been attributed to heavy hunting pressure. The other two cervids are the Red muntjac and the Bornean yellow muntjac, or barking deers—strange-looking, hunch-backed creatures with small, straight, swept-back antlers. Intermediate in size between mouse deer and Sambar deer, they are mostly active during the day, when their short, loud "barks" can be heard everywhere in the forest.

At midnight we stopped to build a fire and snack on the flying foxes in a burned-over clearing that would soon be planted in rice. The bats were skinned and their wings removed. Skewed on sticks stuck in the ground leaning into the fire, the naked bats, their long wingbones curling as they cooked, looked remarkably like gargoyles—especially their shadows, cast by the firelight and the full tropical moon. They were tasty but had hardly any meat on their delicate bones.

After all the effort, we took little except the rubbery bat wings, to be boiled as a side dish; but the hunters, returning wet and bedraggled at 2 A.M., were obviously well satisfied by the quest.

Hunting is not all just manly ritual, though. A 1986 study by Julian Caldicott for the World Wildlife Fund found that hunting supplied, in Sarawak alone, roughly 20,000 tons of meat each year, worth millions of dollars to rural settlements. During some seasons, wild game provides much of the protein served in government boarding schools. Sambur, barking deer and Mouse deer contribute about a fourth of the harvest; the rest is wild pig.

"When there are plenty of pig about," wrote Harrisson, "no one much bothers with any other way. But pigs are puzzling creatures, very mobile, sometimes suddenly moving away even over the mountains into other valleys after better fruit there . . . When pigs are scarce, some strain is put on the comfort of Kelabit life . . ."

Borneo's Bearded pig, or *babi*, is larger than local domestic pigs. It is rather ugly-looking but quite tasty if well cooked. Piglets are dark, but the increasingly hairy adults range from reddish brown to creamy white, with a characteristic brush of long hair toward the end of the long, slender snout. The *babi* move en masse through the forest, leaving distinctive ploughed-up ground as they root for tubers, fungi, worms, insects and carrion. But they much prefer acorns, illipe nuts (of certain dipterocarps) and fallen fruit—figs, durians, mangoes and dozens of lesser tropical delicacies—and will go far to find them.

This nomadic life-style is followed to some degree by all large forest animals who depend on fruit and nuts. Tropical trees flower and fruit unpredictably—some species produce regularly, some sporadically—and fruiting seasons are limited. Consequently, fruit and seed eaters have chronic difficulty matching their population levels to their food supply. Some, such as orangutans and gibbons, cover a limited territory intensively; others, such as hornbills, flying foxes and the Bearded pig, are nomadic over immense areas.

There are, however, general fruiting patterns on which Sarawak's wild pigs rely. They usually end up in the Kelabit Uplands in spring, when acorns and fruit are plentiful. Toward mid-year they move back down into the lowland forest for figs and for illipe nuts. (Illipe nuts are also harvested by Dayaks and shipped to Europe for oil used in making chocolate.)

A Bornean yellow muntjac (barking deer). Its two-spiked antler distinguishes it from the closely related Red muntjac.

Borneo's favorite game animal, the Bearded pig or babi. *Migratory groups follow the irregular mass fruiting of rainforest trees.*

As they move, the pigs are forced to cross rivers, where they are vulnerable—to floods, pythons, crocodiles, and to traditional Dayak and Penan hunters, who wait along the banks at known game trail crossings to ambush them as they enter the water. Though shotguns are now used even by the seminomadic Penan, 40 percent of pig kills are still by spear. When the *babi* are running, few men walk without a spear or gun.

A friend and I were once guided through an almost trackless area of the Kelabit Uplands by a Kayan hunter, son-in-law to the headman of the remote Kelabit longhouse of Ramudu. Ketawan wore running shoes and jogging pants (the better to keep out leeches), but he carried with him a hardwood spear with a thin metallic point lashed with rattan, and on his back a traditional rattan backpack containing a bedroll, a light tarp and a loaf of sticky Kelabit rice wrapped in a banana leaf—the same outfit described by Harrisson half a century before. At and under our feet surged five feisty pig dogs.

In many ways the trip was frustrating. We were hiking in and out of spectacular stream drainages through one of the most remote areas on earth. Yet because of the distance to cover and the difficult terrain, there was no time to explore the streams or spot the forest birds that we could hear all around us.

But there was one animal that found *us.* Despite our "leech socks" (large homemade stockings that tie above the calf), large, energetic leeches—looping end-to-end like an upwardly mobile Slinky toy—often managed to climb above the sock and gorge on blood before being noticed.

Wallace, his fascination mixed with annoyance, noted:

These little creatures infest the leaves and herbage by the side of the paths, and when a passenger comes along they stretch themselves out at full length, and if they touch any part of his dress or body, quit their leaf and adhere to it. They

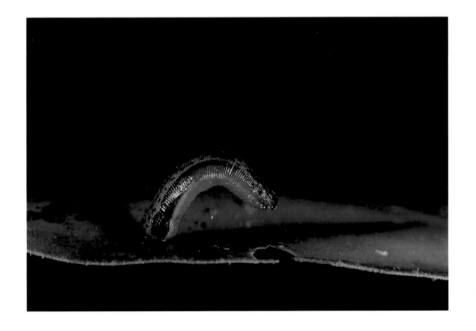

The patient, heat-sensitive Painted jungle leech latches onto passing mammals, including human hikers, for a meal of blood.

then creep on to his feet, legs, or other part of his body and suck their fill, the first puncture being rarely felt during the excitement of walking. On bathing in the evening, we generally found half a dozen on each of us, most frequently on our legs, but sometimes on our bodies, and I had one who sucked his fill from the side of my neck, but who luckily missed the jugular vein. There are many species of these forest-leeches. All are small, but some are beautifully marked with stripes of bright yellow. They probably attach themselves to deer or other animals which frequent the forest-paths, and have thus acquired the singular habit of stretching themselves out at the sound of footsteps or rustling foliage.

A modern scientist, adds more drily: "The land leeches of Malaysia belong to the genus *Haemadipsa*. They have adhesive suckers at the end of the body but the bite is inflicted by a trifid set of jaws, armed with minute, sharp teeth in the anterior sucker. A small quantity of saliva, containing an anti-coagulant, is injected into the wound, and prevents clotting & gives rise to the irritation that follows a leech bite. The body is extremely distensible and can pass through [shoe] lace-eyes." Or, he might have added, pass through or under any known defense or combination of defenses. And so—unless there has been drought for the past few weeks, in which case the little buggers retreat into the damp leaf duff until the first drop of rain, when they sally out, famished for blood—you might as well get use to them.

As we stopped along a rocky stream that made up a good part of the "trail," the dogs up ahead began a wild yipping. Suddenly, a large *babi* boar came crashing down the side of the gully with two dogs on its heels, straight toward us. Ketawan stood in front, holding his spear in a defensive stance. Eager to take part, I reached for my parang.

I pulled at the handle (which two days earlier I had attached to its blade with ShoeGlue—the proper gutta-percha not being readily available). As I raised the handle aloft, unset ShoeGlue dripped down my wrist like butterscotch sauce, the long, lethal blade remaining safely in its wooden sheath. When Ketawan recovered from his mirth, he signaled us back, and bounded up the bank after the grunting, yapping mass of boar and dogs. They all crashed into the riparian brush and disappeared. Soon there was silence.

When we reached him, Ketawan was cleaning off his bloody spearpoint in the stream; the massive boar lay beside him. He removed the boar's guts, filled the carcass with stones, and dragged it underwater where it would be safe from scavengers. He would return the following day to carry it over the long, slippery trail back to his longhouse.

He was properly modest, but his mood had definitely elevated, as it would each time the dogs ran off, even after some elusive monkey or squirrel. When we finally reached our destination, a small Penan settlement called Pa Barang, there was much recounting of the tale and much laughter at my expense. But the young headman, Aye Pet, had himself just returned with a small pig, and we were treated to delicious roast *babi* heart; a tasty ending to a sweaty, leech-infested trek.

THE PENAN

The Penan of Sarawak comprise about 80 settlements with about 9,000 people, in groups averaging 30 or so individuals. They are as mysterious as their name is confusing. Penan itself is a Kenyah term for "upriver people," who live at the headwaters of river valleys, above the navigable water. The parallel Kayan term Punan is also used, but that word is better reserved for two groups of settled Penan in the Belaga District of Sarawak, and can be confused with a Kayan subgroup, the Punan Bah. Groups similar to the Penan in Kalimantan are called Ot Danum, Ukit and Bukitan—all have the same sense of "upriver people."

The Penan groups do not necessarily share a common ancestry. Some may be descended from early Bornean settlers, whose ancient funerary ships are preserved in Niah Caves; others may be descendants of small tribes pushed farther and farther upriver by more aggressive settlers, or may even be offshoots of those very groups. Though their use of blowpipe and their minimal costume—bare feet, loincloth, rattan wrist and calf bracelets, and straight-cut bangs for the men—seem unique, their style of dress and hunting resemble an

An elderly Penan prefers his simple riverside shack to the new longhouse at Long Iman on the Baram River.

unadorned version of the standard Dayak outfit of 50–100 years ago. Many Penan dialects are closer to Kenyah or other neighboring Dayak languages than to other Penan dialects.

What the Penan have in common is a seminomadic life-style. Their diet is based on wild sago-palm starch rather than on rice, and their economy depends on trade with downriver Dayaks. Penan hunt wild pig and deer with spear and shotgun, monkeys with blowpipes and poison darts. They gather sago and wild fruits for food, and forest products such as rattan, cinnamon bark, jelutong (wild rubber), gaharu (incense wood) and damar (flammable resin) for trade. They are considered Borneo's best makers of parangs and of rattan mats, baskets and bracelets. Increasingly, baskets and blowpipes are sold to tourists, especially in new government-subsidized Penan settlements such as the ones near Gunung Mulu National Park.

Almost all of Sarawak's Penan are now settled or "semi-settled" (a situation vague enough to satisfy both the Penan and government officials). In general, Penan settlements consist of a main camp, usually along a river, where bananas are grown, food is stored, and the sick and elderly can stay. The settlement's longevity usually depends on the accessible supply of sago and rattan. Temporary camps are useful as long as the nearby game holds out; traveling camps serve as temporary family shelters for hunting expeditions and for gathering rattan and sago.

Sago is a palm that grows in clumps. One species, growing in the coastal lowlands, has been used by villagers throughout the Sunda islands for centuries and is now cultivated as a cash crop. An unrelated species growing in the rainforest allowed early Bornean settlers to move inland; it still serves rural Dayaks as a back-up source of carbohydrates if the rice crop fails, but, among them, is considered a badge of poverty.

Penan men fell two or three of the thick trunks, marking the immature ones for later harvest, and also collect the edible leaf-bud, called *lekak*. Cut in 3–4

A Penan woman nurses her baby while stripping rattan stems on the longhouse porch.

A Penan woman washes rattan stems in the river before weaving them into baskets, mats and bracelets.

foot (1 m) sections, the trunks are hauled to the nearest stream, where the men and boys chop out the pith while the women and girls press and wash it to extract the starch. Each section contains 15–25 pounds (7–11 kg) of edible starch; up to a dozen sections can be taken from a clump and processed in a couple of days. And so, a year's supply for a family can be processed in a matter of weeks.

Rattans are climbing palms—as important for material goods as sago and pigs are for food. The thin, clumping trunks are armed with formidable thorns; long, wiry runners grow from the ends of the fronds. (The runners snake out into any open space, such as a trail, usually at neck or ankle level. They are sometimes called "back-up vines" since backing up is the only way to extract one's skin or clothing from the grip of their decurved thorns). About half of the 250 or more palm species in Borneo are rattans, more than 60 in genus *Calamus*. Of all these species, though, only six are cultivated, and only a few wild *Calamus* varieties are considered useful for weaving.

Rattan shoots are cut to lengths of about 10 feet (3 m), split and washed in the stream. After drying for two to three weeks they are rubbed with sawdust and further dried for trade or weaving; flexibility may be enhanced by burying the rattan for a few weeks. In peninsular Malaysia, larger, cultivated stalks are boiled in oil, then cleaned and split. The shoot is used for cane furniture, the core for wickerwork.

To the Penan, considered "professors of the rainforest," the forest is home, farm and factory. Native anthropologist Jayl Langub quotes a Penan: "From the forest we get our life. Fruits are important, many different fruits. *Uvud* [sago starch] and *lekak* [sago leaf bud] are necessary; these are our food. From the forest we also get other necessities. Rattan we use to make carrying baskets. And we hunt in the forest. We look for pigs and for deer. With blowpipes we hunt the gibbon and monkey. Just from this land, we get all we need for our life."

But a diminishing forest, government policies which encourage settlement, and a desire for modern goods, better education and health care, all combine to pull the Penan into the sphere of modern Malaysia. With each generation, settlements like Pa Barang move closer to the nearest store, school, church and airfield. And the government is pressing many communities to move into new state-subsidized longhouses. There, the wild supplies need to be supplemented with larger plantings of rice, fruit trees, tapioca and yam; and more emphasis

Traditional Penan elder and modern youths.

is put on crafts such as woven baskets, mats and bracelets to trade for store-bought goods.

As the outlying Kelabit longhouses have shifted toward Bario and Bario children have gravitated downriver toward the schools and career opportunities of towns, the Penan have moved nearer the source of air-transported goods and the Christian fellowship of longhouse Kelabit. After tens of thousands of years, the Penan life-style, dependent on an intact rainforest, may not last beyond another generation.

FORESTS IN THE CLOUDS

Only the bare summit was awesome; why not? This was something entirely different from anything else in tropical island experience. In fact, there is nothing like it anywhere in Southeast Asia, and perhaps in the world. It is, moreover, frequently cold; and therefore very unlike the tropical lowlands below. This and its beauty give immense visual impact, the black contrast with the unflinching green below, impress every mind, and must always have done so.

—Tom Harrisson, in *Kinabalu, Summit of Borneo*

Mount Kinabalu's sheer 2,000-foot (600-m) south wall shimmers above us, illuminated by the bright full moon as we step out from Laban Rata Resthouse, still half asleep at 3:30 A.M. The trail, a steep staircase of rocks, roots and terraced rubble immediately puts our legs to the test. There is no need for flashlights on the open, moonlit trail, but plenty for wool caps, sweaters and gloves. We are still within a few degrees of the equator, but at 11,000 feet (3,300 m) above sea level we have left the steamy tropics far below.

The montane rainforest that towered above us at park headquarters is here reduced to dark, twisted silhouettes no taller than our heads; then to gnarly, dwarfed *Leptospermum* trees; and finally to just the hardy sedges and Heath rhododendron growing along cracks in the dark, bare rock.

The summit itself is bare granite. Huge "exfoliating" slabs peel off the dome like the skins of an onion. Ledges formed by the edges of granite slabs are wide enough to form a solid path along the cliffs, but now and again we must pull ourselves up the long climbing ropes anchored to the rock. These will also guide our way back down should the clouds rise up to cover the summit before our descent.

Yesterday's downpour, which we watched from the resthouse as it cascaded off the summit in broad, foaming sheets, has left only a small pool in a shallow basin. On its surface glistens a thick layer of ice—something of a miracle of nature in the tropics. We cannot resist the urge to hear it crack and tinkle and to feel a small piece melt on our parched tongues.

At 13,455 feet (4,100 m), Kinabalu is the tallest mountain between the Himalayas and New Guinea. During the last ice age, from about 15,000 to

Opposite:
Mount Trus Madi as seen from Mount Kinabalu at sunrise.

"Donkeys Ears" at summit of Mount Kinabalu.

9,000 years ago, Southeast Asia's lone ice cap covered these rocks. Only the slender, jagged peaks above us, now shattered into loose rubble by the daily alternation of freeze and thaw, remained above the ice.

In those days the thick ice cap fed a valley glacier, which flowed northward between the western and eastern plateaus of the butterfly-shaped summit to carve precipitous, mile-deep Low's Gully. Boulders frozen into the base of the flowing glacier worked like sandpaper to grind down the summit rock; scratch lines on the granite surface still mark its direction of flow. The ice cleared all traces of soil from the summit, and constant winds and torrential rains have kept it bare ever since.

To the east, on the other side of Ugly Sister Peak and the twin spires called Donkeys Ears, the sky is now tinged with scarlet. Low's Peak, 200 feet of vertical rubble, seems to rise straight up from the summit dome in a final mocking gesture as we labor upward, panting in the thin air. But finally, at the very top, we are rewarded by a spectacular, almost cloudless, 360° view of northern Borneo.

The rising sun shoots smoky laser beams upwards from behind a pink bank of clouds massed over the Sulu Sea, a hundred miles to the east. To the west, over the coastal Crocker Range, Kota Kinabalu's lights outline its bay along the South China Sea. At our feet, Low's Gully drops off into the void, offering a mixture of vertigo and exhilaration. Beyond, lies the entire northern tip of Borneo. Dominating the southern horizon Mount Trus Madi, Borneo's second-tallest mountain at 8,600 feet (2,600 m) traps the first morning rays in a wispy net of clouds. And in the mist beyond Trus Madi lies the island's mountainous interior.

Twenty million years ago western Borneo lay beneath the sea at the edge of the Southeast Asian continental shelf. On it were deposited thick layers of planktonic diatom shells and river sediments interbedded with sand. By fifteen million years ago, the Australian tectonic plate began to collide with the southeasternmost edge of Asia, fusing the volcanic island arc of eastern Borneo to the continental western half of the island. Titanic collisions crumpled Borneo's layer cake of sedimentary rocks and pushed up a huge central spine of mountains that were once much higher than the current ranges.

Tectonic action has long since shifted southward, to Indonesia's portion of the Pacific's volcanic "Ring of Fire." Bereft of mountain-building forces, Borneo's balance of power shifted toward the mountains' ancient nemesis: water. Supplied by endless clouds from the surrounding seas, rivers of monsoon rain have washed much of the central highlands down onto broad coastal plains.

About two dozen highland peaks still rise 6,000–8,000 feet (1,800–2,400 m) into the clouds—from Tambuyukon and Trus Madi in central Sabah to Murud and Guguang along the Sarawak/Kalimantan border, and south to Mount Raya between the states of West and Central Kalimantan. Beyond that to the south only the low Schwaner Range remain above the vast swamp-forests of the coastal plains that now cover most of the southern third of Borneo. The peaks of the central range average just 2,000–4,000 feet (6,000–1,200 m); and even these highlands have been dissected by a labyrinth of river valleys barely above sea level.

Kinabalu is the one formidable exception to this victory of rain over rock. About 9 million years ago a vast pool of lava collected beneath the Crocker Range. Over a period of some 4 million years it cooled slowly underground, forming a great "pluton" of granite. A million and a half years ago the granite mass began to force its way upward through the crumpled layers of sandstone and shale of the Crocker Range like a mushroom through the forest duff. It is still rising—at the geologically rapid rate of 20 inches (50 cm) per century.

Kinabalu, considered the youngest granite intrusion in the world, is also earth's greatest "batholith" (single, unified rock). One hundred fifty square kilometers of it is exposed as the visible massif; but like an iceberg of incredible proportions, it conceals nine-tenths of its mass beneath the earth.

Freed from the overlying weight of the earth, stresses within the rising granite mass cause the outer few thousand feet of rock to crack and peel. And so the summit's surface rocks like huge, broken roof tiles. The rock's rough texture is created by differing rates of erosion of the varied crystals that make up the granite. Attractive whitish and rosy inclusions decorate the dark slabs of granite rock beneath our feet as we reluctantly retreat down the mountain in a measured race against the banks of fog seeping up the mountain on rising, sun-warmed thermals.

In 1851, Hugh Low, a British colonial official from Labuan (and son of a British horticulturist specializing in tropical plants), was the first European to reach Kinabalu's summit. To say that the mountain was unexplored until then would be to ignore the Kadazan (Dusan) villagers who for centuries have practiced shifting rice cultivation on the mountainsides to about 5,000 feet (1,500 m), and they undoubtedly hunted pig and deer far up the slopes. But until explorers and visitors demanded guides, there was little reason for the local villagers to ascend above the chilly, barren treeline into a zone that was considered the abode of departed spirits. The name Kinabalu, in fact, derives from the Kadazan *Aki Nabalu*—"Place of the Dead."

Low spent two weeks of hard travel from village to village—bartering for food, guides, and porters at each—before beginning his laborious ascent. After a short stay at Paka Cave (elevation 10,000 ft/3,000 m), the highest spot familiar to his guides, his party achieved the barren summit dome. There, Low "gazed down into a circular ampitheater the bottom of which was indiscernible, though I could see down two thousand feet [600 m]." This was later named Low's Gully. He did not attempt the steep peak that now bears his name.

In 1858 Low returned with Spenser St. John, British consul in Brunei and author of the classic *Life in the Forests of the Far East*. On their second attempt, the two reached the summit zone. There St. John scaled what appeared to be the tallest of the scattered peaks; named after him, it turned out to be 16 feet (5 m) short of the ultimate summit.

In 1888, British naturalist John Whitehead, on his second attempt, became the first to reach the top of Low's Peak. More importantly, Whitehead made the first major zoological collections. These included some of Borneo's most colorful montane birds: Whitehead's trogon, Whitehead's spiderhunter and Whitehead's broadbill. Despite his zeal he was almost driven to despair by Kinabalu's unforgiving climate. This from his *Exploration of Mount Kinabalu, North Borneo*: "Just now, at 3 P.M., the sun is shining through a steady shower of rain; this is the first time it has shone upon us in a month. How all-important is our great luminary to our comfort, and what miserable beings we are without his all-powerful rays."

The first detailed account of Mount Kinabalu's flora was by German botanist O. Stapf in 1894. In 1910, British botanist Lillian Gibbs collected more than a thousand plant species, 87 of them new to science, and in the process became

St. John's peak on Mount Kinabalu, topped with lenticular clouds.

Grove of bamboo. These versatile tree-size grasses serve Dayaks in countless ways.

the first Western woman to reach the summit. The same year, one F. W. Foxworthy on "purely a vacation ramble" became Kinabalu's first recreational visitor. A century after Low's first ascent, however, only 53 visitors had reached the summit.

In 1961 and 1964, botanist E. J. H. Corner organized and led two expeditions sponsored by the Royal Society of London to "explore little known sections of the mountain, and particularly its flora, more systematically than ever before . . ." His report, "The Proposed National Park of Kinabalu," led to the National Park Ordinance of 1962 and, ultimately, to the creation of 300-square-mile Kinabalu Park in 1964.

"The people of Sabah," Corner wrote, "possess on this famous mountain what I believe is the richest and most remarkable assemblage of plants in the world. It carries lowland, mountain, and alpine vegetation on a scale that is not seen anywhere between the Himalayas and New Guinea."

Tom Harrisson added, "Kinabalu Park is, without doubt, the greatest single outdoor recreational outlet east of India." There are few other places on earth where you can breakfast in a tropical rainforest, lunch in a montane cloud forest, sleep in a subalpine environment and crunch ice the following dawn. Some 200,000 people now visit the park each year. Of these, a tenth ascend the Summit Trail, and 15,000 achieve the summit.

Mount Kinabalu towers over Borneo's other peaks, nearly a full mile taller than its nearest rivals. Its cloud forest includes most of the plants and animals found on the highest slopes of Borneo's lesser mountains. But above 8,000 feet (2,400 m) its Summit Trail passes through a world unique to Kinabalu.

PORING HOT SPRINGS

Poring Hot Springs, at the park's southeastern corner, is the preserve's lowest area at 3,000–4,000 feet (900–1,200 m). At this elevation there are still buttressed dipterocarps, but the trees are less imposing than those in the lowlands. Emergent giants are missing, and massive lianas are fewer.

Poring means "bamboo," and from such groves Borneo's natives crafted everything from house supports, walls and porch floors to fishtraps, water containers and quivers for poison darts. Wrote Wallace in praise of native bamboos:

> *Their strength, lightness, smoothness, straightness, roundness, and hollowness, the facility and regularity with which they can be split, their many different sizes, the varying length of their joints, the ease with which they can be cut and with which holes can be made through them, their hardness outside, their freedom from any pronounced taste or smell, their great abundance, and the rapidity of their growth and increase, are all qualities which render them useful for a hundred different purposes, to serve which other materials would require much more labour and preparation. The bamboo is one of the wonderful and most beautiful productions of the tropics, and one of nature's most valuable gifts to uncivilized man.*
>
> *The Dyak houses are all raised on posts, and are often two or three hundred feet long and forty or fifty wide. The floor is always formed of strips split from large bamboos, so that each may be nearly flat and about three inches wide, and these are firmly tied down with rattan to the joists beneath. When well made, this is a delightful surface to walk upon barefooted, the rounded surfaces of the bamboo being very smooth and agreeable to the feet, while at the same time affording a firm hold. But, what is more important, they form with a mat over them an excellent bed, the elasticity of the bamboo and its rounded surface being far superior to a more rigid and flatter floor . . .*
>
> *When, however, a flat, close floor is required, excellent boards are made by splitting open large bamboos on one side only, and flattening them out so as to form slabs eighteen inches wide and six feet long, with which some Dyak floor [and wall] their houses.*
>
> *The bridges they construct consist merely of stout bamboos crossing each other at the roadway like the letter* X, *and rising a few feet above it. At the crossing they are firmly bound together, and to a large bamboo which lays upon them and*

Open blossom of Rafflesia pricei, *one of the world's largest flowers.*

forms the only pathway, with a slender and often very shaky one to serve as a
handrail . . .

The outer rind of the bamboo, split and shaved thin, is the strongest material
for baskets; hen-coops, bird-cages, and conical fish-traps are quickly made by a
single joint by splitting off the skin in narrow strips left attached to one end,
while rings of the same material or rattan are twisted in at regular distances.

Water is brought to the houses by little aqueducts formed of large bamboo split
in half. Thin long-jointed bamboos form the Dyak's only water-vessels, and a
dozen of them stand in the corner of every house . . . They also make excellent
cooking utensils; vegetables and rice can be boiled in them to perfection, and they
are often used when traveling. Salted fruit or fish, sugar, vinegar, and honey
are preserved in them instead of in jars or bottles. In a small bamboo case, prettily
carved and ornamented, the Dyak carries his sirih and lime for betel-chewing,
and his little long-bladed knife has a bamboo sheath . . .

There are many other small matters for which bamboo is daily used . . . and
it is probable that my limited means of observation did not make me acquainted
with one-half the ways in which it is serviceable to the Dyaks . . .

Poring's famous hot springs emerge from the ground at 120°F–140°F (50°–60°C) and are run into cement tubs originally designed by the occupying Japanese army during World War II. The tubs attract weary climbers for post-summit therapy, as well as parties of weekend visitors from Ranau and Kota Kinabalu. To the naturalist, Poring's streams and forest offer a window onto Borneo's lower montane forest.

RAFFLESIAS

Poring's primary attraction is the occasional chance to witness the blooming of a rafflesia. The genus *Rafflesia* produces the largest, most massive and most astonishing flowers in the world, including the very largest—*Rafflesia arnoldi* of Borneo and Sumatra, up to 3 feet (1 m) across. Beccari exclaimed: "They are beyond doubt amongst the most marvellous products of Nature in existence, and I can only compare them to vegetable monsters . . ."

Rafflesia plants are parasitic, lacking both leaves and roots. The seedlings attach by suckers only to the trailing stems of a single genus, the wild grave-vine *Tetrastigma*. The flower starts as a small bud, swelling over the course of a few months to the size of a volleyball. Then one day the flower unfolds, the smallest ones a foot (30 cm) across. The hemispheric cavity below the petals features a spiky disk, beneath which are either stamens or ovaries, for the flower is unisexual.

Rafflesia is not designed for beauty. In fact, the five fleshy, petallike lobes, marbled red and white, resemble dead meat, and through a chemical reaction that is still poorly understood, the flower generates a strong odor of rotting flesh. This attracts bluebottle flies, carrion-feeders drawn by the fleshy color pattern and the stench. "The pollinator," writes one botanist, "is exploited by a grand deception and receives no reward for its efforts."

After a few days, the rafflesia flower turns brown and rots. If female and if pollinated, it then releases its minute seeds. These are dispersed by small mammals such as squirrels and tree shrews, which occasionally manage to deposit a viable seed as they scamper along the proper host. It is a tenuous method of reproduction at best.

Rafflesia may be the rarest plant genus on earth. Though its 14 species are scattered throughout Southeast Asia, each is found in only a handful of sites, and two of the species, not seen since World War II, may already be extinct.

Three of the four *Rafflesia* species occurring in Borneo are found in western Sabah, either at Poring or along the Crocker Range. Thirty-four sites have been located and mapped; only nine are presently active.

Rafflesias are endangered both by loss of habitat and by poachers, including local "medicine" collectors who believe the huge flower buds hold special powers. In 1988, a state-level committee in Sabah was set up to monitor and conserve the three local species: *Rafflesia pricei* and *R. tengku-adlinii* in the Crocker Range, and *R. keithi*, found in the Crockers and at Poring.

THE MONTANE FOREST

Kinabalu Park headquarters area, located at 5,000 feet (1,500 m), is in the center of a broad band of montane forest that covers Kinabalu's mid-elevation slopes (4,000–6,000 ft/1,200–1,800 m) and an equivalent zone along the upper slopes of Borneo's lesser mountains.

Despite the decidedly tropical look to the luxuriant forest along the park's fine trail system, the dominant trees here belong to plant families familiar to visitors from the temperate zones: oaks and chestnuts, laurels, magnolias, eucalypts and gymnosperms. Kinabalu is surely one of the richest oak forests in the world, with 70 species—more than 40 just in the genus *Lithocarpus*.

One of Kinabalu's dominant oaks, the trig-oak, *Trigonobalanus verticillata*, "turned out to be one of the great botanical discoveries of this century," according to Corner, whose Royal Society Expedition of 1961 first noted it. The only species in its genus, it appears be the "missing link" between northern beech trees, chestnuts and tropical oaks.

Yet though Borneo has more than a hundred types of oak and more than 30 species of squirrels, its upland oak forests are not particularly rich in squirrels, perhaps because the acorns of the dominant genus, the aptly named *Lithocarpus* ("stone- carpal"), are so hard. Softer fruits are plentiful, and there is no winter for which to prepare by storing acorns. Most squirrels, like the majority of Bornean forest animals, feed on fruits or insects, and on oily dipterocarp seeds.

More than 70 mammal species and 260 birds can be found on the mountain's lower slopes. One reason that Kinabalu is so rich in animal life is that it is so rich in wild figs. Eighty of Borneo's 140 fig species grow on Kinabalu and 13 are endemic. "The fact is," writes Corner, "that Kinabalu has the richest fig-flora of any comparable area in the world." Most of Borneo's mammals are found below 6,000 feet (1,800 m); by no small coincidence, all but one species of fig is similarly limited. The only fig that can survive to more than 10,000 feet (3,000 m) cannot reproduce there because the wasps that pollinate it cannot survive at that altitude.

INSECT LIFE

One of Borneo's more bizarre creatures can be seen along trails right near park headquarters. The trilobite beetle, which vaguely resembles fossils of the long-extinct trilobites, creeps along moss-covered logs, feeding on the decayed wood. I found one nearly 4 inches (10 cm) long, her thorax covered with three dark plates edged in bright orange or crimson. Orange "horns" project from the edge and from under each segment of the nine abdominal segments, which also have pairs of bright orange bumps. Her first thoracic shield is triangular, and from its apex the tiny soft head extends and retracts like a turtle's.

Most beetles undergo complete metamorphosis from larval stage to the familiar winged adult; the trilobite female, however, retains the larval shape throughout her lifetime, merely adding adult genitalia at the final moult. In 1922, Swedish entomologist Eric Mjoberg, then curator of the Sarawak Museum and later author of *Forest Life and Adventures in the Malay Archipelago*, was the first to discover that all of his collected trilobite specimens were female. Where were the males?

Determined to solve the mystery, Mjoberg placed 20 live trilobite females within wire enclosures and paid villagers to watch them. After two years his persistence finally paid off. One morning a tiny male was found mating with one of the females. The drab little male trilobite was no more than a quarter-inch (0.6 cm) long but otherwise a perfectly developed adult beetle. Mjoberg's species is found throughout Sarawak and much of Borneo, but a second, more colorful, specimen is found only on Kinabalu.

Another type of strange animal is surprisingly common along the park trails, yet might never be noticed by a casual hiker: the stick insects. By day, stick insects hide under leaves of trees; they come out at night to feed on the leaf edges. Remarkably camouflaged, many species are sculpted like slender twigs, down to the false bud-scale scars at the tips of their abdomens. Their front legs, when extended forward, add to the disguise. Other species are plumper and covered with thorny spines that can pinch. Some are marked by patterns that resemble patches of lichen. Even the eggs of stick insects are cleverly camouflaged as seeds or as whitish bird droppings on leaves. The only daytime evidence of the insects' presence is the ragged edges of freshly chewed leaves or the occasional sighting of a winged variety by a fortunate hiker.

Stick-insect mimicry can baffle all but the most experienced collector. I was twice invited on collecting trips by C. L. Chan, an authority on the stick insects of Borneo. During our first trip we swept strong beams of light over the

A stick insect, photographed against a contrasting background.

A slender stick insect, complete with false bud scale scars on tip of its abdomen.

A camel cricket.

vegetation along about a mile of trail. Though the conditions were not ideal—an extended drought had dried the normally spongy mosses of the rainforest into crackling carpets—C. L. discovered more than 30 specimens of about 15 species. Photographer Terry Domico (a sharp-eyed naturalist in his own right) and I found a single specimen. On the second trip, park naturalist Tan Fui-Lian and I managed between us five specimens of two species. Chan found 20 species.

Most of the "walking sticks" we collected were brown, 2–4 inches long. One, however, was the green giant *Pharnacea*; its body measures more than a foot (30 cm) in length, and its incredibly slender legs are equally long. It clings to a number of different branches simultaneously, resembling an entire branch rather than a single twig.

The only other insect regularly found on these nocturnal trips is another plant mimic—a bush cricket. From the side it perfectly resembles a shiny young leaf, complete with midrib and leaf veins. Even its long third pair of legs, with which it fiddles its loud, repetitive call, mimic slender leaves, the green midrib being the leg itself. Though it stays hidden beneath a leaf by day, its camouflage makes it much less vulnerable to treeshrews and to hoards of insectivorous birds.

During the day the two most obvious insect groups in the upland forest, as in the lowland forest, are butterflies and cicadas. Some 220 butterfly species have been recorded from Kinabalu's middle elevations. About a third are of Himalayan affinity rather than related to the lowland jungle; another third are endemic, found only on Kinabalu.

Mount Kinabalu is one of the better places to observe Rajah Brooke's birdwing, the handsome butterfly that sent Alfred Russel Wallace into ecstasy. Quite the opposite of trilobite beetles, the males are commonly sighted near park headquarters, while females are rarely seen. For some time this absence of females was a great mystery. It was finally discovered that females feed almost exclusively in the forest's upper canopy. Kiau Gap, along the Kamborongoh Road, is one of the few spots in Borneo where the females can occasionally be observed as they fight strong winds to cross over the ridge. The spot is excellent for finding many other canopy species as well.

Though one may be overwhelmed by the numbers and variety of Borneo's butterflies, it is the brightly patterned moths that most surprise a visitor from the temperate zone, where moths are inevitably small and drab. In fact, the moths of Kinabalu are hardly less spectacular than the butterflies. Of the several hundred species that have been collected here, the most striking is the giant

Atlas moth, with its gorgeously patterned, gracefully curved 10-inch wings. Other moths rival butterflies in color and often have even more intricate patterns. Moths are far more abundant than butterflies at high altitudes, and many local species are recorded only on Kinabalu.

BIRDS OF THE MONTANE FOREST

In many ways the montane forest, while not as rich in bird species as the lowland forest is a much better place for bird-watching. The canopy is lower and more open, giving better visibility, and the cooler weather seems to keep the birds more active throughout the day. The birds also tend to travel rather noisily in mixed flocks.

One day, while hiking near park headquarters, I found myself among a large, mixed flock of raucous Bronzed drongos, loud, gregarious Laughing thrushes, twittering Bush warblers and an exhibitionistic Pied fantail flycatcher. Of the fantail, *Birds of Borneo* says:

> *It is never still, and all day long it dances and pirouettes, filled with an inimitable joie-de-vivre. It turns from side to side with restless jerky movements, and like a ballet dancer before her mirror it tries out new steps and attitudes: down drop the wings, up jerks the head, and all the time the dainty fan of the tail is opened and closed and flirted. Now and again it flits among the leafy branches or emerges from the shelter of the trees, and launches into the air; it seems to tumble, bent on suicide; but a rapid snap at some tiny insect invisible to the naked eye, a swift recovery, and it has returned to the cool recesses of the foliage and is once more bowing and dancing.*

A pair of Malaysian (Gray) tree pies—magpielike birds with long gray-and-black tails, found throughout Borneo's uplands—perched off to the side, benefiting from the flush of insects but not deigning to be part of such a rabble of lesser birds.

A few minutes after the noisy flock had flittered out of sight, both montane barbets—Mountain and Golden-naped—began to call from nearby treetops right at the level of the ridge trail.

The nine species of barbets are the birds most commonly heard in the forests of Borneo, but they are rarely seen. Barbets are medium size, with squat green bodies; the heads of most, however, are unbelievably gaudy, with multicolored patches of bright reds, golds, blues, blacks and yellows, and sometimes all of the above. They nest in holes in trees and feed on fruits and insects in the canopy with their broad, sharp bills. Their strange, monotonous calls—the pattern specific to each species—are characteristic sounds of Bornean forests. "From dawn until about 7 A.M.," writes Smythies,

> *the barbets are busy feeding and are mostly quiet. Then the great barbet chorus rings out, from 7–9 A.M., and is followed by a good deal of calling throughout the day, ending with a second grand chorus at 4–6:30 P.M. when the barbets hand over abruptly to the cicadas. Barbets hum, they do not sing, because the notes are sounded with the bill closed and the throat bulging out; at each note the tail dips.*
>
> *The biological significance of barbet vocalism remains obscure. Why—alone among the birds of Borneo—do they sit in tree-tops and call for hours on end? and apparently at all times of year?*

Pages 152 and 153:
Canopy of the montane rainforest covering the mid-elevation slopes of Mount Kinabalu.

Feeding in the canopy, rarely moving from tree to tree, and motionless while humming, the barbets' *took-took-tooks* are exceedingly difficult to pinpoint. And the birds always seem to notice you, and become silent, before you spot them.

I had finally seen one at Bako—the gaudiest of them all: a Many-colored, or Red-crowned, barbet. Its crown was bright red above a stripe of sky blue; a broad black streak from its jet-black bill through its amber eye contained another patch of red, under which was a patch of bright yellow and below that another patch of red. Its throat was iridescent blue; and all of this atop a body of iridescent forest green. But I had never been able to spot one on Kinabalu, even though they are all around.

Directly above, I heard a loud *took-took-trrroook*, and looking up I clearly saw my first Golden-naped barbet, its metallic blue throat puffing and deflating with each emphatic hum. Then, from the thick woods a male Whitehead's trogon—12 inches (30 cm) of brilliant scarlet head and belly, gray chest and golden back—swooped gracefully out in front of me. It perched on an over-hanging head-height limb, looking back over its shoulder at me, and within a moment was joined by its golden mate—two of the most striking birds I'd ever seen. For the next few minutes the trogons would swoop away as I approached along the trail, only to land farther ahead of me in full view.

Timpohon gate at start of Summit Trail, Mount Kinabalu National Park.

THE CLOUD FOREST

Kinabalu's Summit Trail begins above the power station road at an elevation of 6,000 feet (1,800 m). After a quick dip past Carson's falls, it climbs steeply up the first of many "staircase" sections toward the first shelter. Sweeping up Kinabalu's slopes, clouds swirl through the vegetation for most of the day during most of the year. Yet when the mist clears, the air is translucent, the sky a brilliant blue. The trees are shorter and less crowded here than in the lowlands, and so the cloud forest has its moments of brilliant light.

The bright Kinabalu balsam blooms almost year-round and is the most noticeable herb at mid elevations on Mount Kinabalu.

The most obvious change from the oak forest below is structural. Trunkless pandanus trees grow like monstrous sedges among twisted moss-covered trees. Ten-foot-tall tree ferns spread lacy umbrellas over bright pink flowers of Kinabalu balsam. Rough- backed tree trunks increasingly twist and sprawl in the mist. Where there were liana vines and huge bird's-nest ferns in the lowland forest, now masses of mosses, liverworts and lichens festoon every trunk and branch. This "elfin woodland" is no longer awesome—with huge, buttressed trees and muted cathedral light—but a delightful, infinitely complex world in miniature.

Giant *Dawsonia* moss, the world's largest, carpets the banks along the trail. Wiry *Gleichenia*, a fern found on disturbed sites throughout the lowlands of Borneo, follows the trail almost to treeline. Bright rhododendron flowers flash through the mist.

I had always considered rhododendrons (azaleas) to be a typically temperate family of montane plants (one is the state flower of Washington, where the climate is remarkably similar to Kinabalu's). Actually, rhododendrons are primarily tropical: about 250 species grown in Malesia (Malaysia, Indonesia, the Philippines, and New Guinea). A tenth of this total are found on Kinabalu, and a dozen species are endemic to the mountain or its near neighbors. Especially prominent against the grays and greens of the moss-covered trees are the bright yellow, foot-wide clusters of Low's rhododendron, the pendant orange bells of the spidery Slender-leaved species, the showy Golden rhododendron and the reddish orange tubes of the Copper-leaved rhododendron.

The cloud forest's subtler treasures are often overshadowed by the mountain's robust challenge. Most visitors who start up the Summit Trail aim to reach the peak, or at least attain Laban Rata resthouse's panoramic view. The steep five-or-more-hours climb to the resthouse at 10,800 feet (3,300 m) is strenuous, and Kinabalu's weather is decidedly fickle—springlike sunshine can turn within minutes into chill, slashing rain: a good reason not to dawdle. And though the trail is well marked and well maintained, it is best to watch your footing when the path rises up in front of your face like an attic stairway. All in all, it is easy for one to arrive at Laban Rata happy just to have completed the journey, meanwhile having barely noted the unique world through which one has just passed.

The Slender-leaved rhododendron is just one of Kinabalu's 25 Rhododendron *species.*

Concealed and then revealed by the blowing mist, Borneo's elfin woodlands resemble the setting for a tropical fairy tale—best appreciated at a child's pace and close up. Along a single fissured tree trunk grow a dozen species of lichen, each a different pattern, some leafy, some crustose, some resembling miniature staghorn corals. A dozen kinds of moss cover a single branch, some in a thin carpet, others in thick masses dripping with rough rootlets, the varying hues of green tinged with golden spore capsules. Mosses cover the soil, the stones, the treetrunks and branches. But they hardly monopolize the space. The spongy carpet provides a moist substrate for countless other life-forms—tiny orchids, primitive liverworts and lacy ferns.

Five hundred fern species grow on Kinabalu—about 5 percent of the world's total; more than are found on the entire continent of Africa. Some, tree ferns especially, are reminiscent of earlier ages. The giant tree fern *Cyathea con-*

The Heath rhododendron grows in alpine areas just below Kinabalu's summit.

taminans lines the road near park headquarters, while the shorter-trunked *Cyathia havilandii* follows the ridges up to 9,000 feet (2700 m).

About half of Kinabalu's ferns are epiphytic, ranging from giant Birds-nest ferns on large tree branches to tiny "filmy ferns" covering trunks and rocks. Filmy ferns, whose fronds consist of a single layer of cells, can only exist in the very humid air of the cloud forest or in the spray of waterfalls, since they are as dependent on continuous mist as marine algae are on seawater. And the 40 species round here are almost as unnoticed and unstudied as are small seaweeds in the ocean depths.

Larger epiphytic ferns have rootstocks that work their way up the treetrunks, or their spores lodge in the crotch of branches. The bird's-nest, *Asplenium*, is the largest of these; there are 25 species on Kinabalu of varying sizes. The pendulous fronds of some are 4–5 feet long.

ORCHIDS

Kinabalu's most notable epiphytes, however, are its orchids, which are found in incredible variety. Everywhere along the mossy branches, on rocks or along the trail are dark green, straplike orchid leaves. Many have flowers so small they can be appreciated only through a hand lens, yet some of these are the most intricate of all.

Aside from being perhaps the most beautiful of all plant families, orchids are also considered the most advanced. And, in terms of number of species, they are the most successful, with more than 20,000 species worldwide. Of these, Kinabalu alone has more than 5 percent, almost a third of all Malesian species. According to Corner, Southeast Asia "has by far the richest orchid flora compared to even the tropical belts of South America and Africa." And Kinabalu may be the richest single spot for orchids in all of Southeast Asia, with 1,200 species on its slopes. Most grow exclusively in the cloud forest, and most are epiphytic.

Few wild orchids are as showy as the painstakingly bred hybrids shown in orchid exhibits or worn as corsages. But some of Kinabalu's are sufficiently large and gaudy to be appreciated by even a casual visitor. The *Paphiopedilums*, with their graceful, twisted banners, are among the most spectacular, and *P.*

Opposite:
An epiphytic rhododendron in bloom on Mount Kinabalu.

An endemic Voloneateanum *ground or-chid, Mount Kinabalu.*

rothschildianum was eagerly collected during the latter 19th century. *Paphiopedilum* species have soft, fleshy leaves and grow in shaded nooks between rocks where humus has accumulated.

Another showy species is a spider orchid, *Arachnis (Vanda) lowii.* The botanist who described it called it "the finest plant coming from Borneo," and it is still one of the most prized of all the world's orchids. Wallace noted:

> *This interesting group of orchids is very abundant, but, as is generally the case, nine-tenths of the species have small and inconspicuous flowers. Among the exceptions are the fine* Coelogynes, *whose large clusters of yellow flowers ornament the gloomiest forests, and that most extraordinary plant, Vanda lowii . . . It grows on the lower branches of trees, and its strange pendant flower-spikes often hang down so as almost to reach the ground. These are generally six or eight feet long, bearing large and handsome flowers three inches across, and varying in color from orange to red, with deep purple-red spots. I measured one spike, which reached the extraordinary length of nine feet eight inches, and bore thirty-six flowers, spirally ar-ranged upon a slender thread-like stalk.*

Several *Arachnis* plants may grow together, normally high up on trees near streams. All the flowers bloom simultaneously; the first few are bright yellow with red spots and are strongly scented; lower flowers are creamier with larger red or brown splotches.

Although incredibly varied in shape and color, orchids have a number of distinctive features that characterize the family. Anthers (male pollen sacs) and stamen (female ovaries) are fused into a single "column." Two of the three petals may resemble the three similar sepals, but at least one is modified into a labellum (lip) that serves as a landing platform for insects. The labellum may be further modified as an attractant to pollinators. In some species the lip and other petals form an elaborate trap through which the pollinating insect must pass. Or the labellum may be cleverly shaped and colored to resemble a female wasp. When the male attempts mating, he is collared with a pair of pollinia (pollen sacs). To further entice pollinators, many orchids have both nectaries and scent glands.

Orchid seeds, produced by the millions, are microscopic—ideal for airborne dispersal in the winds preceding jungle rains. They lodge on tree trunks or on

Trichoglottis *orchid, Mount Kinabalu.*

branches high in the canopy. Germination can proceed only in consort with symbiotic mycorrhizal fungi present in the bark of the tree or in the dead moss on trees or rocks. These invade the embryo, providing it with sugars and other nutrients as it develops. Some saprophytic orchids continue to depend on the fungi throughout their lifetimes.

Terrestrial species like the bamboo orchids and grass orchids, notably *Arundina graminifolia* and *Spathoglottis aurea*, common along Kinabalu's road and trails, develop fleshy rhizomes or pseudobulbs or, like *Paphiopedilum*, have fleshy leaves to store water during drier periods. Many epiphytes also develop rhizomes with large pseudobulbs or fleshy leaves for retaining water during dry periods. The roots absorb moisture from bark or from the moss on the tree. Some orchids can even climb trees; they grow continuously from a terminal growing point while internodal roots cling to bark.

The majority of Kinabalu's orchids flower during and after the local rainy season (October to February), but some will always be in bloom. The excellent Mountain Garden behind Kinabalu Park Headquarters exhibits the cream of the species found in the park and will educate the eye to recognize orchid forms before one climbs the mountain.

OTHER PLANTS OF THE CLOUD FOREST

Since the trees of the cloud forest are generally low in stature and grow shorter with elevation, some of the plant types that might grow tall in the rainforest, here sprawl or grow obliquely toward gaps. Even bamboo here has a form (named after botanist Lillian Gibbs) that grows like a lowland rattan, spreading its wiry shoots out in all directions to climb over any available bush or tree. *Nepenthes villosa*, the commonest pitcher plant at this altitude, dispenses with the usual ground pots and aerial pitchers and instead assumes a single, intermediate form on a sprawling vine that rarely reaches more than head height.

N. villosa, found only on Kinabalu between 8,000–11,000 feet (2,400–3,300 m), attains the highest altitude of any Bornean pitcher plant. It is also one of the handsomest. The pitchers range in size from 1-inch babies to giants more than 14 inches (35 cm) tall; they are robust with a particularly well-developed peristome (collar) and fringe. The reddish pot becomes deep crimson with age, and the peristome ranges from red and lime green to a rich, glowing, greenish gold. Once one becomes aware of them, they seem to cover the forest floor and lower trunks between 9,000 and 10,000 feet.

Mount Kinabalu claims 16 of Borneo's 30 species of pitcher plant, making it the richest spot in the world for these tropical oddities. One of the least showy, *Nepenthes tentaculata*, is probably the commonest pitcher in the cloud forest below 8,000 feet (2,400 m), but two of the rarest species, Low's pitcher and Raja Brooke's pitcher, are among the most spectacular. Low's pitcher is narrow-waisted, and shaped, Hugh Low wrote, like an "elegant claret jug." Rajah Brook's is a huge, wine red jug with large, curved lid. Low reported finding one so spacious that it contained a drowned rat. The British botanist Hooker considered "this wonderful plant certainly one of the most striking vegetable productions hitherto discovered, and in this respect is worthy of taking its place side by side with the *Rafflesia arnoldii*."

Unfortunately, Low's and Rajah Brook's pitchers are now rarely seen along the Summit Trail. "The western ascent," notes Corner, "has been much depleted by persons who have removed the plants to sell or in the hope that they would grow in the lowlands, which they do not."

*Slipper orchid (*Paphiopedilum javanicum)*, Mount Kinabalu.*

As suggested by the abundance of pitcher plants, the montane forest has more in common with the kerangas forest than with the rainforest below. Soils are thin and poor in nutrients. And while the rainforest of the lower slopes is closely allied with the Asian mainland, Kinabalu's upper montane plants and animals are more apt to have relatives in Australia or the Himalayas than in the surrounding lowlands.

Seven species of the eucalypt, *Tristania*, the genus with peeling bark which is so characteristic of the kerangas, are found on Kinabalu; and conifers, rare in the rainforest, make up a good proportion of the upper montane trees. The coniferous *Dacrydium*, also common in the kerangas, are dominant trees on Kinabalu's upper slopes; one of the three species here is endemic and grows to 12,000 feet (3,600 m). Another dominant genus, *Podocarpus*, has eight species here, the most common of which has broad, leaf-like needles; two species grow to 10,500 feet (3,200 m). The Australasian conifer *Phyllocladus*, which is common as a tree on ridges to 9,000 feet (2,700 m) grows as a dwarfed bush to 12,000 feet (3,600 m). It may be the world's most primitive living conifer, or even the most primitive gymnosperm.

Kinabalu's upper slopes have been compared to an island in an archipelago of isolated montane habitats stretching from the Himalayas to New Guinea and beyond. Borneo's only buttercup, named after Low, is locally common, but only on the summit of Kinabalu. Its closest relatives are found in New Guinea and New Zealand. "The strangest case of all," writes Harrisson, "is that of a plant, a tiny liverwort named *Takakia* that grows below the rhododendrons in the icy water of the Paka Cave pool." It is known only from Kinabalu, Japan and Alaska.

Some of the smallest but hardiest of all the plants on the rocky summit are the rosettes of the little *Oreomyrrhis andicola*. "As its name implies," writes Corner, "it occurs also in the Andes, from Mexico to Bolivia, and is also found in Malesia to New Zealand. Distributed while Antarctica still linked South America to Australia, this tiny plant tells a long story of snow-capped mountains."

*Mossy pitcher plant (*Nepenthes villosa*) is common as a sprawling vine in Kinabalu's cloud forest.*

FAUNA OF THE MONTANE FOREST

While most montane mammals are limited to the mid-elevation slopes, a few flourish up near the tree line. The Summit rat, is found to 11,000 ft (3,300 m). The strange Lesser gymnure, cousin of the lowlands moonrat (Greater gymnure), grubs around for earthworms and insects right up to the bare rock of the summit. Tree shrews, squirrel-like, long-snouted insectivores considered forerunners of the primates, do particularly well on Kinabalu. One biologist writes, "Nowhere else has such a diversity of tree shrews been found inhabiting a single mountain." At the 10,000-foot (3,000-m) Paka Cave one day I watched a Mountain tree shrew climb up a rotting snag and rip apart the soft wood in search of insects.

Few of Borneo's large mammals venture far up the mountain. Although orangutans have been seen far up the slopes, they are considered foreign to the upper *Leptospermum* forest, and there are no monkeys reported to live above 6,600 feet (2,600 m). But just the night before spotting the tree shrew, I had had the opportunity of seeing a primate far out of its "normal" range.

I had spent the night at Layang-Layang staff quarters, on the Summit Trail at about 8,600 feet (2,600 m). Just below the cabin, on a steep hillside across a deep cut from the trail, I noticed a large magnolia flower on a treetop slightly below me. The four yellowish petals were each about 4 inches (10 cm) long;

the sepals that had covered the erect bud were still attached, looking like additional petals. A similar but unopened bud stood atop the large, dark green leaves of an adjacent tree. Although I had no way to approach more closely, the trees matched Corner's description of "an unnamed magnolia species that occurs abundantly in steep valleys at 9,000 to 10,500 ft."

I heard rustlings in the second tree and suddenly saw a large Maroon langur among the mid-level branches. It wore a long, healthy red coat, with golden "mane" behind its head and neck and a golden "beard" beneath its dark face. Its rump was grayish and became darker gray on the long tail. Its extremities were dark, characteristic of the subspecies *P. r. rubicunda* of eastern Sabah lowlands.

To my surprise, the langur climbed to the top of the tree, plucked one of the unopened magnolia buds and chomped it down in a few bites. It did the same to the other bud. It continued to move around the tree, in and out of view, stopping to eat and groom.

Then a second, previously unseen, langur jumped over from a neighboring tree to join the first monkey. There followed a brief flurry of activity, but no visible interaction between them. After a few minutes, the second langur made an impressive leap of about 30 feet (10 m) into a lower tree and out of sight. The first continued to move around the tree and adjacent ones until the wind picked up and a heavy mist moved up the gorge. The monkey retreated into the trees, and I back to the cabin.

The Maroon is Borneo's most widespread langur, occurring throughout the island's uplands as well as the lowland rainforest. But this was 2,000 feet (600 m) above the upper limit of its known range.

Two days later, while descending from Laban Rata Resthouse, I took a side hike over to the flat circle of bare ground used as a helipad (at 10,300 ft/3,120 m). There, I again heard rustlings, this time in the stunted *Leptospermum* and *Dacrydium* trees directly across a shallow valley. Three langurs, similar in appearance and size to the earlier pair, spotted me about the same time that I sighted them and, with just a quick backward look, disappeared noisily into the trees. A few minutes later, two similar langurs moved up from an area slightly downhill. Seeing me, they took off on the same track as the first three. Their apparent surprise indicated that they were different individuals who had not previously seen me.

When I mentioned these sightings to my friend Steven Pinfield, who has climbed Kinabalu nearly a hundred times and who has descended the mountain's north slopes, he replied that he'd seen another group of Maroon langurs that seem to inhabit Low's Gully to elevations of 10,000 feet (3,300 m).

These sightings raise a number of intriguing questions. The vegetative community on Mount Kinabalu's upper levels is decidedly different from that of the lowland forest, and even from that of the mid-level oak/chestnut zone reaching to 6,500 feet (2,000 m) or so. It includes many species endemic to the mountain's upper level or shared only with upper Trusmadi and Tambuyukon, separated by miles of lowland forest. Most leaves of the trees growing in this zone are decidedly tough and/or waxy. To what degree have these "leaf-eating" monkeys adapted their diet? Do they depend more on seeds and flowers (even insects?) than do their lowland relatives?

The first sighting took place not long before dark and the second, higher sighting, not long after dawn. Presumably, this group spent at least that night in the subalpine zone. Temperatures decrease rapidly with elevation. (Two nights before, at sea level, I had sweated all night, naked under a thin sheet; at Layang-Layang I slept fully clothed inside two lightweight sleeping bags while howling winds and freezing rain beat against the snug cabin.) In order to survive such alpine nights, these langurs must be adapted to an entirely different

Opposite:
Montane rainforest with tree ferns.

temperature regime than are lowland langurs. Are they larger? Their coats warmer? Their diet higher in oils and proteins?

A group of this same subspecies studied in Sepilok Forest Reserve at sea level in eastern Sabah, according to Payne, "occupied about 60 hectares [150 ac] of tall lowland dipterocarp forest." One would imagine that these Kinabalu langurs occupy a considerably larger feeding territory, perhaps covering several square miles. Do the langurs remain at this level, or are they casual visitors? Is the observed group made up entirely of adults or sub-adults, perhaps a group of wandering bachelors? Or are they truly successful colonists, breeding at this altitude?

Borneo's plants and animals inspire such questions at every bend in the trail—from below sea level to the highest spot in Southeast Asia. And even to Borneo's hidden limestone interior . . .

DR. FU YEN'S MYSTICAL EARTHLY PARADISE

I t is pitch black except for the narrow flashlight beams and James' sputtering carbide helmet lamp as we turn right from the first series of passages, squeeze through a narrow slit, stoop along an upward tunnel and descend a short, slippery cliff onto the smooth floor of the cavern. James, our young Mulu Park guide, has been to this recently discovered cave system only once—a year ago—and our confidence was not inspired by his losing his way twice on the forest trail to the cave. George, our Kayan companion, has also visited the cave, once; he has an excellent sense of underground direction, but he is barefoot and has not even brought a flashlight. To all previous Mulu caves we came well-prepared and expertly guided. Here, there is a feeling of danger and exploration that intensifies our perceptions immeasurably.

The cavern we find ourselves in is breathtaking; the center of the ceiling may be 65 feet (20 m) above us, and the floor is of equal diameter. Icicle-like stalactites hang above stout stalagmites. Where stalactite and stalagmite meet, a column stands, as if to hold up the ceiling. On one side, the floor sweeps up to the roof in an operatic backdrop: frozen calcite waterfalls, swirling curtains, fluted columns. Depending on the play of light, one can imagine being in a baroque cathedral, Kubla Khan's Xanadu, or an underground kingdom of gnomes.

The curtain forming another side of the chamber does not reach the floor; by stooping under we can enter a farther chamber. This one is much lower and longer, curving into the blackness, bordered by a mini-canyon cut by a slow-flowing underground stream. We follow it a short way, but then, feeling insecure with our limited supply of batteries, return to the fantasy cave. We should have brought sleeping pads and more food, and especially candles—it would be an experience of a lifetime to spend a candlelit evening here, where it is always midnight; to sleep in this enchanted chamber deep in the earth; and to wake in the morning to total darkness and the musical dripping of water into rock pools.

Our cave lies deep within an immense outcrop of pure limestone exposed along the Melinau River drainage in northern Sarawak near the Brunei border. Until about 5 million years ago, this part of Borneo was seafloor. For about 30 million years the basin filled with thin layers of mud. Pressure changed the mud to shale—16,000 feet (5,000 m) of it, called the Mulu Formation. Then, from about 40 to 20 million years ago the limy skeletons of tiny planktonic diatoms and foraminiferans built up over the shale, creating a massive layer of limestone 5,000 feet (1,500 m) thick: the Melinau Formation. Melinau limestone was covered, in turn, by more than 23,000 feet (7,000 m) of shale and sandstone.

As Borneo was squeezed between the Asian and Australian tectonic plates 15 to 5 million years ago, the Mulu area buckled into a long, steep ridge. Its layer cake of sedimentary rocks was hunched almost vertically up one side of the wavy ridge and down the other. As it was uplifted far above sea level, the ridge top was eroded away, exposing the shale-limestone-shale layers as parallel, mile-wide swaths lying side by side.

Acidic rainwater dissolves limestone, and since Mulu is one of the wettest spots on earth—up to 300 inches (7.5 m) per year—the limestone has been deeply sculpted. In some places unearthly razor-sharp, 150-foot (45-m) pinnacles rise knife-like from the overlying forest. And where the Melinau River has cut the only open pass through the long ridge, the twin peaks, Api and Benarat, tower a mile (1,500 m) above the Melinau Gorge.

Deformations of the land created cracks in the limestone, and through these cracks seeps slightly acidic rainwater, dissolving the limestone and carrying it away. Beneath the water table, barely moving water formed small, tubular passages along the cracks and joints; faster-flowing water enlarged the passages; underground lakes created larger caverns. Once the passages were uplifted to the level of the water table, they were penetrated by surface streams that cut

Opposite:
A sunbeam pierces an interior chamber of the Great Cave at Niah National Park, Sarawak.

Razorlike limestone pinnacles rise to 150 ft (45 m) on the steep slopes of Mount Api, Mulu National Park, Sarawak.

through the impending limestone ridge. The underground streams cut meanders into the cavern floors, enlarged the passages and deposited clay sediments.

Then, when the passages were finally perched above the water table, rainwater dripping through surface cracks into the caverns lost carbon dioxide to the airy chambers. As the water became less acidic, the dissolved limestone (calcium carbonate) recrystallized as calcite on the walls of the caverns and on the surfaces of the sediments. Sheets of water formed curtains of "flowstone"; trickling water produced a ripple effect. Rainwater ran down thin roots, which penetrated the crevices from the forest above; at the tip of the downhanging roots, an occasional crystal of calcite hardened before being washed away by the next drop, forming stalactites from the roof and stalagmites on the floor.

Here and there, surface erosion has broken through the tops of caverns, creating skylights through which the sun illuminates small patches of cave floor and drying winds disturb the moist, still air. But through most of the long, winding passageways, the blackness is unalloyed, and the only sound is the clicking sonar of invisible birds and limy water dripping into rock pools.

EXPLORING MULU'S CAVERNS

It was long known by the Berawan, Kenyah and Kayan living along the nearby Tutoh and Baram rivers that this area was rife with caves. Cave mouths are good for temporary shelter, for fishing and for finding pig, deer and edible birds' nests near the entrances. The ancient Tring people even used isolated shallow caves in the cliffs above rivers for secondary burial sites (in many Dayak cultures, corpses are stored in coffins or large ceramic jars near the house for months or years; then they are ceremoniously taken elsewhere for final repository). But the true extent of the Mulu cave network was discovered only very recently, by scientists whose interest was more abstract, and by cave explorers whose motivations are as inexplicable as mountain climbers' and whose exploits send shivers up the spines of their more claustrophobic brethren.

In 1961, geologist E. G. Wilford visited the area and explored some of the more accessible caves. His booklet on the geology of the caves of Sabah and Sarawak predicted, "Large spectacular caves are most likely to be discovered in the uninhabited and relatively unexplored Melinau area . . . where the Api and Benarat mountains could contain cave systems several miles long." Sixteen years later, when a Royal Geographic Society expedition was organized to study the newly gazetted Mulu National Park, they brought along, almost as an afterthought, six speleologists (cave researchers) out of 130 scientists.

The cavers found an underground world beyond their wildest imaginations: 13 major cavern systems, seven of them more than a mile (1,500 m) in length; all in all, more than 30 miles (50,000 m) of underground caverns. Clearwater Cave alone—one of the most accessible caves just off the Melinau River—consisted of more than 16 miles of passages. The main trunk of Deer Cave turned out to be more than a mile (1.8 km) long and 100–150 feet (30–45 m) in diameter—the world's largest single underground passage.

The dazed explorers wanted more. Two years later an expedition of British cave scientists and Sarawak Forest Department personnel returned to Mulu with the sole purpose of investigating the limestone caves. They feared that the expedition might be an anticlimax after the astounding finds of 1977/78. "But not so!" says their jubilant report, "Caves of Mulu '80." "The eye of faith was rewarded."

Clearwater Cave turned out to be 50 percent longer than it was thought to be—making it the longest cavern in the southern hemisphere. Cave of the

Winds, at 4 miles (6.5 km) in length, was three times the previous measure. Cave complexes were found in two previously unexplored areas; five of the new systems measured from 1 to almost 6 miles (9.4 km) in length.

Although the descriptions of the caverns are properly scientific, an inkling of the awe felt by these experienced cavers is reflected in the names they christened the caverns. From a description of Clearwater Cave:

> *Revival Passage runs northeast while southeast at the same level a scramble over boulders leads into the 800 meters [2,640 ft] of Infinite Improbability Drive. After 500 meters [1,650 ft] of easy going, a scramble up boulders leads to . . . the Secret Garden.*
>
> *The southwesterly high level links to Hyperspace Bypass, a gigantic split-level chamber with two connections at its northern end back into Infinite Improbability, close to where the latter swings north to link with Broadside Chamber. At the southwestern corner of Hyperspace, a ramp leads down into the complex of King Seth's Maze . . .*
>
> *From the top level of Hyperspace, a low passage with a good draught and heavy swiftlet traffic leads into . . . a maze and becomes ever more heavily calcited until a climb emerges at a balcony overlooking the Secret Garden. This remarkable chamber, with a floor area of around one hectare [2.5 ac], is flooded by light from a huge skylight 50 meters [165 ft] above and supports a luxuriant vegetation including small trees. A large gallery drops from its eastern end, then ascends steeply at a spectacular entrance, the Hole in Time, overlooking the Melinau Paku Valley 300 meters [1,000 ft] below.*
>
> *From Junction Cavern, a scramble up boulders into the roof of Revival continues to a small waterfall which is climbed to a junction. To the right, a loop of passage and a short climb through large blocks enters a large chamber followed by an awkward climb into the stalagmite-strewn expanse of Dr. Fu Yen's Mystical Earthly Paradise . . .*

The best was yet to come. A mile into the newly discovered Good Luck Cave—after following a "turbulent torrent," swimming a 50-foot (15-m)-wide whirlpool, and traversing for almost half a mile, sometimes with fixed ropes—the small party emerged from a narrow trench into the astounding Sarawak Chamber. From the center of the cavern light did not reach the far walls, and one of the party even suffered from agoraphobia—fear of open spaces—during its exploration.

Sarawak Chamber proved to be earth's largest known underground cavity, by far. Its major dimensions are 2,300 feet by 1,300 feet (700 m × 400 m); its floor covers 60 acres (24 ha). Its roof is almost 330 feet (100 m) high, its volume more than 16 million cubic yards (12 million cu m). New Mexico's famous Carlsbad Caverns and the world's next two largest caves could fit inside with room to spare.

And on the chamber floor, far past the reach of all predators, the cavers found nesting birds.

DENIZENS OF THE CAVES

Caves have always formed handy shelters. Forest animals—pigs and deer and pythons—find refuge from the rain in the mouths of the caves. Fish and crabs move from the rivers up the underground streams, some species becoming so adapted to the dark that their eyes have atrophied and their skins have grown pale. Bats and birds nest under the sheltering roofs and on the slippery walls;

some swiftlets have become so specialized for cave living that they, alone among all birdlife, developed sonar to fly through the darkness.

The guano deposited by these birds and many species of bats gave rise to a whole community of insects that draw energy from the guano and the corpses of the flying animals, and these small animals attract predators and parasites. Some predators even feed on the birds and the bats nesting or roosting high on the cave walls. All in total darkness.

In our chamber, too, far from the least hint of sunlight, there is life. No bats nest this far in, but Mossy-nest swiftlets knife through the dark, their ecoloca-tion sounding like stones clicking against stones.

George finds a large huntsman spider feeding on a Cave cricket almost as large as itself; Terry rushes to photograph the process. The huge, long-legged Cave crickets climb the walls to feed on swiftlet eggs and nestlings. The beautifully patterned huntsman spiders pounce on the crickets and on smaller insects that feed in the bird guano, which is composed mostly of the exoskele-tons of insects hawked over the rainforest by the wide-ranging swiftlets.

Swiftlets are small swifts, a family superficially similar to swallows but with longer, more slender, scythe-like wings. Like swallows, they are acrobatic aerialists, catching flying insects on the wing. Unlike swallows, they glide with wings open rather than half-closed. They are the only true avian troglobites (cave dwellers). Swiftlet species that nest in caves not only can navigate in total darkness but can find their own individual nest among hundreds of others.

The nests themselves are a unique response to the cave's damp, slippery walls. During breeding season, swiftlet salivary glands enlarge enormously. The swiftlets fashion their nests from the copious saliva, which hardens into "nest cement" in contact with the air. One species uses saliva exclusively while others use it to bind moss, grasses or feathers.

One would not think that the tasteless saliva of birds would be particularly valuable. But to believers in traditional Chinese medicine, swiftlet saliva, in the form of bird's-nest soup, is an invaluable elixir to ensure male potency. So, for at least 1,200 years, high-quality Bornean swiftlet nests have been worth more than their weight in gold. Consequently, there are those willing to risk their lives to collect them.

The most highly prized nests are those of the Edible-nest (Brown-rumped) swiftlet, whose whitish yellow nests are made of almost pure saliva. The best caves for them are along the Baram River and are often owned (and subse-quently leased out) by upper- class Kenyah and Kayan. The second-best nests

A Huntsman spider devours a large Cave cricket.

Small fruit bats in a Mulu cave.

are from the largest and most common species—the Black-nest swiftlet—whose nests are collected in quantity from the most famous of all Bornean caves, the Great Cave at Niah, 80 miles (130 km) due west of here near the coast.

THE GREAT CAVE AT NIAH

This unusual species of gnat larvae catches smaller flying insects by suspending sticky threads from the ceilings of caves.

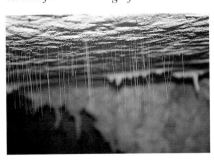

The Great Cave is awe-inspiring. Its entrance overhang measures 800 feet (245 m) wide by 200 feet (60 m) high. Its immense inner chamber, in the center of a labyrinth of smaller side-caves, is 200 feet (60 m) high, topped by a distant skylight through which some of its flying inhabitants exit and return. The walls and ceilings are covered with a dozen species of bats roosting upsidedown by their tiny feet and wing-hooks, and with thousands of swiftlet nests—White-bellied near the entrances, Mossy-nest in the depths, Black-nest between the extremes.

Black-nest swiftlets, which make up most of the commercial harvest at Niah, are larger than their 2-inch (7-cm)-deep, "half-saucer" shaped nests; characteristically facing in against the wall, their tail and long, folded wings stick out into the air. The nest, which takes two months to construct, is formed of saliva mixed with the bird's feathers; it holds a single egg. If the nest is removed before the egg is laid, the bird will make another. The first nest is collected in October;

the swiftlet pair, in theory, is left in peace to raise their egg in the second nest, which is harvested after the nestling fledges.

A spidery forest of poles up to 200 feet (60 m) long hang from the roof of the Great Cave entrance and from the ceiling of the inner chamber. These are climbing poles, formed of sections of belian (ironwood) connected by dowels through holes drilled in the flattened ends. High up against the dark cave roof the pole tips, and occasional crosspieces, are wedged into crevices in the rock.

The steel-nerved local men who shimmy up these poles carry beeswax candles, hand-rolled around a piece of cloth. (The candles burn clean and have a predictable lifespan; they won't break if dropped, and there is no bulb to burn out.) For removing the nests they carry a *penduluk*, a telescoping bamboo pole, to which is lashed a steel blade and a beer bottle to hold the candle. Nests scraped from the ceiling are gathered by a helper on the cave floor far below. The nests are then sold to middlemen who have them cleaned (by hand) of feathers or other nest material; most are ultimately shipped to Hong Kong or Taiwan.

In 1931 Niah hosted an estimated 2.2 million swiftlets, mostly Black-nest; by 1962, after collection had been regulated by the Sarawak Museum, populations rose to about 4 million. By 1974, however, numbers dropped to 1.3 million, and have continued to fall. How much of this is due to overharvesting of nests, how much to disturbance by harvesters and visitors, and how much to nearby deforestation (which may affect the populations of insects on which the birds feed) is unknown.

Each swiftlet weighs only a half-ounce (15 g), but the total mass of Niah's million birds equals almost 20 tons. From a circle of forest with a radius of about 15 miles (25 km) from the caves, the swiftlets gather almost 10 tons of flying insects each day. A million or so insectivorous bats—Wrinkled-lipped and Naked (free-tailed) bats; Fawn, Cantor's, and Diadem roundleaf bats; the

Main entrance to the Great Cave at Niah National Park, Sarawak.

Black-bearded tomb bat; the Bornean horseshoe bat; and the Lesser bent-winged—may double this with their droppings. Indigestible exoskeletons of the insects are deposited within the cave, along with corpses of dead bats and birds, fallen nestlings and remnants of the insects feeding on the guano.

A number of fruit- and nectar-eating bats also roost in the caves—Geoffrey's and Bare-backed rousettes; Dusky and Spotted-winged fruit bats; and the Cave nectar bat. The guano of these fruit eaters adds moisture and sugars to the rather dry mix of insect remains.

The bat and swiftlet guano supports a surprisingly complex web of cave animals. Predictably enough, four species of flies and three cockroaches are commonly found in the guano along with 17 beetle species; but less expected, there are three kinds of small clothes moths that feed on and lay their eggs in cave guano. One of the most fascinating of the guanobites is a small millipede named *Orphnaeus*, common in Deer Cave. When disturbed, it exudes a brightly luminous green slime that remains behind in the dark as the millipede crawls to safety.

Feeding on the moths, flies, beetles and cockroaches are a number of ants, spiders, scorpions and pseudoscorpions, centipedes and an assassin bug. Two rare geckos, found so far only in Niah and Deer caves, also catch flies and moths. The large Cave cricket feeds on guano as well as on the eggs and young of swiftlets; it in turn is eaten by the huntsman spider and the large Long-legged centipede, which has a sting powerful enough to wound an unfortunate caver. Four kinds of earwigs specialize in feeding on the oils and flaking skin of the numerous Naked bats.

Aside from birds and bats and the occasional gecko, the only vertebrate to penetrate the caves is the Cave racer. A large, handsome, nonpoisonous snake, it is pale green with a broad black eye-streak and diamond pattern and grows to more than 6 feet (2 m) long. The only snake commonly found in caves, it preys on bats and swiftlets, which it can catch in total darkness. British biologist Philip Chapman, one of the Mulu explorers, has "heard it utter a hoarse mewing call when threatened and this would seem to be the only known instance of vocalization, other than hissing, among the snakes." Perhaps its ears are more highly evolved than other snakes; most others can hear only low vibrations.

BATS

Though the Mossy-nest swiftlet penetrates far into the caves, the bats tend to roost near the cave openings. Their large wings and fluttery flight are not well suited to narrow passages, and perhaps there is little advantage to adapting their highly sensitive moth-hunting sonar for crude navigational needs. Only the rousettes—fruit-eating bats that have no need of sonar for hunting—have developed a simple sonar of tongue clicks similar to those of the cave swiftlets.

Fruit and nectar bats have not evolved the elaborate facial structures that send and receive the sonar pulses; and so, their faces have foxlike or mouselike snouts and large eyes, giving them the look of typical mammals. Borneo's insectivorous bats, however, have developed incredibly complex sonic structures in front and above the nose (and their eyes are correspondingly reduced to tiny dots), giving them faces that many humans find hideous.

Horseshoe bats have an elaborate noseleaf, which consists of a roughly horseshoe-shaped anterior noseleaf and a connecting process ending in a tall upward-pointing tube called a sella. Above and behind this is a complex posterior noseleaf, which rises to a long pointed tip. Their large, pointed ears

Opposite:
Leaf-nosed bats in a Mulu cave.

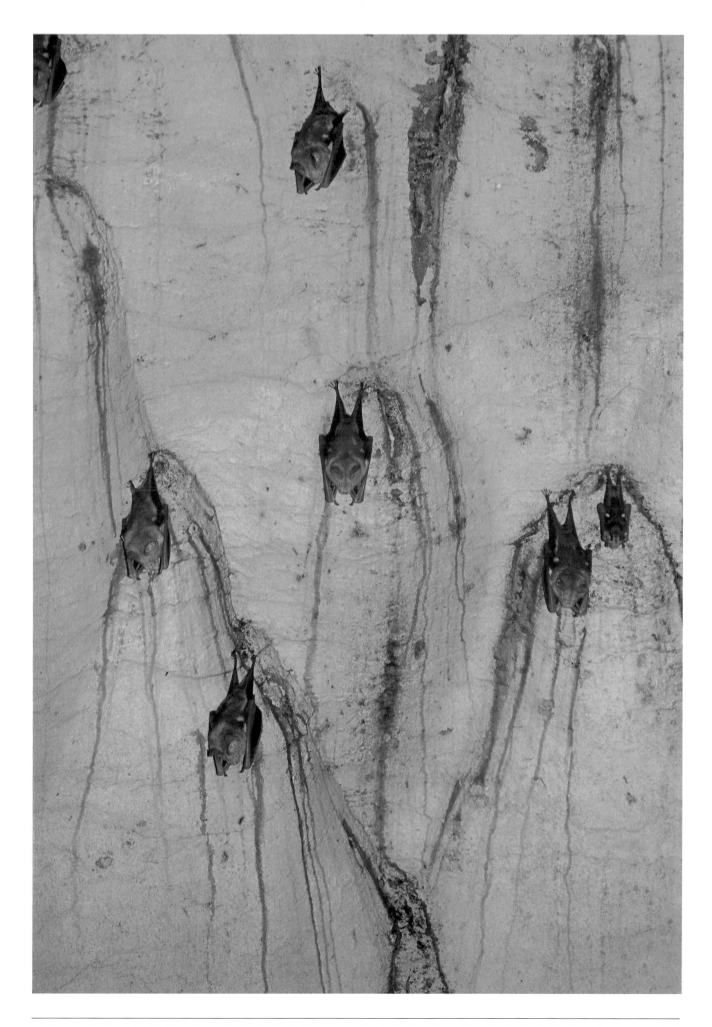

The Great Cave at Niah in daylight. The candle of a bird's nest poacher can be seen high against the cave's ceiling.

are fronted by a flap called the antitragus. Roundleaf bats have a more solid-looking but equally complex sonar structure around the nose.

The two common species of free-tailed bats—the Wrinkled-lipped and the Naked—are distinguished by a thick tail that protrudes from the membrane that stretches between their legs. If the Wrinkled-lipped bat is not particularly unappealing—aside from its large, round, forward-pointing ears and piglike nostrils—the larger Naked bat is downright ugly. Its long, pointed, cupped ears reach out over a long snout with a short, underslung lower jaw and a triple chin. Its loose gray, hairless skin crawls with symbiotic earwigs that feed on the bat's skin oil, keeping it clean.

These free-tailed bats, though, are the principal performers in two of nature's most spectacular daily shows. Every evening, the mouth of Niah's Great Cave becomes a rush-hour of incoming swiftlets and outgoing bats (reversed in the dawn commuter rush). An estimated 200,000 Naked bats, along with tens of thousands of others of different species, flutter out of the huge cave entrance as thousands of swiftlets return from the forest canopy for their evening roost.

Perched above the cave entrance, or circling above it, are the Crested goshawk and Jerdon's baza—a hawk that has replaced the Bat hawk, decimated by nest collectors in the belief that it reduced the swiftlet population. The hawks dive on the bats as they orient themselves and on the swiftlets as they linger in front of the cave mouth picking off the day's last few insects.

For an observer seated on a large rock near the Great Cave entrance, looking out from the limestone cliff into which the cave is carved, the swiftlets, bats and hawks create an exciting three-ring aerial circus, as dusk falls on the rainforest below.

An equally stunning sight is provided by the bats of Mulu's Deer Cave, where 300,000 Wrinkle-lipped bats fly from the southwest entrance or from smaller holes above the entrance. They fly "in huge, wheeling flocks or long, sinuous clouds," in Chapman's words. "The whooshing roar of hundreds of thousands of wings can be heard as far away as Long Pala and the sight and sound is unforgettable as the bats fly fast and high above the forest to unknown feeding grounds west of the Park." Adding to the spectacle are the high-soaring Bat hawks, which dive into the mass of exiting bats like a barracuda into a school of reef fishes, picking out single victims from the wheeling thousands.

Once over the rainforest canopy, the bats themselves will hawk moths in a similar fashion, picking them from the clouds of insects hovering over and among the trees. By sunrise—as swiftlets zip out from the cave for the day's hunt—the bats will bring back a small part of the forest's energy to the caverns below the roots of trees, refueling the mysterious, sunless life of Borneo's interior.

EARLY HUMAN INHABITANTS

Niah's Great Cave is famous not only for its wildlife but for its unique position in the archaeology of Southeast Asia.

Assuming that such an imposing overhang as the Great Cave's mouth would be a logical shelter for the earliest of Borneo's human inhabitants, in 1957 Tom Harrisson organized a major dig sponsored by the Sarawak Museum. The following year, the skull of a sub-adult human was found at a depth of 106 inches (265 cm). Since each 2.5 inches (6.3 cm) of cave sediments represents about 1,000 years, the skull was estimated to be about 40,000 years old, making it the oldest human remains in Southeast Asia.

The find drew the world's attention to Niah and encouraged its listing as a National Historical Monument (later to become a national park in 1974). Assisted by British zoologist Lord Medway (now Earl of Cranbrook), the team identified a long sequence of human usage and associated animals eaten by the inhabitants. The finds include oyster shells from about 37,000 years before present (BP) and 30,000-year-old remains of orangutan, monkeys, pig, wild ox, rhinos, bear, tapir, hornbills, lizards, turtles, rats and bats—all presumably eaten by the human cave dwellers.

Human tools include a 12,000-year-old axe blade and a more advanced quadrangular adze from 4500 BP; well-made, polished tools and a ceremonial jar from 3600 BP; beautiful shell jewelry and buttons from 2500 BP; bronze nails

Aboriginal cave paintings on the walls of Painted Cave, Niah National Park.

A secondary chamber within the Great Cave at Niah.

and a three- color-ware urn more than 2,000 years old, along with fishing nets and mats. The team also excavated remains from 166 burials: 38 were Mesolithic (between 2000 and 4000 BP), the rest were Neolithic (from 2,000 years ago until historical times).

Equally spectacular were the finds from a nearby, much smaller cave whose walls were covered by paintings in red haematite. Painted Cave proved to be an ancient cemetery, containing dozens of crumbling "death ships," wooden funerary coffins carved and decorated like small boats, placed on posts. The wall paintings include "dancing" figures, the head of a hornbill, fighting cocks, and so forth, and seem to represent animal and human spirits and voyages of the dead, but these have not been interpreted in detail.

The finds at Niah caused a reappraisal of early modern man. If the assigned dates are correct, civilized people did not appear in Europe from Africa 40,000 years ago and then spread out from there to Asia. They were well-established in Southeast Asia by that time, perhaps having moved down the Indochina Peninsula. And, in fact, the Punan (settled groups related to the Penan) claim the funerary ships of Painted Cave as those of their ancestors. Thus, Borneo not only hosts the last large tracts of the world's richest and most ancient rainforest but is also cradle of one of the earth's oldest cultures.

FATE OF THE RAINFOREST

The dipterocarp forests have become one of the world's major sources of hardwood timber . . . and exploitation is taking place at an ever-increasing pace.

—T. C. Whitmore

The winter of 1982–83 saw a periodic anomaly in world weather known as El Niño. On Borneo, the monsoon rains simply failed to appear. The last half of 1982 passed with less than 40 percent normal rainfall in East Kalimantan and Sabah; almost no rain fell between February and May.

As the drought progressed, evergreen trees cut down their transpiration rates by shedding their leaves like deciduous trees—the crumpled leaves lay on the duff like tinder. Peat soils dried and crumbled, toppling many of the shallow-rooted trees. Massive amounts of logging debris left by the rapidly expanding timber industry covered huge areas with dry debris. But to native dryland rice farmers, to plantation concessionaires, and to the growing number of farmers brought to Kalimantan by Indonesian government transmigration schemes, the dry spell was a golden opportunity to burn off the logs and stumps from newly cleared fields.

Fanned by the hot, dry wind, the small burns coalesced into raging forest fires, which soon spread from cleared areas into secondary forest. They began to ignite even the huge trees of the intact rainforest—previously believed to be impervious to fire. During the first few months of 1982, a large chunk of Borneo's rainforest was ablaze.

For close to three months the fires raged. Heavy rains in May finally doused the worst ones, but by then the fires had consumed 9 million acres (3.5 million ha) of East Kalimantan, more than a third of which was lowland dipterocarp rainforest or peat swamp forest. Half of the newly established Kutai National Park was destroyed. The loss in timber value alone in Kalimantan was estimated at $5 billion; the loss of wildlife and nontimber forest products was incalculable. In Sabah, 2.5 million acres (1 million ha) burned, including the eastern and southern slopes of Mount Kinabalu. Taken together, the fire—documented by satellite imagery—was the largest ever recorded on earth.

Government officials and foresters blamed the conflagration on slash-and-burn farmers, and, no doubt, it was the farmers who started many of the burns. But scientists studying the fire argue that El Niño droughts have taken place every 50–100 years without such consequences, and a similar one in 1877, before widespread logging and agricultural clearance, was not accompanied by forest fires. Clearly, the combination of unregulated logging and agricultural clearing has created conditions that threaten the very existence of the rainforest.

Fire is not the only threat to the integrity of Borneo's primary rainforest. Logging itself, especially the way it is currently practiced, damages far more than the relatively few high-quality trees it intends to harvest. In one study in Sarawak, of every 26 dipterocarp trees cut per hectare, 33 other trees were destroyed or damaged. Forty percent of the soil was exposed in the process, setting back regeneration and exposing the thin forest soils—often compacted by heavy equipment—to erosion. Up to 15 percent of the harvest area was totally denuded and compacted for forest roads, which now snake through Borneo's forests into the highest mountain ranges of the most remote interior regions.

The roads themselves have a further effect on wildlife, by opening remote areas to hunters in four-wheel-drive vehicles. First come the loggers themselves, since life in the logging camps offers little other recreation. Then urban hunters follow the roads deep into the rainforest. Canopy animals, whose habitat has been reduced by the logging activities, now find the canopy broken into islands separated by cleared areas. Terrestrial animals, which tend to use the new roads for travel, are especially vulnerable to hunters.

The ultimate destruction of the primary forest comes when a logged area is transformed into large agricultural plantations. Much of eastern Sabah is being transformed into oil palm plantations.

Kalimantan has been the recipient of agricultural transmigration schemes designed to spread Java's dense population through the less populated Indones-

Opposite:
Bole of a large dipterocarp tree.

Logging and slash burning, Sabah.

A large patch of rainforest cleared for an oil palm plantation, Sabah.

ian islands. Unfortunately, southern Borneo's thin rainforest soils are not the fertile volcanic soils of Java, and some of the transmigrants were even settled in sterile heath forests. Borneo's population was already at ecological maximum. Even where Kalimantan is capable of more intensive agriculture by the skilled farmers of Java and Madura, the distance to markets and the lack of good transportation make cash farming problematic.

LOGGING

To fully understand the plight of Borneo's forests it is helpful to have an overview of timber harvesting throughout the entire region over the past few decades.

Logging of the dipterocarp forests of Southeast Asia has been driven by resource needs of Japan, Europe and the United States, and has largely been financed by large Japanese trading houses such as C. Itoh and by American

Log barge on the Niah River, Sarawak.

timber companies such as Weyerhauser. The Philippines, especially the southern island of Mindanao, were logged in the 1960s (the local dipterocarps were
termed "Philippine mahogany"). As the forests of the principal islands became
depleted, the industry shifted southward to Kalimantan and Irian Jaya (Western New Guinea) with the encouragement of the Indonesian government.
Japanese-financed logging began there in 1963, and by 1971 Indonesia
supplanted the Philippines as Japan's largest log supplier—principally from
East Kalimantan. When the Indonesian government began to restrict
Kalimantan's export of raw logs in 1978 (banning them completely in 1986)
and opted instead to export finished plywood, the international timber industry
shifted to Sabah. During the past few years, as Sabah's forests have run out of
the most desirable species, Sarawak has taken up the slack.

Together, Sarawak and Sabah export 9 billion board-feet (20 million cu m)
of raw logs, more than 2 billion board-feet (5 million cu m) of sawn wood, and
1 million cubic meters of plywood. Kalimantan supplies another 5 million cubic
meters of plywood. Taken together, Borneo's 6.5 million cubic meters of
exported plywood represents more than 22 billion board-feet (more than 50
million cu m) of raw logs.

By 1988 Malaysian Borneo was supplying four-fifths of all the tropical logs
on the world market and 90 percent of Japan's hardwood log imports.
Kalimantan supplied 95 percent of Japan's tropical plywood imports (along
with most of the European Community's imported plywood). All in all,
three-quarters of Japan's tropical timber products now come from Borneo.

Most of the raw logs imported by Japan from Borneo also eventually become
plywood. One would expect that beautiful hardwoods would be used for
exterior veneers over softwood cores. But in fact Borneo's dipterocarps have
been sold at such a low price that they are sometimes used as plywood core
between exterior softwoods imported from North America. Even more disturbing is the fact that most of the tropical plywood is utilized by the construction industry—as concrete forms (*kon-pane*), which are used a few times and
then discarded.

In the 1970s Indonesia decided that it was more beneficial to turn its raw
timber into higher-value finished products such as plywood. The gamble has
proved successful enough that Malaysia's central government is now pressing
Sabah and Sarawak to limit exports of raw logs and to invest instead in
downstream processing facilities; Sabah has recently announced a limit on
exported logs.

Most logs will be shipped to Japan to be peeled for plywood and used as forms for concrete construction.

By the time the processing industries come on-line, however, the forests may already be depleted of quality timber. There will then be dozens of plywood and furniture mills crying for raw materials (as in the U.S. Pacific Northwest), putting further pressure on Borneo's remaining forests. Kalimantan now has about 150 plywood mills; some have now begun to import logs from Sarawak.

Meanwhile, Japan—keeping its own extensive softwood forests in reserve, due to slower growing conditions and higher labor and harvesting costs—is looking as far away as Brazil for future supplies of hardwood logs to feed its local plywood and saw mills.

The artificially low price of imported dipterocarp logs is due to forces at both ends of the supply line. A recent review by the World Commission on Environment and Development found

> *Many tropical countries with large forest resources have provoked wasteful "timber booms" by assigning harvesting rights to concessionaires for . . . only a small fraction of the net commercial value of the timber harvest. They have compounded the damage . . . by offering only short-term leases, requiring concessionaires to begin harvesting at once, and adopting royalty systems that induce loggers to harvest only the best trees while doing enormous damage to the remainder. In response, logging entrepreneurs in several countries have leased virtually the entire productive forest area within a few years and have overexploited the resource with little concern for future productivity, while unwittingly opening it for clearing by slash-and-burn cultivators.*

Timber sorting yard. Sarawak now supplies a large percentage of all tropical hardwoods on the world market.

Even though the logging industry has neither planted nor tended the forest (and in most cases need not replant it), the capital outlay on heavy equipment is high. Profits are maximized only if high-interest loans are paid back in minimal time. Logging concessions tend to be granted as political spoils which can be revoked with changes in government; shifting political alliances can also

transform one party's "legitimate" concessions into another's "flagrant corruption." And so, the pressure is on the concessionaires to extract the timber and get out as fast as possible.

At the importing end, countries such as Japan opt to protect their own forest reserves—while trying at the same time to keep their local mills supplied—by encouraging imports. "Some industrial countries typically import unprocessed logs either duty-free or at minimal tariff rates."

The result of these pressures is that the rainforest is logged off in a wasteful manner at a rate far above sustainable yield, and the forest ecosystem is damaged to a far greater extent than is necessary. By keeping stumpage fees (cost of the trees that the state charges the concessionaire) artificially low, the exporting states are deprived of maximum revenues and sustainable income (and consequently cannot afford a forestry staff capable of managing the forests properly).

Yet, though the price of Bornean hardwoods is low, the short-term income is large due to the sheer volume of the harvest. Sarawak, for instance, derives 30 percent of its public revenues from log exports. Although Sabah and Sarawak are being pressed by the federal government to export "downstream" processed products such as plywood and furniture, it is a painful process to restrict exports while switching over.

Furthermore, since there is only a very hazy concept of "conflict-of-interest" in Bornean politics, there is little difference between the large-scale loggers and the politicians who represent them (and who are often themselves large-scale concessionaires).

Publicly, the response of local politicians to environmental criticism of rainforest management has been to adopt a fortress mentality. Internal protests, such as blockades by the Penan and others, are considered to be entirely the doing of "outside agitators" such as Bruno Manser. European and Australian environmental groups are "fanatical crusaders" who are making Sarawak "a

After a heavy rain, the Segama River turns muddy.

scapegoat." Western governments, who are accused (often correctly) of allowing their own forests to be destroyed for economic development, are said to have no right to criticize. No attempt is made to separate Western and Japanese governments or logging industries—which helped set up Borneo's—from the environmental groups that are criticizing the same industry in the United States, Canada, Australia and the Philippines as well as in Borneo.

Officials assure that the way to transform Borneo's economy from "primitive" to "modern" is to transform the forest into agricultural plantations. Yet Borneo's proven ability is to grow trees. Despite its generally fragile, nutrient-poor soils, the island has evolved an integrated forest ecosystem capable of producing some of the most magnificent trees on earth. Plantation commodities such as cocoa, rubber and palm oil tend to become overproduced throughout the tropics, often depressing the price to below production costs.

Attractive, durable hardwoods, on the other hand, will surely demand much higher prices in the future—as furniture, hardwood flooring and decorative paneling—than they now do for disposable concrete forms and plywood fill. If properly managed (with sustainable yields, less destructive forest practices, longer-term contracts, realistic stumpage prices), the dipterocarp forest—including its rattans, wild pigs and deer, illipe nuts, river fishes and other forest products—and the mangrove forest, a nursery for fish and shrimp, could produce stable incomes for generations.

The International Tropical Timber Organization (ITTO) was founded in 1983, based on a United Nations Conference on Trade and Development's International Tropical Timber Agreement. The ITTO's stated goal is "proper and effective conservation and development of tropical timber forests with a view to ensuring their optimal utilization while maintaining the ecological balance of the regions concerned . . ." The advisory body now includes 42 nations as members, including most producers, such as Malaysia and Indonesia, and most consumer nations, including Japan and the United States.

ITTO scientists who visited Sarawak at the invitation of the Malaysian government in 1990 reported that official timber harvest in that state was more than 50 percent above sustainable yields. Illegal logging ups the harvest further, since even government officials acknowledge that forestry personnel are too few in number and are insufficiently trained and equipped. They lack the status to challenge rule-breaking by legal concessionaires or the power to stop deprivations by logging pirates.

Recently, the drying up of reservoirs in populated states of western peninsular Malaysia has been linked to deforestation of surrounding states, whose catchment areas supply Malacca and Kuala Lumpur. The Malaysian Department of Environment's 1989 Annual Report found that nine rivers in Sarawak and 14 in Sabah were seriously polluted by soil erosion.

Borneo's environmental degradation is hardly unique. Deforestation is a worldwide problem with predictable consequences. If Borneo's forests are not managed more carefully, temporary timber booms will be followed by long periods of timber bust. Soils will be compacted or washed away. Polluted rivers will lose their freshwater fishes, shrimp and terrapin, and will degrade the nearshore reefs and saltwater fishery. Overlogged watersheds will be subject to cycles of flood and drought. People as well as wildlife will suffer.

Opposite:
The species composition of secondary forest will be much different than the primary forest it replaced.

WILD PRESERVES

Wildlife species—and the growing numbers of "eco-tourists" they attract—depend on the setting aside of sufficiently large forested areas, preserved in

Rural Dayak farmhouse with banana plants and coconut palms.

their natural state. If the areas are large enough to accommodate viable populations of orangutans, gibbons, hornbills and other large popular animals, they will also protect thousands of lesser-known species. Such areas may also be able to accommodate hunting pressures by Penan and rural Dayaks dependent on wild game and on forest products such as sago and rattan.

Much of Borneo is as mysterious now as it was a hundred years ago, and much may forever be a mystery. Magnificent forests are being destroyed that contain plants and animals we will never know. Dayak culture is changing at such a rapid rate that firsthand knowledge of jungle plants gained over hundreds of generations is fading into oblivion. In Borneo, as with much of the natural world, there is a critical race between preservation—based on sound ecological research—and the double-edged transformation called "development."

So far, the records of Sabah, Sarawak and Kalimantan are mixed when it comes to preservation. Some magnificent areas of forest and scenic beauty have been set aside as parks and are being managed well and adequately protected: Sabah's Kinabalu and Tunku Abdul Rahman national parks and Sarawak's Mulu and Bako are world-class in scope and facilities. Kalimantan has created national parks around the Gunung Palung and Tanjong Puting research stations; Kutai National Park shows great promise if it can recover from encroachments and the damage caused by the fires of 1983–84.

Large areas of forest have also been set aside—on paper at least—as wildlife reserves. The prime example is Sarawak's huge Lanjak-Entimau Wildlife Sanctuary and the connected Gunung Bentung/Kiramun Nature Reserve across the border in East Kalimantan. Malaysia has recently proposed that the two reserves become the world's first transnational park.

Other large reserves are on the drawing board. The next few years will show how serious the governments are about setting aside land for wildlife and parks. But dwindling forest reserves and growing populations surrounding these areas will threaten even the best-managed parks with encroachments from logging (legal or otherwise), slash-and-burn farming, and overhunting.

The following is a list of Borneo's national parks, selected wildlife sanctuaries and active research sites as of 1992:

Coastal Parks

The Melinau River runs clear from its unlogged watershed in Mulu National Park, Sarawak.

BAKO NATIONAL PARK (1957)
Sarawak's oldest national park. Located on a peninsula 23 miles (37 km) northeast of Kuching. Covers 11 square miles (2,742 ha).
> **Ecozones:** Sand beaches and beach forest; mangroves; freshwater swamp; kerangas forest; rainforest.
> **Animals:** Long-tailed macaque; Bearded pig; Water monitor lizard; Silvered langur; Proboscis monkey; many coastal birds.
> **Trail system:** Well-marked 18-mile (30-km) network of 16 interconnecting trails.
> **Access:** One-hour bus ride to Kampong Bako, followed by 20-minute boat ride.

SANTUBONG NATIONAL PARK (in final stage of gazetting)
Just west of Bako. Covers 7 square miles (1,700 ha) of Santubong Peninsula. Site of early Indian and Chinese trading communities at mouth of Sarawak River.
> **Ecozones:** Beach forest and mountainous area of peninsula.
> **Animals:** Proboscis monkey; langurs.
> **Access:** Road and boat.

An Estuarine crocodile basking at the river's edge.

TUNKU ABDUL RAHMAN PARK (1974)
Includes part or all of five nearshore islands off Sabah's Kota Kinabalu.
> **Ecozones:** Coral reefs; rocky coast; beach forest; mangroves; lowland dipterocarp forest (Gaya Island).
> **Access:** 15–30 minutes by boat from downtown Kota Kinabalu or Tanjung Aru Beach Hotel.

TIGA ISLAND PARK (1978)

Three small islands off western Sabah about 30 miles (50 km) southwest of Kota Kinabalu. Main island has research station run by Sabah Parks and National University of Malaysia (Sabah branch). Unusual "mud volcanoes."

Ecozones: Coral reefs; beaches; variety of lowland forest types.

Animals: Megapode bird, roosting White-bellied sea eagles, and large population of Lesser frigate birds (in season); Amphibious sea snakes on Pulau Kalampunian Damit.

Access: Fishing boats from mainland; visiting scientists may be transported by park officials.

TURTLE ISLANDS PARK (1977)

A group of small islets in the Sulu Sea off Sabah's east coast, 20 miles (36 km) north of Sandakan.

Ecozone: Nesting beaches for marine turtles, primarily the Green sea turtle.

Access: Private boat operators from Sandakan.

SIMILAJAU NATIONAL PARK (1978; still being developed)

Beach and coastline 20 miles (36 km) northeast of Bintulu in Sarawak; covers almost 30 square miles (7,000 ha).

Ecozones: Beach and mangrove forest.

Access: Road from Bintulu.

SAMUNSAM WILDLIFE SANCTUARY (1979)

Covers 23 square miles (6,000 ha) along the lower reaches of the Samunsam River near Sarawak's coastal border with West Kalimantan; proposed extension would more than triple the size.

Ecozones: Beach, mangrove and kerangas forests.

Animals: Sarawak's largest population of Proboscis monkey (about 160 individuals); Silvered and Banded langurs.

Access: Visitation by special request only; difficult transport.

Lowland Forest

SEPILOK FOREST RESERVE (1931)

Covers 17 square miles (4,300 ha) in eastern Sabah, 8 miles (13 km) northwest of Sandakan. Site of Orangutan Rehabilitation Center.

A large Common birdwing butterfly sips nectar from a forest flower.

Borneo's frog fauna is one of earth's most diverse.

Ecozones: Dipterocarp and swamp forest. Decent trail system and good birding.
Animals: Orangutan; langurs; forest birds. Confiscated species include orangutans and (at times) Two-horn rhinoceros, Asian elephant, Bornean gibbon, Sun bear, Clouded leopard.
Access: Taxi or tour bus from Sandakan.

NIAH NATIONAL PARK (1974)
Covers 12 square miles (3,140 ha); 60 miles (100 km) southwest of Miri in Sarawak. Site of Niah Caves.
    Ecozones: Lowland forest with limestone outcrops.
    Animals: Swiftlets; cave bats; Cave racer snake; hornbills. Varied wildlife and good birding along river trail and boardwalk to caves.
    Access: Road (rough but being upgraded) from Miri or Bintulu.

LAMBIR HILLS NATIONAL PARK (1975—Day use only)
Between Miri and Niah Caves in Sarawak. Covers almost 30 square miles (7,000 ha). Good but limited trail system. Canopy observation tower.
    Ecozones: Lowland forest with streams and waterfalls.
    Access: Good road from Miri.

GUNUNG MULU NATIONAL PARK (1976)
Covers 200 square miles (53,000 ha) surrounding Mount Mulu in Sarawak near the Brunei border. Good trail system, but much of the area must be accessed by longboat.

A clump of spiny rattan palms. Its slender climbing shoots bear catclaw thorns.

Ecozones: Extensive limestone cave system and jagged limestone peaks. Lowland and hill forests. Rivers.
Animals: Large populations of cave bats and swiftlets. Large mammals appear to have been hunted out by nearby Penan settlements but good birding (large hornbill populations).
Access: By express boat from Miri or Marudi; then longboats. Arrangements simplified (and often less expensive) by going through tour agencies in Miri. Airstrip under construction.

DANUM VALLEY CONSERVATION AREA (1984)
Covers 170 square miles (438 sq km) 53 miles (85 km) west of Lahad Datu in eastern Sabah. Includes modern Field Studies Center. No formal protection, but the quasi-governmental Sabah Foundation (Yayasan Sabah), which controls the surrounding logging concession, has placed the Conservation Area under a management committee that includes Sabah Forest Department, the National University and eight other agencies. Self-guided nature trail and 18 miles (30 km) of marked but primitive trails (some restricted). Dormitory beds available (space limited). Tourist facilities being developed.
Ecozones: Lowland and hill forest on the Segama River.
Animals: Varied wildlife includes primates; Mouse and barking deer; civets. Occasional sightings of Asian elephant, Banteng, and Clouded leopard; signs of almost-extinct Asian Two-horned rhinoceros.
Access: Rough logging road limited to Sabah Society four-wheel-drive vehicles. Arrangements must be made in advance with Yayasan Sabah office in Lahad Datu.

TABIN WILDLIFE RESERVE (1984—undeveloped)
Covers 465 square miles (120,521 ha) on the Dent Peninsula in easternmost Sabah.
Ecozones: Many forest types.
Animals: Important sanctuary for Two-horned rhinoceros and Asian elephant. May be degraded by surrounding activities.
Access: Almost inaccessible (only by private four-wheel-drive vehicles). Permission needed.

KUTAI NATIONAL PARK (1980)
Covers almost 800 square miles (200,000 ha); north of Samarinda in East Kalimantan. Excellent potential but partly damaged by logging and forest fire in the early 1980s.
Ecozones: Lowland and hill forests.
Animals: Varied.
Access: Road from Samarinda but status of visitation uncertain.

A Buffy fish-owl prepares to hunt.

TANJUNG PUTING NATIONAL PARK (1988)
Covers more than a thousand square miles (305,000 ha) in southern Central Kalimantan. Site of orangutan research and rehabilitation center founded by Birute Galdikas.
Ecozones: Extensive swamp forest; lowland rainforest.
Animals: One of Borneo's highest orangutan populations.
Access: Difficult. Need permits from state authorities. Visits can be arranged through Earthwatch program (Watertown, Massachusetts, USA).

GUNUNG PALUNG WILDLIFE RESERVE (1986)
Covers 350 square miles (90,000 ha)—existing and proposed in West Kalimantan. Site of forest ecology research station directed by Harvard University's Mark Leighton.

Opposite:
A visitor to Sepilok Orangutan Rehabilitation Center has her hands full with this pair of baby orangutans.

A jungle stream in Kinabalu National Park.

Ecozones: Varied lowland and hill forests.

Access: Difficult. Invitation from station and government permits needed.

Upland Areas

KINABALU PARK (1964)

Northeast Sabah. Covers almost 300 square miles (75,000 ha) on the slopes of 13,500-foot (4,100-m) Mount Kinabalu, tallest mountain in Southeast Asia. World-class park with a range of accommodations, excellent trail systems and wildlife. Trails include popular Summit Trail and one being developed to link headquarters to Poring.

> **Ecozones:** Upland oak forest; cloud forest; unique summit zone. One of the world's most diverse collections of orchids, ferns, tropical oaks and chestnuts, rhododendrons, pitcher plants. Rare *Rafflesia* blooms at Poring.
>
> **Animals:** Contains all montane mammals of Borneo; most montane birds; interesting insects.
>
> **Access:** Paved (but steep and winding) road from Kota Kinabalu. Minibuses, taxis and tour buses. Overnight visitors make reservations at Sabah Parks headquarters in Kota Kinabalu.

CROCKER RANGE NATIONAL PARK (1984)

Covers 540 square miles (140,000 ha) of Crocker Range in western Sabah. Some areas affected by shifting agriculture.

> **Ecozones:** Hill forest and river valleys. Contains most of the known sites of *Rafflesia* in Borneo.
>
> **Access:** No development or easy public access at present but local nature societies and private nature guides may offer hikes.

LANJAK-ENTIMAU WILDLIFE SANCTUARY (1983)

Covers 650 square miles (170,000 ha) on Sarawak-Kalimantan border south of Sibu. Contiguous with Gunung Bentuang/Karimun Nature Reserve on West Kalimantan side of border and with proposed Batang Ai National Park to the south. Malaysian government has recently proposed upgrading the two reserves to national park stature. Together they would be twice the size of West Malaysia's Taman Negara.

> **Animals:** Orangutan; Bornean gibbon; White-fronted, Hose's and Maroon langurs. Many others.
>
> **Access:** Difficult.

BUKIT RAYA/BUKIT BAKA NATURE RESERVES (1978)

On border of West and Central Kalimantan. Together they cover more than 800 square miles (210,000 ha) with a proposed extension of more than 2,000 square miles (590,000 ha). Includes 7,500-foot (2,278-m) Bukit Raya, highest point in Kalimantan.

> **Access:** Difficult.

SELECTED BIBLIOGRAPHY

Anderson, J. A. R. "The Structure and Development of the Peat Swamps of Sarawak and Brunei," *Journal of Tropical Geography* 18 (1984).

Argent, G., A. Lamb, A. Phillips, & S. Collenette. *Rhododendrons of Sabah*. Sabah Parks Publication 8, (1988).

Ave, J. B., & V. T. King. *People of the Weeping Forest*. Leiden: Nat. Museum of Ethnology, 1988.

Barclay, J. *A Stroll Through Borneo*. London: Hodder & Stoughton, 1980.

Beccari, O. *Wanderings in the Great Forests of Borneo*. Oxford: Oxford University Press, 1989.

Bennett, E. "Cyrano of the Swamps." *BBC Wildlife* 2/88 (1988).

————. "Proboscis Monkeys in Sarawak: Their Ecology, Status, Conservation, and Management." Kuala Lumpur: WWF Malaysia, 1986.

Bennett, E., J. O. Caldecott, M. Kavanagh, and A. C. Sebastian. "Current Status of Primates in Sarawak." Kuala Lumpur: WWF Malaysia, 1988.

Bock, C. *The Headhunters of Borneo*. Oxford: Oxford University Press, 1985.

Caldecott, Julian. "Hunting and Wildlife Management in Sarawak." Kuching: WWF/National Parks & Wildlife, 1986.

Chan, L., M. Kavanaugh and Cranbrook. "Proposal for a Conservation Strategy for Sarawak." Kuala Lumpur: WWF Malaysia, 1985.

Corner, E. J. H. "The vegetation of Mount Kinabalu." In *Kinabalu, Summit of Borneo*. (Luping, Chin, & Dingle, eds.). Kota Kinabalu: Sabah Society, 1978.

Cox, J., and F. Gombek. "A Preliminary Survey of the Crocodile Resource in Sarawak, East Malaysia." Kuala Lumpur: WWF Malaysia, 1986.

Cranbrook, Earl of (ed.). *Key Environments Malaysia*. Oxford: Pergamon Press, 1988.

Francis, C. *Pocket Guide to the Birds of Borneo*. Sabah Society/WWF Malaysia, 1984.

Galdikas, B. M. F. "My Life with Orangutans." *International Wildlife* 6 (1990).

Hanbury-Tenison, R. *Mulu, The Rainforest*. London: Weidenfeld and Nicolson, 1980.

Harrisson, T. *World Within: A Borneo Story*. London: Oxford University Press, 1986.

Henrey, L. *Coral Reefs of Malaysia and Singapore*. Kuala Lumpur: Longman Malaysia, 1982.

Howes, J. R. "Evaluation of Sarawak Wetlands and their Importance to Waterbirds," Reports 1–4. Kuala Lumpur: Interwader/NPWO/WWF Malaysia, 1986.

Inger, R. F. *The systematics and zoogeography of the Amphibia of Borneo*. (Fieldiana: Zool., V52.) Kota Kinabalu: Sabah Society, 1990.

Inger, R. F., and P. K. Chin. *Freshwater Fishes of Borneo*. (Fieldiana Zool., V45.) Kota Kinabalu: Sabah Society, 1990.

Jacobson, S. K. *Kinabalu Park*. Sabah Parks Publication No. 7, 1986.

Kavanagh, M., Abdul Rahim Abdullah , and C. J. Hails. "Rainforest Conservation in Sarawak: An International Policy for WWF" (Project 3262). Kuala Lumpur: WWF Malaysia, 1989.

Kemp, A. C., and M. I. Kemp. "Report on a study of hornbills in Sarawak." Kuala Lumpur: World Wildlife Fund Malaysia, 1974.

King, B., M. Woodcock, and E. C. Dickinson. *A Field Guide to the Birds of South-East Asia*. London: Collins, 1975.

Kurata, S. *Nepenthes of Mount Kinabalu*. Sabah National Parks Publications No. 2, 1976.

Luping, D. M., W. Chin, and E. R. Dingle (eds.). *Kinabalu, Summit of Borneo*. Kota Kinabalu: Sabah Society, 1978 (New edition due in 1991).

MacKinnon, J. *Borneo*. Amsterdam: Time-Life Books, 1975.

———. *In Search of the Red Ape*. New York: Holt, Rinehart and Winston, 1971.

Melingreau, J. P., G. Stephens, and L. Fellows. "Remote Sensing of Forest Fires: Kalimantan and North Borneo." *Ambio* 14 (6), 1985.

Morrell, R. *Common Malayan Butterflies*. Kuala Lumpur: Longman Malaysia, 1960.

Morrison, H. *Life in a Longhouse*. Singapore: Summer Times Publ., 1988.

Nectoux, F., and Y. Kuroda. *Timber from the South Seas: An Analysis of Japan's Tropical Timber Trade and its Environmental Impacts*. WWF International, 1989.

Payne, J. "Orangutan conservation in Sabah." WWF Malaysia, 1988.

Payne, J., & G. Cubitt. *Wild Malaysia*. London: New Holland Publ. Ltd., 1990.

Payne, J., C. M. Francis, and K. Phillips. *A Field Guide to the Mammals of Borneo*. Kuala Lumpur: Sabah Society/WWF, 1985.

Phillips, A., and A. Lamb. "Pitcher-Plants of East Malaysia and Brunei." *Nature Malaysiana*. V13 (4), Oct., 1988.

Richards, P. W. *The Tropical Rain Forest*. London: Cambridge University Press, 1952.

Ripley, S. D. *The Land and Wildlife of Tropical Asia*, 2nd ed. Hong Kong: Time-Life Books, 1980.

Roberts, T. R. "Freshwater Fishes of Western Borneo (Kalimantan Barat, Indonesia)." San Francisco: Cal. Acad. of Sci., Memoir #14, 1989.

Rubeli, K. *Tropical Rainforest in South-East Asia: A Pictorial Journey*. Kuala Lumpur: Tropical Press, 1986.

St. John, S. *Life in the Forests of the Far East*. (2 vols.). London: Smith, Elder, and Co., 1862.

Shelford, R. W. *A Naturalist in Borneo*. Oxford University Press, 1985.

Smythies, B. E. *The Birds of Borneo*. 3rd ed. Kuala Lumpur: Sabah Society & Malayan Nature Society, 1981.

Stuebing, R. "Sea Snakes of Pulau Tiga." Kota Kinabalu: Univ. Kebangsaan Malaysia, n.d.

———. "Megapodes on Pulau Tiga." Kota Kinabalu: Univ. Kebangsaan Malaysia, n.d.

Stuebing, R., Ismail Ghazally, and H. C. Ling. "Distribution and Abundance of the Indo-Pacific Crocodile in the Kilas River, Sabah." *Proceedings of Int. Conf. on Forest Biol. and Cons. in Borneo*. Kota Kinabalu: 1990.

Sutlive, V. H., Jr. *The Iban of Sarawak*. Prospect Heights, IL: Waveland Press, 1988.

Sutton, S. L., T. C. Whitmore, and A. C. Chadwick. *Tropical Rain Forest: Ecology & Management*. Oxford: Blackwell, 1983.

Tung, V. W. Y. *Common Malaysian Beetles*. Kuala Lumpur: Longman Malaysia, 1983.

Wallace, A. R. *The Malay Archipelago*. New York: Dover Publ., 1989.

Whitaker, R. "Preliminary Survey of Crocodiles in Sabah, East Malaysia." Kuala Lumpur: WWF Malaysia, 1984.

Whitehead, John. *The Exploration of Mount Kinabalu, North Borneo*. London: Gurney and Jackson, 1893.

Whitmore, T. C. *Tropical Rain Forests of the Far East*, 2nd ed. London: Oxford University Press, 1984.

———. *Palms of Malaya*, 2nd ed. Kuala Lumpur: Oxford University Press, 1977.

———. (ed.). *Biogeographical Evolution of the Malay Archipelago*. Oxford: Clarendon Press, 1987.

Whitten, A. J., S. J. Damanik, J. Anwar, and N. Hisyam. *The Ecology of Sumatra*. Bogor: Gadjah Mada University Press, 1984.

Whittow, G. C. *Malaysian Wildlife: A Personal Perspective*. Kuala Lumpur: Eastern Universities Press (Univ. Malaya), 1986.

Wood, E. "Ecological Study of Coral Reefs In Sabah, Part 2." *Sabah Soc. J.* (VIII) 1 1970.

Wood, E., and D. George. "Semporna Marine Park Survey." Kuala Lumpur: WWF Malaysia, 1981.

Yong, H. S. *Malaysian Butterflies—An Introduction*. Kuala Lumpur: Tropical Press, 1981.

PHOTO CREDITS

All photographs are by Terry Domico except the following:

Green sea turtle, Andy Dalton, p. 29

Proboscis monkey, John Hyde, p. 56

Langanan Falls, Mark Newman, p. 82

Rhinoceros hornbill, Mark Newman, p. 91

Sepilok Orangutan Rehabilitation Center, Mark Newman, p. 106

Clouded leopard, Mark Newman, p. 129

Barking deer, Mark Newman, p. 133

Mount Trus Madi viewed from Mount Kinabalu, Mark Newman, p. 140

Rafflesia pricei, Tengku Adlin, p. 146

INDEX

Numbers in italic indicate illustrations and captions.

Gray treepie—*See Malaysian treepie*
Great argus pheasant (*Argusianus argus*), 123–124, *124*
Great Cave (Niah National Park), 103, 130, 136, *166*, 172–174, *173*, 174, *176*, 177–178, *178*
Great egret (*Egretta alba*), 54
Greater gymnure—*See moonrat*
Greater mouse deer (*Tragulus napu*), 132
Greater racket-tailed drongo (*Dicrurus paradiseus*), 123
Greater sand-plover (*Charadrius veredus*), 52
Great Kayan Expedition (1862), 9
Green broadbill (*Calyptomena viridis*), 91
Green sea turtles (*Chelonia mydas*), 28–30, *29*
guano, 171, 174
gulls, 34
Gunung Bentung/Kiramun Nature Reserve, 188
Gunung Mulu National Park, 72, 191–192
Gunung Palung Wildlife Reserve, 192, 194
gutta-percha latex, 4
Gyrinocheilus (fish genus), 79

H

Haemadipsa (leech genus), 135
Hampala (fish genus), 74
Harrisson, Barbara, 16, 106
Harrisson, Tom, 8, 15–16, 30, 106, 131, 145, 161, 177
Hawksbill sea turtle (*Eretmochelys imbricata*), 29
headhunting, 8–9
Heath rhododendrons (*Rhododendron ericoides*), 141, *156*
Helmeted hornbill (*Rhinoplax vigil*), 89
herons, 54
Hinduism, 2–3
honey, wild, 7
honey bear—*See Sun bear*
hornbills, 82, 89–91, 133
    Black, 91
    Pied, 82
    Rhinoceros, 80, 83, *91*, 91
    Wreathed, *90*
horseshoe bats, 174, 176
horseshoe crabs, 48–49
Hose's langur (Gray leaf monkey) (*Presbytis hosei*), 98
Hospitalitermes (termite genus), 126
House swift (*Apus affinus*), 38
hunting, 131–136
huntsman spider (*Heteropoda*), *171*, 174

I

Iban (ethnic group), 8–9, 11–12, 41, 91, 128
ice ages, 5–6, 141–142

illipe nuts, 7, 133
Indonesia, 1–2
Inger, Robert, 71–72
In Search of the Red Ape (John MacKinnon), 20
insects
    Kinabalu Park, 148–151
    mangroves, 54–55
    rainforest, 108–111
    tropical streams, 73–74
International Tropical Timber Organization (ITTO), 186
Iridomyrmex myrmecodiae—*See under ants*
Irrawady dolphin—*See Snubfin dolphin*
Islam, 3
Itoh, C. (Japanese firm), 182
ITTO—*See International Tropical Timber Organization*
ivory, hornbill, 4, 89–90

J

Javan rhinoceros—*See Lesser one-horned rhinoceros*
jellyfishes—*See Mastigias jellyfishes*
Jerdon's baza (*Aviceda jerdoni*), 176

K

Kadazan (ethnic group), 9, 19, 143
Kalampunian Damit Island, 32
Kalimantan (Indonesia), 1–2, 181–183
Kampong (village), *18*
Kantu (ethnic group), 9
Kapuas River, 6, 64–65
Kayan (ethnic group), 9, 70, 136
Kelabit (ethnic group), 7, 9, 131, 134
kelip-kelip—*See firefly beetle*
Kenyah (ethnic group), 9, *10*, 70
kerangas forest, 39–42
Kiau Gap, 150
Kinabalu, Mount, 17, 19, 91, 141–145, *142*, *144*, 179
Kinabalu balsam (*Impatiens platyphylla*), *155*
Kinabalu Park, 145, 148, *154*, 188, *194*, 194
Kinabatangan River, 20, 71–72, 80
King cobra (*Ophisphagus hannah*), 75, 119–120
kingfishers
    Collared, 38
    Ruddy, 36
    Rufous-backed, *35*
Kissing gouramis (*Helostoma temmincki*), 78
kite—*See Brahminy kite*
Klias Peninsula, 17
Komodo dragon, 34
Kota Kinabalu (city), *3*, *4–5*, 18–20, 142
kraits, 120
Kuching (city), 11–12, 15
Kutai National Park, 179, 188, 192

L

Labuan Island, 12, 17
Lambir Hills National Park, 191
Land and Wildlife of Tropical Asia, The (S. Dillon Ripley), 50
Land Dayaks—*See Bidayuh*
Langanan Falls (Sabah), *82*
langsat, 7, *20*
languages, 6–7
Langub, Jayl, 138
langur, 55, 98
    Banded, 55
    Hose's, 98
    Maroon, 162, 164
    Silvered, 55, 80, 98
Lanjak-Entimau Wildlife Sanctuary, 188, 194
laughingthrushes (*Garrulax*), 151
Lawangan (ethnic group), 9
leaf-nosed bats, *175*
Leakey, Louis, 106
Leatherback sea turtle (*Dermochelys coriacea*), 29
leaves, *114*, *115*
leeches, 134–135, *135*
Leighton, Mark, 89
lekak (edible leaf-bud), 137–138
leopard—*See Clouded leopard*
Leptospermum tree (*Leptospermum flavescens*), 141
Lesser adjutant stork (*Leptoptilos javanicus*), 54
Lesser bent-winged bat (*Miniopterus australis*), 174
Lesser frigate bird (*Fregata ariel*), 34
Lesser gymnure, 161
Lesser mouse deer (pelanduk) (*Tragulus javanicus*), 131, 132
Lesser one-horned (Javan) rhinoceros, 130
Lesser pygmy flying squirrel (*Petaurillus emiliae*), 96
Limbai (ethnic group), 9
lionfishes (Scorpaenidae), *25*
Lithocarpus tree, 148
Little green heron (*Butorides striatus*), 54
Little green pigeon (*Treron olax*), 91
liverwort—*See Takakia liverwort*
lizards
    Flying, *94*, 95
    geckos, 174
    Monitors, 34, 36
loaches, 79
lobster—*See mud lobster*
Loggerhead sea turtle (*Caretta caretta*), 29
logging, 68, *181*, 181–186, *183*, *184*
longan, 7
longboat, 7, 7–8
longhouse, 7, 9
Long-snouted (Forceps) butterfly fish (*Forcepiger longirostris*), 26
Long-tailed (Crab-eating) macaque (*Macaca fascicularis*), 43

Wanderer butterfly (*Valeria valeria*), 109–110
Wanderings in the Great Forests of Borneo (Odoardo Beccari), 12–13
warblers, 54, 151
Weaver ant (*Oecophylla smaragdina*), *54*, 54
Weyerhauser Company, 183
whip coral, 24
Whiptailed stingray, 64
White-bellied sea eagle (*Haliaeetus leucogaster*), 32, 38
White-bellied swiftlet (*Callocalia esculenta*), 172
White-breasted wood-swallow (*Artamus leucorhynchus*), 36
Whitehead, John, 90–91, 144
Whitehead's broadbill (*Calyptomena whiteheadi*), 144
Whitehead's spiderhunter (*Arachnothera juliae*), 144

Whitehead's trogon (*Harpactes whiteheadi*), 144, 154
white mangroves (*Avicennia*), *44*, 48
White-rumped shama (*Copsychus malabaricus*), 112
Whitmore, T.C., 117
wildlife preserves, 186–194
Wilford, E.G., 168
Wood nymph butterfly—*See Smaller wood nymph butterfly*
woodpecker—*See Golden-backed woodpecker*
wood-swallow—*See White-breasted wood-swallow*
Wooly-necked stork—*See Storm's stork*
World Within: A Borneo Story (Tom Harrisson), 8, 16
wrasses (Labridae), 27–28
Wreathed hornbill (*Rhytoceros undulatus*), 90

Wrinkled-lipped bat (*Tadarida plicata*), 173–174, 176–177

Y

Yellow glassy tiger butterfly (*Danaus sita*), 110
Yellow-lipped sea krait—*See Amphibious sea snake*
Yellow-ringed (Mangrove) cat snake (*Boiga dendrophila*), 55
Yellow-vented bulbul (*Pycnonotus goiavier*), 54

Z

Zebra barb (*Puntius fasciatus*), 76
zooxanthellae, 25–26